MORE PRAISE FOR *WORK & FAMILY*

"In our twenty-six years of working to promote the use of voluntary flexible work schedules as a means of helping employees balance work and the rest of their life, two events stand out related to the *Wall Street Journal*—the first time that paper used the term 'job sharing' and its inauguration of Sue Shellenbarger's column on "Work & Family." What a delight to see so many of these wonderful articles collected together in book form. They not only document the needs that people have in today's demanding workplace, they also represent an articulate and effective force for change."
—Barney Olmsted and Suzanne Smith
Co-directors, New Ways to Work
Authors of *Managing in a Flexible Workplace*

" 'Can you have a family and work?' is one of the most frequently asked questions on every Take Our Daughters to Work® Day and one that Sue addresses in this book. Our daughters, sons, parents, and employers everywhere will find Sue Shellenbarger's readable essays full of answers from parents, other experts, and contemporary research. These essays are written for working parents by a working parent."
—Marie C. Wilson
President, Ms. Foundation for Women

"By her articles in the *Wall Street Journal*, which she began in 1991, Sue Shellenbarger was among the first people to alert the corporate world to work-family issues, and to provide employees with the wealth of her and others' experience. This collection from those articles is a wonderful compendium of concerns and innovations in this domain."
—Lotte Bailyn
Author of *Breaking the Mold: Women,
Men, and Time in the New Corporate World*

"Sue Shellenbarger's columns remind us that we can and must be a success at home and at work. This book brings together many of the columns we have clipped out of the *Wall Street Journal* and urged our colleagues and family to read."
—Alan G. Merten
President, George Mason University

"A born storyteller, Sue Shellenbarger has managed the difficult task of introducing passion into the pages of the *Wall Street Journal*, becoming the advocate of all working parents. Her stories have been a powerful influence in raising the consciousness of business leaders. And they have taught all of us more about living than the stock market tables that appear in the back of the *Journal*."
—Milton Moskowitz
Co-author of *The 100 Best Companies to Work for in America*

WORK

&

FAMILY

Essays from the "Work & Family" Column of
The Wall Street Journal

Sue Shellenbarger

BALLANTINE BOOKS • NEW YORK

Library of Congress Cataloging-in-Publication Data
Shellenbarger, Sue.
    Work & family : essays from the "Work & Family" column of
    The Wall Street Journal / Sue Shellenbarger. — 1st ed.
        p.   cm.
    ISBN 0-345-42226-0 (alk. paper)
    1. Dual-career families—United States.   2. Work and family—United States.
3. Parents—Employment—United States.   I. Title.
HQ536.S4823   1999
306.872—dc21   98-11673
                                                                        CIP

Text design by Ann Gold

Manufactured in the United States of America

First Edition: April 1999

10   9   8   7   6   5   4   3   2   1

To Richard, whose love and laughter have sustained me,
and to Maggie, Rich, Luke, Cristin and James, from whom
I have learned so very much.

Contents

IV   The Highwire Walk

V   At Work

VI Employers Reach Out

VII Caring for the Aged

VIII   *Across the Generations*

Preface

Few issues are more universal than tension between work and family. From the hard-pressed manager with no time for children, spouse or aged parents, to the single assembly-line worker with no child care for a night-shift job, tens of millions of Americans endure work-family conflict daily.

Worries about family needs are flooding the workplace because no one is home during the day anymore in most American households to attend to family. Three-quarters of mothers of children under 18 and two-thirds of caregivers to the elderly also hold paid jobs.

Even those who do stay home to care for loved ones are touched by our collective anxiety over work and family. The American obsession with work as a centerpiece of personal identity compels all of us to develop a rationale for the roles we choose vis-à-vis the workplace. Thus at-home parents define themselves in terms of the choices they have made about working, calling themselves "formerly employed mothers" or "sequencers" to make the point that they, too, could work if they chose to.

Evidence that families in our society, particularly children, are in trouble has deepened our psychological dilemma. Growing concern about poor-quality child care, high juvenile crime and suicide rates and a troubling incidence of teen pregnancy, depression and drug use have helped give rise in the 1990s to what historian Neil Howe has called a "parenthood revival."

And societal values are changing. Severed by corporate layoffs from a lifelong bond with one employer, many American workers, men in particular, are turning inward and homeward to find new meaning.

When *The Wall Street Journal* created the "Work & Family" column in 1991, no one was covering work-family conflict in a systematic way. Women's progress in the workplace in the wake of the feminist movement had drawn consistent and deserved media attention.

And the public, riveted by sociologist Arlie Hochschild's book *The Second Shift,* was beginning to realize that juggling work and family in this new, no-boundaries context was a black hole for human energy, sucking the creativity and vitality out of primarily women. But media coverage of work-family matters was confined mostly to scattered stories about a child-care center here, a job-sharing setup there. Little attention was given workers' day-to-day emotional struggles, emerging family solutions, cross-generational tensions or the byzantine workplace stresses that were arising on this new work-and-family landscape.

The "Work & Family" column was born of the wreckage of my own career. As a stepmother who, with my husband, shared joint custody of three wonderful children with his first wife, I had strong hints throughout the 1980s that combining work and family was tough. But nothing compared with the conflicts I experienced after the birth of my first natural child in 1987. As chief at the time of *The Wall Street Journal*'s third largest domestic bureau in Chicago, I felt a compelling responsibility for the careers and professional growth of the 15 reporters and editors there. I loved, and still love, journalism and had reaped more intellectual growth and stimulation from my career than from any other facet of my life up to that point. However, I also was driven by the most powerful imperative I have ever felt: The instinctive drive to make sure that my baby was nurtured well.

My worries about the constant compromises I kept making to combine work and family had me tossing and turning through sleepless nights. Try as I might—and notwithstanding my employer's unstinting support and commitment to helping me resolve my conflicts—I simply couldn't make newsroom rhythms and staffers' needs mesh with the responsibilities of motherhood as I interpreted them. For the first time in my career, I had encountered a problem that I couldn't solve by working harder or smarter.

In successive steps, I left management to return to reporting, then scaled back to a part-time schedule. After the birth of my second child in 1990, I left my position at the *Journal* to become a full-time freelancer and regain the sense of control over my life that I wanted. Throughout my effort to reconcile work and family imperatives, I, like millions of others in similar situations, felt isolated and alone.

It was at that step, as I regretfully left *The Wall Street Journal* staff, that my colleague and mentor at the paper, Larry Rout, a senior editor, suggested I consider writing a new column on work and family for the Marketplace Page of the paper. My managing editor quickly embraced the idea, and "Work & Family" was born in its early form, as a periodic collection of news briefs. I continued to write "Work & Family" and cover workplace issues for *The Wall Street Journal* as a freelancer and, in 1994, returned to the staff as a full-time telecommuter. The column was well received by readers, and in October of that year, with the support of then-Marketplace Page Editor Cynthia Crossen, we expanded it to its current one-topic form and increased its frequency to three times a month from once every three weeks.

Editors watched closely to see if the column was substantive enough to warrant a permanent slot. One of my acquaintances remarked, "How can you sustain a column about work and family for more than three weeks? What could you possibly write about?" In fact, the inner conflicts and personal growth that millions of Americans were experiencing over work-family matters proved a rich lode of material that today, nearly five years later, still runs as deep as ever.

I built the column on a foundation of people's heartfelt personal stories and try each week to touch some universal human chord—some element in our strivings that would bring us all together. I believe that's the main reason the column survives and thrives. In the work-family stories of other people, readers find relief, at least temporarily, from the sense of aloneness we often experience while trying to support families, raise good children and do right by our elders.

Hundreds of letters have poured into my home office over the years, telling how the column has prompted readers to examine their life choices, change parenting techniques or look for a new employer. "I cried when I read your column because I want desperately to be at home with my son but can't afford it," one woman wrote in response to a column about the backlash against working parents. Executives write and call with questions about how to

improve the quality of their workplaces. "Congratulations on causing us to think about child care in a new way," wrote a Connecticut
man in response to a profile of a child-care provider. Another column, on how a CEO responded to the death of his wife, led a Colorado executive to write, "You've made leaders think."

Today, "Work & Family" is one of five regular Marketplace Page
columns that are among the best-read features in *The Wall Street Journal.* Other columns cover personal technology, health, careers and
front-line business strategies, and each has a strong voice and personal, subjective viewpoint. The 100 "Work & Family" columns in
this collection were all published between 1994 and 1998 and are
organized into eight topic areas, including starting a family, creating
a home, raising kids, balancing life day-to-day, negotiating workplace demands, understanding employer policies, caring for aged
family members and fathoming the effect of different generations'
work-and-family views on each other.

As the columns show, the context for our work-and-family struggles is changing fast. The "conspiracy of silence" that once sur-
rounded family concerns at work, as the late Felice Schwartz of
Catalyst, a nonprofit New York research and advocacy concern, ob-
served, is ending as more workers give voice to their conflicts. Old
gender-role taboos are crumbling and technology is shattering the
boundaries of the workplace, giving workers more choices than ever
in how to combine work and family. Families are changing in form,
children's developmental needs are better understood, workplace
policies are evolving and flexible-work opportunities have never
been greater.

Through all the changes, the mission of the "Work & Family"
column remains the same: To help individual readers align the
moment-to-moment reality of their daily lives with their most cherished personal values and responsibilities. In that, I hope, they
might attain that elusive Holy Grail of the modern age: The inner
peace that comes with leading a balanced and well-examined life.

Acknowledgments

I am so grateful to so many people for helping me create and sustain this column that I can only acknowledge a few of them. Above all, two managing editors of the *Journal* made it possible for the column to grow and flourish. Norm Pearlstine, now at Time Inc., saw merit in the idea, understood the readers I wanted to reach and encouraged me as I struggled to launch the column. The current managing editor, Paul Steiger, was enthusiastic about the column from its outset, when he was deputy managing editor. He has been incredibly helpful through the years and continues to advise and support me in every way. His belief in the mission of the column has inspired and sustained me many times.

Ron Alsop, editor of the Marketplace Page at the column's inception, provided advice and encouragement. Cynthia Crossen, Marketplace Page editor at the time of the column's 1994 expansion, risked devoting more space to "Work & Family" at a time when several hot topics were competing for readers' attention. She also helped me find my voice, and the intellectual courage, to give the column a distinct tone and flavor. Her successor, Kathy Deveny, helped me make the column more topical and hard-hitting. Mike Miller, current editor of the Marketplace Page, has provided a steady stream of creative ideas, insights and suggestions that have kept the column ahead of the news.

My column editors through the years, Don Arbour, Bob Muller, Rose Ellen D'Angelo and Stephanie Capparell, have honed my thinking, style and word choice and provided front-line reactions that helped me clarify my points. They also wrote all those clever, succinct headlines—all while keeping a sense of humor on deadline. Artist Carol Lay provides the ingenious, offbeat cartoons that attract so many readers to my work. Her drawings have made me laugh aloud over my morning coffee more times than I can recall.

Inside the *Journal,* many colleagues have been instrumental in the column's success. Dan Hertzberg, deputy managing editor, has been generous in his encouragement and support. Senior editor Larry Rout provided the idea for the column, the encouragement to keep it going and periodic suggestions and perspective. Carol Hymowitz, also a senior editor, has been a steadfast source of courage, ideas and insights.

In the field of work-family research and services, dozens of professionals have provided insights over the years in long, patient interviews and conversations. Though these sources are too numerous to name here, a few pioneers in the field have offered some of the most spirited and valuable discussions, including Dana Friedman, Fran Rodgers, Faith Wohl, Ellen Galinsky, Kathleen Christensen, Paul Rupert, Arlene Johnson, Diane Burrus and Jim Levine.

The idea of turning these columns into a book would never have hatched without the encouragement and advice of Walt Mossberg, the *Journal*'s pioneering personal technology columnist whose example has been an inspiration and a model to me. Jim Pensiero, an assistant managing editor of the *Journal*, helped implement the plan. And my editor, Susan Randol, helped define, design and polish it. Without these three people, there would be no book.

My family, of course, has made this volume possible in the most fundamental way. My eternal respect and gratitude are due my parents, Frank Shellenbarger and the late Martha Jane Shellenbarger, for their remarkable example of successful integration of hard work and a profound commitment to family. To my beloved stepchildren, Margaret Wade and Richard and Luke O'Connor, and children, Cristin and James O'Connor, I owe whatever parental depth, wisdom and restraint may be reflected in this volume.

Finally, I could never have sustained this work without the love and support of my husband, Richard O'Connor. Whatever creativity and energy I invested have been fueled by his unfailing belief in me. It has made all the difference.

Part One

STARTING A FAMILY

Seven months pregnant and a bureau chief for *The Wall Street Journal,* I once called a dozen reporters together for a staff meeting.

I settled my expanding bulk into a chair, my tentlike maternity dress billowing around me, and began summarizing for my staff the highlights of a managers' meeting I had attended in another city. On one issue, I remarked, "I'm going to try to tread lightly."

Carol Lay

Rolling his eyes, one reporter burst out: "Now THAT is going to be a real trick!" We all laughed, and my pregnancy, a matter none of us had discussed much, suddenly became OK to talk about.

With pregnancy, parental leave and inaugural ventures into the child-care market, many parents must find entirely new ways of relating to the worlds of work and home. They encounter both logistical and emotional challenges in managing lives split anew between competing responsibilities. The columns here offer perspective on some of the lessons parents too often learn the hard way: Planning ahead for parenting needs, finding the right child care and supervising it well, and managing the child-care breakdowns that can wreck even the best-laid plans. As the stories related here suggest, a little planning and sharing of experiences can help working parents achieve the sense of wholeness and competence we all strive for.

Employees, Managers Need to Plan Ahead for Maternity Leaves

Today's stripped-down workplace affords little time for motherhood.

When Tammy Hutchison, a pregnant computer-systems salesperson, was ordered to get bed rest by her doctor to avoid a premature birth, her boss called a week later: Had she had the baby yet?

When she explained that the point of resting was to avoid having the baby, he urged her—only half-joking, she says—to get up and jog around the block to speed things along, because he really needed her at work. When she had her baby five weeks later, on a Sunday, he was on the phone again, saying, "Great! We'll see you back here on Monday," she said.

Making time for prenatal care and maternity leave is causing problems for employees and managers. With a raft of federal laws, from the Family and Medical Leave Act to the Pregnancy Discrimination Act, protecting the 2.1 million working women who give birth each year, relatively few employers still fire women for getting pregnant.

But more subtle obstacles face pregnant women, who may be under pressure at work, rushed through maternity leave or denied comparable jobs or promotions when they return to a changing workplace.

Ms. Hutchison shortened her maternity leave to two months from a planned three. She says she found that when she returned to work, amid layoffs, a promotion that had been promised her, but not announced before she left, had been given to someone else. She sued her employer and the case was eventually settled, the terms of which are confidential, says Peggy Garrity of Santa Monica, Calif., the attorney who handled the case.

Such job pressures rob some new mothers of the joys of childbirth. Though a financial analyst for a New York employer tried to lay plans during her pregnancy to cover her work during her maternity leave, her boss and coworkers kept sending new duties her way. Calls from the office began nine hours after she gave birth, and she worked 15 to 25 hours a week throughout her 13-week leave. At one point, her boss "ripped into me for a half-hour" for not finishing some research.

Sometimes, she was so tied up on conference calls that she would have to let her baby lie crying when he awakened from a nap. "I can't tell you how many times I was in tears during my maternity leave, and it was supposed to be the happiest time of my life," the analyst says.

At worst, job pressures bear even greater risks. A study of 584 women at the University of California, Davis, shows that women lawyers who work more than 45 hours a week are three times more likely to experience miscarriage in the first trimester of pregnancy than women who work less than 35 hours.

If women are stressed or skip doctors' appointments, they may run a higher risk of giving birth prematurely, says Mary Scanlon, an assistant vice president at Cigna HealthCare, Hartford, Conn., which has studied prenatal-care issues. U.S. employers' health-care tab for such births: $5.6 billion a year.

One reason pregnant women are sometimes treated irrationally is the persistence of old stereotypes, such as the notions that all pregnant women lose interest in their jobs and eventually quit. In fact, a study of 140 bank employees found pregnant workers' performance ratings actually improved during pregnancy, says researcher Hal Gueutal, an associate management professor at State University of New York, Albany. Cigna says 80% of women return to work after maternity leave.

Also, it really is difficult, even for the most supportive manager, to cover maternity leaves. Jonathan Rubin, a father of two whose wife is a pediatrician, has no shortage of empathy for working mothers. Yet as manager of a pricing unit for Cigna, he admits it took a lot of planning and creativity to cover the leave of a pricing manager in his unit.

First, he scouted out an employee to fill in for the manager and convinced her boss to give her up for three months. Then, he and his team worked longer hours to cover the month it took to bring in the replacement. Finally, when the pricing manager returned and asked for a four-day work week, Mr. Rubin again bent the schedule. Although he says he "struggled to grasp, OK, what's the right thing to do?" he wanted to retain a skilled worker.

Cigna has developed a training program to support "expectant managers," debunking stereotypes and stressing managers' role in enabling women to take care of their pregnancies. At Owens & Minor, which put 100 managers through the training, the program "heightened awareness," says Henry Berling, executive vice president.

Cigna and Mr. Rubin give the following tips:

- Discuss and reach agreement with a pregnant worker on plans for covering her work while she's out; the best time is usually the sixth month of pregnancy.
- Openly discuss any worries coworkers have about covering for a woman on leave; draw on all resources, including other managers and units, to distribute work fairly.
- Be patient with new mothers' efforts to balance their expanded responsibilities.
- Weigh short-term scheduling hassles against the long-term benefits of retaining an employee; covering a mother's job for three months can be preferable to training a replacement for six.

—June 11, 1997

How to Screen Out a Working Parent's Worst Nightmare

As I prepared a few years ago to hire the first of what seems like several hundred child-care providers I've employed as a working mother, I called a nanny agency in a distant state that a friend had recommended.

I mailed information on our needs, then listened as the agency's owner described by phone a teenager she claimed would be a good fit. "When do I get to meet her?" I asked.

After a pause, she said, "Most people just take who we send."

Unfortunately for working parents, just taking who the agency sends is increasingly risky these days. If your stress level from juggling multiple roles isn't high enough yet, consider this: The need for careful screening of nannies and sitters has never been greater. A recovering job market is reducing the pool of applicants for child-care jobs. And more people with questionable backgrounds are applying for them. While most of the 300 or so nanny agencies in the U.S. are run by well-meaning people, and some provide excellent service, only about 10% to 30% do thorough background and criminal records checks on the people they place, according to estimates by several background-check services and nanny agencies.

Some agencies make false claims about screening. Though one young woman came highly recommended by a Chicago agency that claimed it had checked her references, Suzanne Shelton-Foley, owner of a Chicago marketing and public-relations firm, had an uneasy feeling about the applicant. When she called the references, it was clear that no one else had contacted them. "I can't believe she used me as a reference," one woman told her, adding that the applicant had "a serious cocaine problem" and that she had fired the woman after she vanished from the job for days without notice.

Such lapses can be more than an inconvenience. A California family employed a nanny through an agency for more than a month, allowing her to drive the children around, before an acquaintance of the nanny's told them her license had been revoked for drunken driving, and she had been convicted of theft. A background check confirmed the report, and the family fired the nanny, says a former agency owner familiar with the case.

Inadequate screening is one issue raised by a book to be published next month called *Circle of Fire* by Joyce Egginton, which revisits the 1991 burning death of a Westchester County, N.Y., infant, left in the care of a Swiss au pair. The book alleges that the nanny, who was acquitted of criminal charges in the case, set the fire in the home, and that some of her Swiss references were false and hadn't been checked by the agency that placed her. Laura Brevetti, a New York attorney for the nanny, says the book doesn't raise any new evidence and that the jury made the right decision.

The au pair program, a cultural-exchange initiative under which a handful of designated agencies bring young, mostly European women to the U.S. for 13 months, has met mounting criticism for inadequate screening of both nannies and the families who employ them. The U.S. Information Agency, which oversees the program, published new regulations last week requiring for the first time a criminal records check and a personality profile on applicants, among other things.

So what's a parent to do? If you use a nanny agency, it's important to ask exactly how much checking of candidates has been done. Agency fees range widely, from $800 to $3,000, and the quality of service is just as uneven. Some take only a cursory application. Others screen out 99% of the people who call. Two professional groups, the International Nanny Association, Norfolk, Neb., and the Alliance of Professional Nanny Agencies, Austin, Texas, set tough screening and ethical standards for member agencies.

If you're hiring on your own and have any doubts about a candidate's background, or if your agency doesn't do background checks, you can order one from a private background service for $50 to $250. But you must be willing to ask the candidate up front for a lot of personal information, including past addresses. A thorough check should include a state-by-state review of driving and criminal records for the past five to seven years, a Social Security number check and a credit check, says Lynn Peterson, owner of PFC Information Services, an Oakland, Calif., information broker.

Leaving out even one component can be risky. Denise Collins, owner of Aunt Ann's Agency in San Francisco, recalls screening a young woman whose application reflected 10 years' child-care experience and glowing references from three families. But while a criminal-records check in San Francisco, where the applicant said she had always lived, revealed no problems, a credit check showed other residences. A records search in those places revealed the woman had a felony drug conviction and, just a year earlier, had served prison time for assault with a deadly weapon. Her references were phony, too; one praised her performance as a nanny during the time she was in jail.

Even the best background check, of course, doesn't paint a full portrait of a candidate's personality and character. Increasingly, parents find that only careful, probing interviews of all references, even if an agency has already contacted them, can determine whether a nanny is suited for the job. In my case, I did hire that teenager the agency sent—and seven years later, I'm still getting calls from other parents for references.

—November 30, 1994

Child-Care Crunch Puts Parents Between the Kids and the Boss

It is one of parents' most painful dilemmas: Your boss changes your work hours, and you can't find child care.

You hit the phones to call child-care providers and find too-short hours or sky-high fees everywhere. A gut-wrenching mental image of your kids, home alone as you leave for work, clouds your thinking. You plead for understanding with your boss, who looks pained but offers little help.

Despite your best efforts, you just can't be at work when the boss wants. Then, you get fired.

Court dockets nationwide bear evidence of a trend: More workers are getting disciplined or fired because they can't find child care. Diane Mutchler, a Federal Express agent in Pittsburgh and mother of three, was fired after she failed to report to a night-shift assignment for lack of child care. Joy Newland, a clerk for a Minot, N.D., drug wholesaler and mother of three, lost her job because her boss assigned her to an "on-call" evening shift during hours no child-care provider would accept. David Prickett, a single father and mechanic for a Minneapolis circuit-board maker, was fired because he couldn't find child care for his shift.

After two decades of exponential growth in day care and working parents, why are employees still being forced to choose between their children and their jobs?

The answer is that the rules of the workplace are changing, and the child-care system isn't keeping up. As if turning your kids over to someone else every day weren't complicated enough, workers are losing control over their hours, too. Weekend and night work, forced overtime and involuntary part-time work with unpredictable hours are on the rise as employers fine-tune schedules to cut costs or improve service. But most child-care providers are mired in the 9-to-5 era, excluding part-timers and fining parents for picking up children late.

The clash poses one of the saddest no-win situations in today's workplace. Employers can't win when an employee lacks child care to comply with a schedule change. Their best hope, as a human resources executive at a New York financial services concern with 24-hour customer-service operations says, may be that "we've never had to fire anybody" for it.

But "companies sometimes forget that these employees live in the community," says Michael Lotito, West Coast managing partner for the law firm of Jackson, Lewis, Schnitzler & Krupman. Picture the egg on an employer's face, he suggests, if friends and neighbors ask a fired parent, " 'Hey, I thought you were working for ABC Corp.' And they say, 'Well, I was, but I couldn't find child care. So I go to my supervisor and he says he doesn't care about my kid—he's got a department to operate.' "

Employees can't win either. Many depend on child-care arrangements so fragile that they collapse at the slightest schedule change. In a handoff much like "a football game," a New York father says, he and his wife, who work back-to-back shifts at a pharmaceutical plant, meet at 3:15 P.M. daily at the plant. She watches their son in the car while he changes into his work uniform. He watches their son while she changes out of her uniform. She punches out at 3:30 P.M., they kiss goodbye, and he punches in a few seconds later.

Few people notice such stresses—until a parent panics and the problem erupts in its ugliest form. In a much-publicized case a few years ago, Chante Fernandez, an Elizabeth, N.J., single mother and full-time secretary, locked her five-year-old daughter in her car while she worked weekends at a second job at a nearby mall.

Defending her decision as "an act of desperation" after a fruitless search for weekend child care, Ms. Fernandez told police she badly needed the paycheck. Her fine on misdemeanor charges was suspended.

Such incidents "happen more often than anyone has record of," says Joan Zorza, senior attorney for the National Center on Women and Family Law. The dearth of child-care services, child-care advocates say, is society's failing. "The employer feels, 'Why should I be burdened? I haven't done anything,' " Ms. Zorza says. "In a sense, the employer is right."

But being right adds up wrong when employers are paying the

bill anyway—in lost workers and higher payroll taxes, as state courts increasingly hold employers responsible for unemployment compensation in child care–related firings. The best solution, consultants say, is for employer and employee to work together—with the employer helping look for child care and asking for volunteers to swap hours. Federal Express won't comment on Ms. Mutchler's case. But the company says it balances employees' needs with those of its operation and provides as much notice as possible to workers whose shifts are changed. It also recently added an employee child-care referral service.

"The employer is obliged not to be judgmental and to be willing to talk, investigate, evaluate different approaches," Mr. Lotito says. "After you go through all that, you may still have to say, 'There is nothing that I can do for you. But that doesn't mean I don't care.' "

The real question, perhaps, is whether anyone can care enough in today's workplace. With employers still more inclined to stretch workers further, clashes over child care are "only going to get worse," predicts the New York human-resources executive. The trend "is putting tremendous strain on people. We're only seeing the tip of the iceberg."

—October 12, 1994

Quality Day Care
Through the Eyes of a Child

W hen Seija Surr recalls her time in day care as a child, she doesn't remember whether she learned any words or what her teachers talked about.

Instead, the 27-year-old editor for a San Francisco publishing house recalls what she felt, saw and tasted—her affection for a favorite teacher, the sweet rainbow candy the teacher handed out, her purple blanket against her cheek at nap time, the cold metal jungle gym outside and her fear of falling from it. "It's funny, the kinds of things you remember—the social and tactile experiences more than academic things," she says.

What matters most to the nine million U.S. children in day care isn't licenses, computers, shiny toys or rainbow paintings on the walls, studies show. It is the quality of each child's experience. In that touchyfeely bit of truth lies a conundrum that bedevils parents and regulators alike: Things that can't be seen outside the classroom or regulated—how a child is treated and what he or she feels, hears, sees, tastes and touches while parents are absent—also have the biggest impact on the child's happiness and progress.

A child's moment-to-moment interaction with the adult in charge is the most potent factor. In a study of several child-care centers in Bermuda, the way teachers talked to children had the biggest effect on their happiness and skills. Teachers who gave kids information— "Oh, look at that firetruck, see how red it is"—and support—"That's great! You did such a good job"—fostered better progress than those who gave mostly orders or criticism, says Sandra Scarr, a professor at the University of Virginia and chairwoman of KinderCare Learning Centers, a child-care chain.

A secure relationship with the adult in charge gives a child confidence, says Carollee Howes, a professor and leading child-care researcher at the University of California, Los Angeles. "The child will feel, 'This person will take care of me, and I can explore this rich environment.' " Conversely, a broken relationship disrupts learning. Ms. Surr's most poignant memory of day care is her distress at losing a favorite teacher to another class.

If intangibles matter so much, how can a parent assess day-care choices? Some measurable traits, including those regulated by most states, can at least improve the odds for kids. Classroom ratios of one adult for every three to four infants, four to six two-year-olds and seven to 10 three-year-olds are recommended by the National Association for the Education of Young Children, a Washington, D.C., accreditation group. (Most states allow more children per adult.)

Though group size isn't regulated in many states, it's important. "One of my most terrible experiences was being in a room with 36 toddlers in diapers with nine caregivers," Dr. Howes says. "The ratio was 1 to 4, but there were simply too many people in a very, very stuffy room." The association recommends groups of six to eight for infants, eight to 12 for two-year-olds and 14 to 20 for three-year-olds.

Teacher training and education are linked in research to faster learning and socialization among kids. Also helpful are a structured program and orderly rooms with a variety of materials and activity spaces.

But none of these yardsticks guarantees a good experience for kids. After enrolling my toddler in a day-care center with good ratios and a stable staff, I was puzzled when he came home a wreck every day. A visit to the center revealed that teachers were swapping classrooms several times a day, so kids never knew who would be caring for them. Lacking stability, my son stopped talking much with anyone there, storing up his frustration for home.

Also, high-quality care is so scarce in many places half to three-quarters of parents who use day care feel they have no choices and must settle for what they can find, studies show—that parents lapse into denial about their kids' experience. A study by Debby Cryer, an investigator at the University of North Carolina, found that parents "significantly overestimated the quality of care their kids received," she says. In one center, researchers saw that none of the infants was fed on time, held or even diapered until just before the parents came. But though parents suspected problems, "almost all said they thought their child was the lucky one who got most of the attention," Dr. Cryer says.

Amid mounting concern about child-care quality, the national association has seen a sharp rise in centers seeking accreditation: 4,000 have gained accreditation, a third more than a year ago, and 7,000 more have applied. Accredited centers must submit annual reports; complaints prompt visits by the association. The group sets exacting goals for teachers' interactions with kids, including showing respect, affection, encouragement and emotional support. Employer support is rising, too. The American Business Collaboration, an employer group, is financing training for day-care center directors, urging them to have staffers spend more time on the floor with kids and include softness and texture in their surroundings.

And in comforting news, research shows that one factor parents can at least partly control—the quality of family life—matters most to children. A three-state study of 720 families shows that while day-care quality affects kids' development, family factors such as parental stress and income are as much as 20 times more powerful. "In the long run," Dr. Scarr says, "it's the families that are most important."

—January 18, 1995

Good, Early Care Has a Huge Impact on Kids, Studies Say

I f anyone had any doubts, new research out this month should erase them: The importance of the quality of care a child receives in the first three years of life is monumental.

A report set for release April 17 at a White House conference will show the nurturance a child receives can actually affect the capacity of the brain. Aided by new brain-imaging technologies, says Ellen Galinsky of the Families and Work Institute, New York, neuroscientists are finding that good nurturing and stimulation in the first three years of life, a prime time for brain development, activates in the brain more neural pathways, or synapses, that might otherwise atrophy, and may even permanently increase the number of brain cells.

Separately, a study sponsored by the National Institute of Child Health and Human Development, the broadest and deepest childcare research yet, shows high-quality care has effects so far-reaching that they even color the mother-child bond.

In tracking 1,161 children to age three so far, researchers said last week that high-quality care by nurturing, stimulating providers improves kids' scores on cognitive and language tests. It helps mothers behave more positively and sensitively to them. Also, for low-income mothers, good care can help them relate better to their children.

All this has chilling ramifications for the roughly three million kids three and under in poor-quality child care (based on Families and Work Institute estimates that about one-third of child care is potentially damaging). For those children, child care may

- Hurt intellectual and verbal skills.
- Increase their mothers' negativity toward them.
- Put those with poor or depressed mothers at greater risk by further eroding the mother-child bond.

• Deprive them of the stimulation needed to develop their brains to the fullest.

None of this will come as a surprise to experienced working parents, who know child-care quality has profound effects not only on kids' development but on the whole family. When Linda Foster, a management consultant, was looking for ways to stimulate her toddler's verbal skills, a skillful day-care teacher suggested she find some puzzles with pegs on the pieces that he could grasp easily. The result: Ms. Foster had a focal point for play with her son that helped the two sit down and talk for longer periods.

Two sisters who shared caregiving duties for management-consultant Anne Pauker's three children took them to visit family and friends working at the police station, where all the adults made a fuss over them. The kids "bonded with the [caregivers'] whole family," Ms. Pauker says. The outcome: happy, confident children.

The flip side: Bad child care is the developmental equivalent of a train wreck. Kellee Harris, who owns a sports-marketing firm, saw a day-care center transform her calm, happy three-month-old into a clingy, anxious baby in just two weeks. The baby was always sitting alone in a swing when Ms. Harris or her husband came. When the couple realized no one was holding or interacting with her, they immediately found better care.

And when Ms. Pauker's three-year-old started napping more than usual during a stint with a different caregiver, she concluded her child was depressed and fired her sitter. Only months later did the child ask, "Mom, why did [the former sitter] hit me?" As her child gradually opened up, Ms. Pauker learned the sitter had spanked her and frequently told her she was bad. More groundbreaking research, by Arthur Emlen at Portland State University and the Oregon Child Care Research Partnership, a consortium, confirms that parents do a fairly good job of differentiating between good and bad child care. In studies of 862 children, the factors parents saw as important—such as whether a child feels safe in care and gets a lot of attention, and whether a caregiver is open to new learning—correspond to ways experts evaluate care. Many parents use poor-quality care, Dr. Emlen found, not because they don't recognize it as bad, but because they feel helpless or believe they lack other choices.

The big picture that emerges suggests it's high time for an era of empowered child-care consumerism. The need for quality child care isn't going away; three decades after the advent of modern feminism, 55% of all working women's paychecks are deemed indispensable, providing half or more of family income.

We know a lot about how to improve child care. The Families and Work Institute found in Florida and elsewhere that quality can be improved without too much trouble, by raising providers' training and educational support and trimming group sizes—changes that, in those studies, didn't price anybody out of the market.

As important, based on the NICHD's and Dr. Emlen's research, is the ability of the family to find and manage care. Helping parents search for better care, understand their choices and exploit all resources could spawn more confident consumers, Dr. Emlen suggests.

American consumers are usually pretty savvy about seeking out good deals. A little support for families could go a long way toward relegating at least one notorious lemon—bad child care—to the scrap heap.

—April 9, 1997

Weighing the Risks of Watching a Nanny With a Video Camera

Is it a good idea to hide a camera in your home to videotape a nanny at work with your children? Beyond the nightmarish TV newsmagazine stories about child abuse, several factors suggest it's time for parents to re-think the issue.

Legal questions about videotaping are heating up. Criminal cases against nannies are rising as more parents press charges using video-taped abuse as evidence. At the same time, Lewis Maltby, head of the American Civil Liberties Union's workplace-rights unit, attacks secret taping in speeches before nanny groups as immoral and potentially illegal. He expects a test case soon to challenge taping without a nanny's consent. Even some nanny agencies are acknowledging the trend by insisting that nannies be asked in advance to consent to videotaping.

Though I've long opposed videotaping, two cases recently have shown me that it can be valuable in some situations. Neither of the couples involved had thought they ever would videotape their nannies or even want to. Both are glad they did.

In one case, a human-resources manager for a publishing concern had no problems with his nanny. An expert in hiring, he knew he had screened her well. He videotaped her only because he wanted to test an in-home camera that his company was considering offering employees as a child-care benefit. He and his wife were stunned by what they saw. The nanny failed to talk or play with the baby for hours and lay on the couch most of the day. She interacted with the baby for "all of 10 minutes" and scolded him by slapping him on the hand and tugging his hair, says the manager, who fired her.

Separately, an East Coast executive, also experienced in hiring, used a reputable agency, checked references and chose a nanny with a good six-year record. Later, she got glowing reports on the nanny from a baby-exercise instructor and a neighbor who saw her with her baby during the day. The baby seemed delighted to see the nanny.

But the baby had some puzzling bruises; a pediatrician said she might be falling against furniture. After asking the nanny to watch the baby carefully, the mother videotaped her. She still has night-mares about the Jekyll-and-Hyde performance she saw; "the nanny's personality changed dramatically" after the parents left, the mother says. She screamed at the baby, left her unattended for hours and slapped the baby across the face.

Parents all want their nannies to be Mary Poppins; they dream of making the nanny "a member of the family," and sometimes that happens. But let's get real. Being a nanny is a tough job; many are inexperienced and untrained—and sometimes have been under-paid and badly treated as well. A nanny's performance depends partly on her emotional connection with her best instincts, a link easily broken by an outbreak of abuse or misfortune in her own life. And the job's demands change over time, from coddling an infant to stimulating a schoolchild.

Thus it shouldn't be surprising that parents might want tools for monitoring performance. Many child-care centers already use video cameras. In private homes, the cameras can be bought, rented or in-stalled by professionals.

Of course, secretly planting a hidden camera in the philoden-dron bears risks. Your nanny may be doing fine, and discovering the camera may shatter her—or his—trust.

Also, you could become a test case for the ACLU. While federal law permits videotaping a nanny at work with a child in common ar-eas of a home, the practice becomes illegal under wiretapping law as soon as any personal conversations are captured on audiotape, for instance, if the nanny makes a phone call, Mr. Maltby says. Taping a nanny in a bedroom or bathroom is an invasion of privacy under common law. State laws on these issues vary.

A better route is to acknowledge the possibility of videotaping up front by disclosing it to nannies, preferably before hiring, and get-ting written consent. What many parents who videotape find, says Richard Heilweil of Babywatch, a Spring Valley, N.Y. provider of videotaping systems, isn't abuse but simply poor performance.

There are arguments against this option, too. If you doubt a nanny enough to need videotape, many say you should fire her. Probably true, but easier said than done. As a mother of nine years, I'd fire a questionable nanny in a heartbeat. Would I have acted as decisively as a new mother? Probably not.

Others say a nanny won't behave normally if she thinks she's being videotaped. It's true, I suppose, that a really bad nanny could take a child into a bedroom to avoid the camera. But that view is too cynical even for me. A videotaping agreement is more likely to make most nannies more self-conscious about performance, and that's a good outcome.

Critics also say talk of videotaping will poison the parent-nanny relationship. Maybe. But if it is cast in a constructive light, as a tool to monitor and improve performance, many nannies will learn to accept it. "I've come full circle" on videotaping, says Jacqueline Foote Clark. A former opponent, Ms. Clark, head of A Choice Nanny Franchise System, Bethesda, Md., now says, "If we see it as a helpful tool and use it as a helpful tool, our industry will be cleaner and our children will be better cared for."

—October 16, 1996

When Blizzards Hit, Day-Care Worries Snow Parents Under

When big storms hit, most people's work schedules are shaken or derailed. But working parents hit a special kind of stress overload.

Rugged weather like this week's Eastern blizzard often leaves schools and day-care centers closed and sitters stranded at home long after businesses, markets and offices reopen. Business deadlines hold firm, meetings at the office go on, deals get done and global customers demand service—all while families' house-of-cards child-care arrangements are tumbling down around them.

Child-care breakdowns set two-paycheck couples at war over who stays home with the kids. Deborah Swiss, a Boston author and gender-equity consultant, bumped into a friend Sunday who said she and her husband, anticipating the storm, had already slugged it out over Monday's child-care arrangements. "I've taken the last two snow days. And no matter what my husband says, he's staying home this time!" she said, her two young children in tow. Admitting defeat, her husband was working Sunday to get a jump on the week.

But even carefully made plans don't always avert stress. A New York couple agreed Monday that the husband, a bank manager, would stay home with their four-year-old and work on his laptop so the wife, a human-resource executive, could speak at a meeting.

But while the husband planned to take part by phone in a scheduled meeting at his own office, his home telephone lacks a "mute" button—a career-threatening flaw with a noisy preschooler nearby.

He tried to arrange for his son to play in a neighbor's apartment, but the child rejected the matchups he suggested.

Worse yet, the banker's boss had missed the voice mail he sent to report in from home that morning and was irate. "I got in. How come you're not here?" the boss demanded by phone.

"He's having stress," his wife sighed in a telephone conversation from her office. Father and son "will be a little grumpy when I get home," she predicted.

Even workers with older children and good home-office setups face multiple distractions. On a snow day last week, Marcia Brier, owner of MCB Communications, a Needham, Mass., marketing consulting firm, was deep in a complex conversation with a tax lawyer about limited-liability companies when her nine-year-old daughter slipped her a note asking for waffles for breakfast.

"I'm a good juggler, but that was a tough one," she says.

Then, the schools in Ms. Brier's area reopened two hours late the next day, threatening her plans to attend a 10 A.M. business meeting. Her husband couldn't help because he had to go to his law office. After trying to field business calls while looking for a place for her daughter to stay for two hours, she solved the problem with the help of a friend. But "it threw me into a tailspin," she says.

Working-parent guilt can assume draining proportions in such situations. Facing a deadline today on an important 100-page report, Tani Takagi, director of grants for a nonprofit foundation, felt bad about asking her sitter to brave the storm to come to her New York home Monday to care for her children, ages six and one. But her husband, a corporate lawyer, was expected at his office and couldn't help; and though Ms. Takagi was able to work on her home computer, she needed to concentrate. The sitter came, but Ms. Takagi felt so guilty, she let her leave early—then worked through much of the night to make up for lost time.

Chastened by severe child-care problems during the dozens of school shutdowns that marked 1993's hard East Coast winter, a few employers have taken steps to provide snow-day care. For the first time, NationsBank this week opened all five of the snow-day child-care programs it set up in 1994 at different sites, says Kimberly Hains, the company's work and family program director. "This will be a real test," she said.

Meanwhile, workers forced to sit out stormy workdays are often too stressed to enjoy it. When hurricane-force winds hit the West Coast last month, knocking out electricity in my neighborhood for four days, blocking streets with downed trees and shutting down everything but the workplace, I got a big dose of such anxiety.

A telecommuter without electricity or child care for my kids, ages five and eight, I tried to forget my looming deadlines and enjoy the unstructured time with them.

Forced away from my computer, I helped a neighbor salvage her belongings after a tree smashed her roof. The kids and I walked through the neighborhood, agog at the 100-foot Douglas firs felled by the storm, and the whole family spent evenings around the fireplace telling stories. Like this week's giant snow, the cold, dark silence was a sobering reminder of our interdependence and our relative frailty before Mother Nature.

Accepting our human limitations in these high-pressure times, though, takes conscious effort. I had a hard time relaxing during the West Coast shutdown; I found myself awakening at 2 A.M. and trying to work by battery-powered lantern.

Others exercise better self-control. Facing deadlines and worried about losing power, Ms. Swiss at first resisted her daughter's urging Monday to leave her computer and help build a snow fort. Then she reconsidered. Take time off, she told herself, "and you might be energized." And guess what? "I did it," she said. "And it was fun."

—January 10, 1996

Part Two

CREATING A HOME

Never before have Americans exercised so many different choices about how to set up their families.

Stereotypes about the American home typically make room for only two kinds of arrangements: The so-called "traditional" family with a man out working and a woman caring for the household, and the two-career pair with both spouses working days

Carol Lay

outside the home, then rushing around evenings to cram family life into a few hours. Laboring on the margins of this rigid worldview is the stressed-out single mother.

But a clearer look shows new family types blossoming, with many giving rise to creative and novel ways of combining work and family. One-third of dual-earner couples work back-to-back shifts, allowing their kids to be in full-time parental care. In other homes, husbands stay home while wives play breadwinner. Some workers start home-based businesses to integrate work and child-rearing, a fast-growing trend. In profiles in this section of Mike and Stephanie Bursek, John Morrissey and Christine Young, and John and Beth Makens Long, you will meet such families.

Others make even more offbeat approaches work. Dismayed by the effects of heavy business travel on his family, Joe Healey bought a 10-ton motor home and took them along on his travels. And in a quietly heroic achievement, Suzy Kellett, finding herself the single mother of quadruplets in her 20s, supported her four sons and daughters both financially and emotionally for the next 21 years, nurturing them to successful adulthood.

The crumbling of traditional gender roles is giving families unprecedented freedom in dividing household labor, the focus of several columns in this section. Finally, several others show how diverse family types have become a lightning rod for our national angst over the state of children, raising a painful backlash against working parents.

Couple Orchestrates Complex Dance Needed in Two-Career Home

I t's an hour before dawn and the outlines of the mountain behind Rick and Barbara Mauntel's Phoenix home haven't yet emerged from the darkness.

But Mr. Mauntel has already showered, dressed for work, read the paper and had coffee. At 6 A.M. he awakens Jeffrey, four years old, and Jillian, two. As Ms. Mauntel gets ready for work, her husband dresses the kids and makes them breakfast, then drops them at day care before heading for his job as a project manager at Motorola.

Ms. Mauntel's turn comes at 6 P.M. She will leave her job as a Motorola payroll manager to take care of the children, feed and bathe them before books and bedtime. Later, the couple will "fight for the computer" in their home office as both try to get some more work done before bed, Mr. Mauntel says.

Theirs is the complex dance of the dual-earner couple, their lives interwoven in every detail of work and family. Neither makes meeting or travel plans at work without checking with the other. Neither makes day-care plans for the kids without talking it over. And neither could reach valued long-term goals, including a secure retirement and college education for the kids, without the role-juggling of the other.

Traditional gender roles with their tidy division of labor are a hazy memory for the Mauntels; both had mothers who worked. But while Motorola provides far more support than most employers—a flexible work environment and such benefits as sick-child care—the couple lacks the extended-family network nearby on which their parents relied.

They also have higher-pressure jobs than their parents. Mr. Mauntel, 42, the engineer son of a health inspector and a home economist, manages an R&D team that competes with semiconductor makers world-wide to build more efficient chips. Ms. Mauntel, 39,

the CPA daughter of a trucking-company manager and a deli-
catessen manager, oversees paychecks for 15,000 employees.

Their careers wax and wane on each other's support. Ms. Mauntel coasted briefly in a job as a tax-department analyst at Motorola
after Jeffrey was born so she could manage all the child care. But "I
paid the big price for that" with a slowdown in career growth, she
says. To help her regain momentum, Mr. Mauntel started sharing
the load at home; she has since been promoted twice. Without his
support, she says, "I couldn't do it. There's no physical way."

As her career takes off, his "is starting to plateau a little" with all
his juggling, he acknowledges. A manager for 12 years, with a prestigious string of patents for his team's inventions lining his office, he
has little to worry about in terms of his professional standing.

But some friends his age are vice presidents, including some who
admitted to him bypassing having children for career. Asked if that
frustrates him, he says, "I don't think about it . . . I'm not saying I'm
not ambitious. But there's more to life than just the job."

Quite a bit more, based on the Mauntels' daily routine. Each carries a mobile phone and pager, with private pager signals to each
other like "911-911-911" for emergencies. When a day-care center
wanted them to pick up Jeffrey at midday, it was Mr. Mauntel who
dropped everything to go. When Ms. Mauntel's job demands long
hours, he backs her up, slipping out of meetings at 5:15 P.M. to
check on her plans.

The same give-and-take marks their child-care choices. When Jeffrey once had trouble adjusting to a day-care center, Ms. Mauntel fa-
vored easing his stress by switching to a new center for a half-day
and hiring a nanny for afternoons. But Mr. Mauntel balked at the
$15,000-a-year cost. Frustrated, she typed a proposal with child-care
alternatives evaluated as Option 1, Option 2, etc. and presented it to
him, manager-style, for a decision. He agreed to her preference.
And Jeffrey is now faring better.

"Some people take vacations to Hawaii. We spend our money on
child care," she says.

Both feel guilty a lot, worrying that they spend too much time
away from their jobs—and their kids. As Mr. Mauntel drops them off
at day care one recent morning, Jillian clings to his leg, then drops
sadly to the floor as he leaves. "They say she's fine five minutes after

I leave," he says, his brow furrowed with worry. "But I never get to see that part."

Both battle constant fatigue. Though they talk by phone a half-dozen times a day, they are often too tired by dinner to talk. After trying to make conversation one evening, Ms. Mauntel told her husband, "Listen, I'm just going to go down to the store and call you." Free time is spent with the kids; neither can remember the last time they went out as a couple.

But clearly, the Mauntels are moving to the same background music: the knowledge that meeting their long-term financial goals requires two incomes. To fortify that perspective, Mr. Mauntel often retreats near midnight to the patio behind their Santa Barbara–style house, sets up his telescope among the brittlebush and potted rosemary there, and gazes at the stars.

A photo he took of the Orion Nebula graces his office wall, among pictures of the kids. "It's restful. It's quiet," he says of his hobby. And it's guilt-free; "it doesn't take time away from the family, because they're sleeping.

"And who knows? Maybe someday the kids will be interested" in the stars, he says. "I can't teach them without knowing it myself."

—February 28, 1996

Chicago Couple Finds Rewards in Defining New Family Roles

One recent day, Christine Young was busy doing what a growing number of women do: Trying a case. In a courtroom in downtown Chicago, the 5-foot-2-inch assistant district counsel for the U.S. Immigration and Naturalization Service called out objections and grilled witnesses with a rigor that has earned her the nickname "The Pit Bull."

Eleven miles south in Beverly, a Chicago neighborhood, her husband John Morrissey, also an attorney, was doing what few men do: Taking care of the kids all day. In their rambling Victorian house, the 6-foot-2-inch former rugby star cuddled 1½-year-old Fallon, comforted five-year-old Liam when he bruised his knee and worried about how the children will fare if he goes back to work full time.

The couple has turned traditional gender roles upside down, a radical thing even in the '90s. Taking a few days' paternity leave may be stylish in some circles, but quitting your job, as Mr. Morrissey did, is not, bringing isolation and sometimes ostracism. But Mr. Morrissey, 34 years old, and Ms. Young, 36, have found their arrangement rewarding, creating not so much an altered version of the traditional family as a new kind of family, with both parents deeply involved with their children.

They have taken their share of static; with others, they find their arrangement is a kind of Rorschach test on gender roles. When Ms. Young a few years ago asked Mr. Morrissey's father, the immigrant patriarch of a traditional Irish clan and founder of a construction company, what he would think of a man who stayed home with the kids, the elder Mr. Morrissey replied, "I would think he was a sissy." (He quickly backtracked, saying, "If John did it, I would think it was fine.")

After seeing Mr. Morrissey with Liam every day, one newsstand operator assumed that the child's mother was dead and started giving Liam candy. At the park, mothers sidle away from Mr. Morrissey and the children, and some insist on talking to Ms. Young when they telephone. Both parents suspect Fallon has missed out on play dates.

There are other costs. To stay home, Mr. Morrissey, who formerly handled appeals for the Illinois attorney general, gave up a job he had just attained in the trial division, a post he had worked years to get. But staying home meshed better with his long-term goal of a solo practice, and the couple's incomes were about equal.

When he told his family the news, he worried that his traditional brother, whose wife stays home with the kids, would say, "Great, I'll buy you a couple of skirts." (He didn't.)

But for both Mr. Morrissey and Ms. Young, the unconventional arrangement is healing old wounds. Before Fallon was born, they tried the usual two-jobs-and-a-day-care-center route with Liam, but a string of hair-raising child-care experiences—including one center where Liam, then 1½, was strapped into a chair alone and left to cry—upset them both. Now, Ms. Young says, she enjoys peace of mind.

As a child, Mr. Morrissey wished for more time with his entrepreneur father. And Ms. Young was hurt by lifelong estrangement from her father, who divorced her mother when she was a child. The experience, she says, left her believing that "the most important thing about a man was that he be a great father."

One recent afternoon at home, Mr. Morrissey meets Liam's bus from camp, listens intently when his son complains, "I hurt my leg," then studies the invisible bruise, brow furrowed, until the pain stops. Fallon, just up from a nap, turns her face into her father's shoulder to avoid a stranger's gaze while Liam pats his sister's back, leaning against Mr. Morrissey's knee.

Ms. Young remains very involved with the kids as well, bathing and reading to them at night and spending more time with them on weekends. This is a distinguishing trait of families with stay-at-home dads, says a recent study of 93 families by Robert A. Frank, a doctoral student at Loyola University of Chicago. While the fathers lend a strong male influence and become better at nurturing, the working mothers also stay deeply involved.

Such couples seldom reverse household roles completely, Dr. Frank found. "Why are you cooking dinner, Dad?" Liam asked on his father's first evening at the stove. The rest of the family wondered the same thing after Mr. Morrissey, working from his new *Dad's Own Cookbook*, misread a fish-stew recipe, spent $60 on ingredients and produced enough to feed 55 people. Now, Ms. Young plans menus and Mr. Morrissey prepares them.

For Mr. Morrissey, attaining his own career goal of a solo law practice has been harder than he expected. Fitting client work into nap times and evenings is hard, and he lost one client when Liam screamed for help in the bathroom while he was talking on the phone. (He has since set up an office nearby and gets occasional child-care help so he can work.)

But for him and Ms. Young, the balance works. Mr. Morrissey's example has even won over his brother, who recently declared, "I'd love to stay home with the kids."

Though Mr. Morrissey loved his job, caring for the kids has been more rewarding, he says. "If someone walked up to me and said, 'I took over your job and I [argued a case before] the Supreme Court,' I'd say, 'That's great, but I took Fallon to the park today,' " he says. "Sometimes when I'm sitting there in the park and the kids aren't fighting and the sun is shining, I think, 'It doesn't get any better than this.' "

—August 16, 1995

For the Burseks, Best Parent Regimen Is Back-to-Back Shifts

It's 2:15 P.M., around the time many people in corporate life are just getting back to the office from lunch.

At the Seattle home of Stephanie and Mike Bursek, it's time for The Hand-Off.

Ms. Bursek is getting home from her job as a trainer for Eddie Bauer, and Mr. Bursek is about to leave for his, as a color-camera specialist in a printing plant. His eight-hour shift caring for the couple's two preschoolers is ending, hers is beginning. Spencer, age four, and Audrey, one, bounce happily underfoot.

"What about diapers?" Ms. Bursek asks.

"Changed at 12:20," her husband replies.

"Bottles?"

"Three."

"Lunch?"

"Pizza, watermelon and Cheerios. Audrey ate well," he replies. The rapid-fire talk continues as Ms. Bursek runs to the bedroom to change from suit to tunic and tights. Twenty minutes later, Mr. Bursek kisses his wife and heads for work.

They won't see each other awake again for 24 hours.

In a huge but mostly overlooked piece of the American child-care picture, one-third of all dual-earner couples with children under five work back-to-back shifts, says Harriet Presser, a University of Maryland professor and an authority on shiftwork. The setup tends to be good for kids. It's evident to a visitor that the Bursek children are happy, confident and secure.

But "what may be good for the children may not be good for the marriage," Dr. Presser adds. Not only do the parents both work a "second shift," but they lack time together, contributing to what she is calling a "substantially higher" divorce rate than average.

That's news to the Burseks, who have been tag-team parents for four of the 7½ years they've been married. Their example sheds light on what it takes to make this tough setup work:

An overriding desire to be with your kids. Initially, the Burseks put Spencer in a child-care center. Though he did fine and the center provided good care, it was "heartbreaking" for both parents, Ms. Bursek says. "It was such a long time away from him." Though she loved her job, she was ready to "chuck it all."

As it happened, Mr. Bursek's employer moved him to nights and he started keeping Spencer home some days. The easygoing Mr. Bursek, who was one in a family of four boys, discovered a delight in fatherhood that surprised them both. On long outings he called "Two Guys Doing Stuff," he and Spencer watched deer on Mount Rainier or studied fingerlings at a fish hatchery. Ms. Bursek had to buy a pager to keep in touch. "I fell in love with Mike all over again, watching him," she says. "He was so enthusiastic." Spencer thrived and they made the setup permanent, allowing Ms. Bursek to enjoy her job again, she says.

The Burseks' desire to be with their kids trumps just about everything else in their lives. Though Mr. Bursek, who is 35, loves to tinker with "anything with an engine," he has mostly set his hobby aside. "My kids need a father more than I need a Harley."

Flexible goals. Ms. Bursek, 33, has a flair for fashion and dreamed of a career as a buyer. But after Spencer was born, she gave up a hard-won post as an assistant buyer at Eddie Bauer, the retailer based in Redmond, Wash., for her current 35-hour-a-week job as merchant-education specialist. Unexpectedly, she discovered she loves the work. She acknowledges she could probably be making $30,000 more a year on the fast track, based on the progress of her peers. That's only partly offset by the more than $1,000 a month they save on child care. (Spencer attends preschool part-time.) Their 1,000-square-foot house is cramped, and they drive old cars. But their combined income "in the high 70s," she says, covers the essentials, such as visits to both sets of grandparents in California.

Control over work time. If Ms. Bursek didn't get home from her 6:30 A.M. to 2 P.M. workday by 2:15 P.M., Mr. Bursek would have been late to his 3 P.M. to 10:30 P.M. shift at the *Seattle Times,* a job he loves. That requires her to exercise a degree of control over her time rare among professionals. She credits her bosses at Eddie Bauer with giving her the support she needs. If work spills over, she goes in on an occasional Sunday.

Planned fun. The Burseks swap babysitting with friends now and then. Mostly, though, weekends are prime family time. Mr. Bursek prepares special dinners. Saturday is "Wrestling Night" with the kids. Sometimes, they take a spin in his latest toy, a 1958 Edsel; for effect, Ms. Bursek dons cat's-eye shades and a pony tail. "We're always looking for a reason to laugh," she says.

None of that changes the fact that the Burseks mostly see each other asleep during the week—a hurdle both say can be surmounted only by a strong partnership, and a shared belief that their setup is ideal for their kids. "It is hard. It really is; there's no way to sugar-coat it," Mr. Bursek says. Asked what it takes, he lists: "One, patience. Two, patience. Three, understanding."

After answering more questions, he pauses. "By the way, could you also put in the fact that I love my wife very much? Can you squeeze that in there somewhere?"

Consider it done.

—February 25, 1998

Single-Parent Woes Times Four Didn't Dent Her Career or Family

A treacherous storm struck while Luke, Tyler and Abby Kellett were climbing Mount Hood earlier this year. Subzero temperatures and 50-mile-an-hour winds buffeted their tent, threatening to rip it off the glacier where they camped.

But using "all the smartness they had," says their mother Suzy Kellett, the siblings secured the tent, checked it through the night—and survived. Most important, she says, "they stayed very confident, very calm."

As a single working mother of 21-year-old quadruplets, Suzy Kellett, 51 years old, knows something about staying calm in a storm, and she has taught the quads—Luke, Tyler, Abby and Gwen—to do the same. Unruffled by crises that always seem to come in threes and fours—such as the time three quads landed in the hospital in a single week with playground injuries needing stitches—Ms. Kellett charted a steep career ascent in the film sector and built a strong family.

Though single-parent families take a lot of criticism these days, the Kelletts' story shows how successful such families can be when trust, firm rules and a strong parental example of resiliency are present.

A former teacher, Ms. Kellett dreamed in her 20s of raising a family with her husband in their house near Sun Valley, Idaho. But when her husband left her alone with 10-month-old quads, she retreated to the Northfield, Ill., home of her parents, Patty and John Boylston.

She soon landed a receptionist's job for a magazine and rose through a series of research and editing posts. Adapting "like a chameleon" to opportunities, she moved to the Illinois Film Office, a public agency that recruits filmmakers to the state, and soon won the prestigious job of agency director, where her hours were long but more flexible. She lured the makers of such box-office hits as

Risky Business and *Home Alone* to Chicago. Having the quads, says Ms. Kellett, now head of the Washington State Film Office in Seattle, "made me strive much higher in my life than I would have" without them.

All the while, she and her mother pieced together child care, hiring live-in sitters. She often piled the quads into the car to scout movie locations; "look for a yellow house with a porch," she would say. When they were eight, the family moved to a town house near her parents.

The Kelletts faced all the pressures typical in working families, times four. Ms. Kellett agonized over her frequent business trips, putting letters on each child's pillow before she left. At home, she had to spend so much time on "maintenance," such as shopping for $200 in weekly groceries, that she feared the kids "were raising themselves." She adds, "I knew I had to figure out creative ways to keep this family together."

She taught them to help one another, down to buttoning each other's shirts before kindergarten. "For this family to work without a daddy, we've got to work together. It's going to be tough, but we can make it," she told them. With the challenge, Abby says, "she made us feel special."

The children grew so used to sharing everything, including a bedroom at their grandparents', that moving to a home with separate rooms for boys and girls was a shock. Enraged at the sight of his sisters' locked door, Luke took a running start and knocked the door off the hinges. "Having actual possessions? In this family?" Tyler explains. "If he hadn't done it, I would have."

Ms. Kellett nurtured that closeness. Drawing on the power of darkness to create a sense of safety, Ms. Kellett held "tea times" at 9 P.M. in their darkened living room or in the field behind their town house. "There was richness in those conversations in the darkness," she says.

She set simple but firm house rules, never broke a confidence and welcomed the quads' friends into their home, which became known as "Camp Kellett." Each night, she sat by each child's bed and, again in darkness, gently probed each one's concerns. "She wouldn't wait for us to come talk about our problems," Luke says. "She'd ask. She always assumed there was something."

Echoes of their mother's drive began surfacing in the quads' lives. Noting that "Mom always had a script in her hand," Gwen started critiquing movie scripts in seventh grade and as a teenager became a performer, singing at country clubs and hotels. Gwen's rules of thumb, learned from her mother: Adapt. Don't waste time. And do what you want to do. After Ms. Kellett promised the quads they could attend any college if they stayed on their high school honor roll, they did. With help from her ex-husband and parents, the quads are seniors now at the universities of Washington and Colorado, pulling down good grades in tough science-related fields.

Though they are living apart now, the Kelletts' bonds remain strong. When the quads met at Luke's frat party at University of Colorado, they spent the evening sitting in a circle together on the floor while the party swirled around them. "We can still sit around in a pitch-dark room and laugh for hours," Abby says. And their love of family life, in the nontraditional form they know, seems certain to endure. All want spouses with careers; Tyler, an aspiring teacher, would like to be a stay-at-home dad for a while. And they insist they wouldn't mind having quadruplets. "I dreamed I had quads, and the doctor said, 'These are all yours,' " Gwen says. "I said, 'Oh no! Oh no!' " But when she awoke, she realized, "I would want it just the way we had it."

—September 18, 1996

Couple Unites Career and Family with Help from a Mobile Home

T he 10-ton motor home rolls like a battleship through the night and plows to a stop before me outside the Kansas City, Mo., airport terminal. Entry steps unfold from its 34-foot side and a door opens, spilling a rectangle of light on the pavement. Curious, I climb the stairs.

Inside is Joe Healey's life.

Not just his vacation home, mind you, but his whole life: his full-time office, his home, his wife's home, their three kids and the kids' home school, down to their damp P.E. garb hanging in the cramped bathroom.

For Mr. Healey has achieved perhaps the ultimate integration of work and family. Instead of leaving his family behind when he travels for his work as a professional speaker, he takes them along in the RV. The Healeys have trekked 34,000 miles through 39 states in the past 13 months, with Mr. Healey making 10 speeches a month and his wife Jill home-schooling Joseph, 11 years old; Jennifer, eight; and Josh, seven, in the RV's 320-square-foot interior.

It seems impossible. Wouldn't anyone go crazy?

Yet this family, I learn during my visit and subsequent interviews, is anything but frazzled. The children are cohesive and charming. Ms. Healey is pleased with the fruits of their lifestyle. And Mr. Healey, who posted 1996 income of more than $100,000—a record for him—says the sense of life balance he has gained enriches his work. "That's the part that has been amazing to us," he says. Living like nomads "hasn't been the challenge that people think."

Previously, as an entrepreneur running a dry-cleaning chain, then a self-employed speaker traveling heavily, Mr. Healey saw far too little of his family to suit any of them. Still, when he floated the idea of traveling together, Ms. Healey reacted at first as any normal person might: "You're nuts," she said.

But upon reflection, she says, the potential benefits, including family time together and "field trips" for the kids, changed her mind. They bought and equipped the RV with a desk in the shotgun seat, where Mr. Healey can work on the road; the couple share the driving. A wall desk and a fold-out table provide school space. A section of the side wall slides out to expand the interior. The RV also has enough printing, computer and communications gear to command battalions on the march.

To ease cabin fever, Mr. and Ms. Healey spell each other with the kids; when Ms. Healey needs a break, she takes an evening alone at a bookstore. The kids use their in-line skates, and the family uses pools and exercise rooms in hotels where Mr. Healey appears. He addresses corporate, government and public audiences on time management, technology and communication skills, booked partly through National Seminars of Shawnee Mission, Kan.

Navigating the RV to Mr. Healey's clients isn't easy. En route to Long Island, fellow travelers misdirected them straight into a Manhattan traffic jam. With the RV stranded like a beached whale amid incredulous, honking New Yorkers, Mr. Healey jumped out at a stoplight and found one kind soul who led them out of the mess.

The logistics can be trying. After the family had planned a day at the beach, a snafu in the RV's wiring forced Mr. Healey to spend two hours fixing it. Then, the kids locked the bathroom from the inside; finally, the RV steps caught and bent on a highway guardrail. After pounding a counter in frustration, Mr. Healey spent two more hours on repairs. Exhausted, the family retreated to an RV park.

Shortly after that, Mr. and Ms. Healey discussed returning home. But the children, led by Joseph, staged a presentation on why they should continue, citing the "great education" they were getting from exposure to new people and places, from St. Patrick's Cathedral in New York to the Grand Canyon. In a letter, Joseph wrote, "I do not know of any other parents that . . . support [their children] like you do." The Healeys hung in.

In ensuing weeks, benefits blossomed for the adults. Ms. Healey says she loves the family time and watching her children learn. Mr. Healey, instead of rushing through airports, spends evenings talking with Joseph about Abraham Lincoln, a shared interest discovered on a Springfield, Ill., visit, or reading Garrison Keillor aloud. "One of the great things," Ms. Healey says, "is just laughing together before we go to bed."

Always successful as a speaker, Mr. Healey began leavening his talks by revealing more of himself, including family stories; audiences respond warmly. The rock-tumbler of family life also has helped him cultivate inner peace. When more mishaps (a windstorm, a plumbing leak and another accident with the RV steps) fouled their day recently, the children looked at Mr. Healey wide-eyed, expecting him to explode and pound the counter. But Mr. Healey took it in stride. "Let's just go on," he said calmly. His children cried, "Daddy, that's really good!"

The Healeys' odyssey will end this summer, when the family will settle in Pittsburgh near family and enroll the children in school. In some ways, Mr. Healey is a little sad. Sprinting through the Kansas City airport with me as I catch a plane home, he says, "You know, this reminds me. Running through airports is something I haven't missed. Not at all."

—March 26, 1997

One Entrepreneur Who Shapes
Success to Fit Family Needs

A visit to Beth Makens Long's four-bedroom Tudor house in Orland Park, Ill., a Chicago suburb, offers no clue that she runs a $17 million business from the basement.

Her home is unpretentious, her office well-equipped but utilitarian, with outdoor carpeting and plain furniture. Evenings and weekends, her children, Conor, three years old, and Meaghan, two, clamber over her desk and tap out games on her computers.

But Ms. Long, 36, earns $100,000 to $200,000 a year from that office as a manufacturers' rep selling capital equipment at $500,000 and up to the utility industry. She could move into an office suite and hire a staff if she wanted; in the past, she has done twice her current annual sales. But she is holding her business in check and tailoring her strategy to harmonize with family needs.

Many people start businesses to gain control over their lives, only to find themselves again consumed by their work, either by success or by the struggle to survive. Ms. Long is avoiding that trap, controlling her business's growth while keeping it well-positioned for the future.

That achievement, her story shows, is far more than a single decision or event, but a day-to-day process of weighing business against personal goals.

As an entrepreneur, Ms. Long says "that spirit just drives you" to expand the business. The daughter of a man who always had several companies going at once, Ms. Long in her 20s jettisoned a "stifling" first career in banking in favor of sales. "I want to sell. I want to sell big stuff," she told her father. He introduced her to a friend who taught her to sell really big stuff: boilers, scrubbers and other parts for power plants, steel mills and paper factories, drawing 1% to 10% on sales as big as $40 million. Working 80-hour weeks, she became the firm's top producer.

After the friend died, Ms. Long started her own business in a suburban office and expanded it to $30 million in sales with two employees. She also met and married John Long, a utility executive, then merged her company with a bigger mechanical-contracting firm. Through two pregnancies, she continued to go flat-out, bagging a $275,000 order from her hospital bed the day after Conor's birth. She hired a live-in sitter and returned to work in six weeks.

But by Meaghan's birth, she had wearied of her employer's demands that she work 8-to-5 weekdays and attend numerous meetings, despite the long evening hours she had to put in with clients. As she held her new baby, "I realized I had missed the first 1½ years with Conor," she said. "He liked the babysitter better than me. I decided if I was going to work that hard, it was going to be for myself and my family."

In January 1995, she resigned and started Connemara Ltd., named for Conor and Meaghan.

The business grew so fast that by last spring work again was consuming her; she was taking on more and more product lines. "I said to John, 'I'm doing fantastic.' And he said, 'Yeah, I know. When is the last time you took a day off with the kids?' " Once, when she and John continued to work, mobile phones at their ears, on what was supposed to be a day off at their Lake Geneva, Wis., condo, Ms. Long had a moment of truth. "Our 2½-year-old and 3½-year-old are bobbing in the water and we're both doing business. It was the silliest scene." She turned to him and asked, "What are we doing here?"

Back home again, she sent "Dear John" letters to customers telling them politely she was dropping several lines. "They couldn't believe it," she says. One customer asked her, "Beth, what are you doing? You could make $100,000 a year just on this one line."

But that $100,000 would cost her 10 hours a week of precious time with John, Conor, Meaghan and her stepdaughter Kristin, 19, who visits often. "It was hard. There's a part of me that says, 'Go for the gusto. Why limit yourself?' Then I go back to, when you die no one ever says, 'Gee, I wish I had worked harder.' "

Time is increasingly precious as her kids get older. "If you don't catch these few moments, pretty soon they'll be off to high school and you'll have missed it," she says. Early morning is prime "cuddle time" with Conor and Meaghan. "If somebody says, 'How about that 8 o'clock meeting?' I say, 'How about that 9 o'clock meeting?' " One recent morning, she and the kids piled into the car to chase a fire engine. Other days, they have lunch dates.

All the while, she positions her business to stay vital. Though she recently turned down a high-paying job with a consulting firm, she offered to sell the firm's utility-consulting services, in anticipation of growing demand amid deregulation. She has invited a friend into the business as a partner, to give her more flexibility to build new lines.

Friends sometimes needle her. "Beth, you could be a millionaire!" one said. But if she focused exclusively on work, she thought, "I'd have all these trophies and when I died, there'd be five people who cared enough to come to my funeral." She paraphrases a quote credited to the late Jacqueline Kennedy Onassis that has become a kind of personal mantra: "If you screw up raising your kids, nothing much else you do in life matters."

—August 28, 1996

More Men Move
Past Incompetence Defense
to Share Housework

I f you ever want to start an argument at a party, just ask a group of dual-earner couples, "Now that you're all working full-time, do you split the housework evenly, too?"

Chances are, the men will say they do their fair share at home. The women will say they don't. The only thing couples are likely to agree on: The way they divvy up housework is changing.

As women assume a more crucial role as family breadwinners, many are renegotiating the traditional household roles that kept them working a "second shift" at home for decades after feminism opened doors at work. (Nearly half of married working women, or 48%, provide half or more of their household's income, says a 1995 poll by Families and Work Institute and others.) Though every couple is unique, men generally are helping out more at home; in a 1991 survey of 4,806 corporate employees by the University of Dayton and Utah State University, men and women agreed that men share housework more than what was shown in a 1986 survey. A study by Rosalind Barnett of Radcliffe College found dual-earner men doing 45% of the household chores (though women still do most of the repetitive, mindless tasks like cleaning). Also, fathers are spending 66% as much time with children as mothers, up from 50% in 1981, says Joseph Pleck of the University of Illinois.

But the shift to shared housework is far from complete. Most couples today are in what sociologists call the transition stage—evolving between "traditional" roles, with women taking sole responsibility for homemaking, and "egalitarian" roles, with men and women sharing equally the burdens of homemaking and earning money, says Leah Potts Fisher of the Center for Work and the Family, Berkeley, Calif., who runs workshops for couples on such issues.

In many households, that evolution is happening fast. Craig and

Amy Corbin of Orlando, Fla., began their marriage five years ago on some traditional assumptions. "From the beginning, the understanding was that his career was primary, and when kids came along, I would take a back seat," says Ms. Corbin. But when Ms. Corbin's career as an auditor at Deloitte & Touche took off, both began valuing her job more, not only financially but for her self-esteem. To allow both to "pursue our careers 110%," they worked out a housework-sharing system, says Mr. Corbin, a senior claims specialist for an insurer. They divide responsibility so each works about the same amount of time daily on housework and care for their 17-month-old daughter. When one devotes more time, he or she gets free time on the weekend.

Such sharing can give a major boost to a woman's career. When Deloitte invited Ms. Corbin, an audit-staff supervisor, to take on an enticing three-month project in Hartford, Conn., her husband, well-practiced at housework and child care, told her, "I think we can make this work," and encouraged her. Ms. Corbin accepted and is commuting home weekends; she gives her husband broad credit for affording her "the opportunity to take assignments like this one."

Sheer overwork is forcing many women to break the traditional female silence on the issue. When Diane Nobles, a vice president at Caremark and mother of two preschoolers, took on major new job duties 1½ years ago, she had to admit, "I can't do everything anymore," she says. She asked her husband, a management consultant, for more help; now he does most of the laundry, among other things.

"A few years ago, I would have bottled it up inside and stewed about it," she says. "But I can't afford to do that anymore. I've got enough other stress points without worrying about the laundry."

More women are rejecting what one calls the incompetence defense—men's plea that they just can't do housework right. When one accountant criticized her husband of five years for leaving her all the housework, a situation she said was slowing her progress on the job, he protested that he would only "screw it up," says Cathy Feldman of Blue Point Books, the Santa Barbara, Calif., publisher of *I Work Too,* a collection of dual-earner interviews.

The accountant replied: "I'm not touching anything for the next five years, and I'm going to put 100% into my career. I guess you'll just make a mess until you learn to do things right," Ms. Feldman says. Left to his own devices, the husband learned fast and started doing more.

Other women are learning to accept less than perfection. After Jayne Oliva and her husband divided chores, he washed the clothes but left them sitting crumpled in the laundry basket. Ms. Oliva, a self-described neatnik who runs her own medical-practice consulting business, restrained herself from folding it; instead, she bought "large quantities of underwear." Now "he has learned that I won't jump in, and eventually he gets to it."

Ms. Fisher urges couples to hold meetings to divvy up chores. Ms. Oliva has weekly talks with her husband, calendar in hand, to plan home duties.

From Ms. Fisher's perspective, the trend seems likely to accelerate. Younger couples in her workshops are more at ease sharing housework, and the next generation may be even more egalitarian, she says; "I see my teenage son confiding to his buddies, 'The really cool girls want men who can cook.' "

—February 21, 1996

Good News at Last
in the Battle of the Sexes:
Men Are Helping More

I t's fashionable these days to highlight the ways—beyond the obvious—that men and women are different. Women communicate differently from men, linguists say. Women's brains work differently, neuroscientists say. Men are from Mars, women are from Venus, says author John Gray.

Now come workplace researchers telling us something really different: Men and women are a lot more alike than you may think.

The time men and women put in caring for family and doing housework, their reactions to work-family conflict, the ways they want to structure work around family—all are growing so similar that seasoned researchers are flabbergasted.

"Phenomenal" is how longtime workplace researcher Ellen Galinsky, of Families and Work Institute in New York, describes the changes in men's roles documented in the institute's National Study of the Changing Workforce, released today.

"We saw so little gender difference that it really took us aback," says veteran researcher Marcia Brumit Kropf at Catalyst in New York, of its recent study of working couples.

The notion of the '90s man as more sensitive and attuned to relationships isn't new. But up to now, the documented changes in men have been mostly attitudinal—showing, for example, that men feel stressed over work-family conflicts previously thought to affect only women.

Now, studies show that men are actually changing their behavior. Most of the changes cut across demographic groups and encompass men in both single- and dual-earner households, suggesting a mainstream shift among men toward greater involvement in nurturing. Here's the evidence:

Men are spending more time with their children. The Changing

Workforce survey of 2,877 workers shows that fathers are spending a half-hour more each workday, and one hour more each day off, caring for and doing things with their children than in 1977.

- More men than women plan to provide care for elderly relatives. A survey of 1,015 Americans by the National Partnership for Women & Families, previously the Women's Legal Defense Fund, shows 56% of men and 53% of women expect to do so in the next 10 years.

- Men are doing more housework. The amount of time that employed, married men spend on cooking, repairs, laundry, bill-paying and other housework has risen nearly an hour per workday since 1977, regardless of whether they have working wives. The time that employed, married women spend fell by a half-hour, leaving only about a 45-minute daily gap between men's and women's chore time, the Workforce study shows. The gap in 1977 was three times that.

- Men drink alcohol and get depressed just as often as women when work and family clash. That's the conclusion of a four-year study by Michael Frone of the Research Institute on Addictions in Buffalo, N.Y., and others. The sexes are also equally prone to high blood pressure.

- Men want the freedom to join women in "sequencing" their careers—slowing job progress during family-focused stages of life, then speeding up again without prejudice from employers. A Catalyst study of 852 partners in dual-earner households found 65% of men want to do so, compared with 72% of women.

Andy Artis of Boise, Idaho, can attest to that. After throwing himself into work for 10 years, the former TV-station business manager took a cut in pay and benefits to take a job that allows time with his kids, ages nine and 11. As an ad-agency marketing director, he sets his own hours, staying home mornings to see them off to school and taking a break evenings to coach their teams.

Now 37 years old, Mr. Artis sees this relatively low-key career phase as lasting only about 10 of the remaining 35 years he plans to work. "During this window of time that I have some influence in my children's lives, they're my top priority," he says.

Changes this sweeping call for a new male icon, a Betty Friedan or Oprah Winfrey for the guy set. I asked experts whether any male cultural emblems of the recent past—Alan Alda? Robert Bly? Mrs. Doubtfire?—embody men's changing roles.

None of the above, says Mike Lafavore, editor in chief of *Men's Health*, a 1.5-million circulation magazine that has rocketed to a top spot among men's periodicals by knowing the '90s man cold. To his readers (median age 34), the new man is more like Jack Nicholson or Tom Hanks—seeking challenges and enjoyment both on and off the job, including "trying to be better parents, and getting closer to our wives, our children and to our friends." (Personally, I favor Tom Hanks; no way would Jack Nicholson ever change a diaper.)

Whatever the icon, the implications are far-reaching. Even in male-dominated industries, employers that ignore work-family concerns are apt to have increasing trouble filling openings. Assuming a healthy economy, growing numbers of men will flee workaholic corporate cultures, for family's sake. On a personal level, the implications are simpler. No matter how isolated we may feel in our work-family conflicts, there's consolation in knowing that the values that unite men and women are more powerful than the differences that divide us.

—April 15, 1998

Three Fathers Reflect
on the Exhausting Joys of
Bigger Role at Home

B ucking traditional gender roles is never easy. The growing number of men who are doing so, as noted here last week, are highly motivated to play a bigger part in home and family life. Here, three of them reflect on the challenges:

In moments of introspection, Paul DiGiammarino, a 43-year-old American Management Systems Inc. executive, admits to conflicts over his expanded role at home. To make more time for family, he stepped down last year as co-head of the $100 million AMS unit he had co-founded to fill a vice-president slot. Since then, he feels torn between two missions: a private one as a father, and a public one as a builder of businesses. "Could the economy be as successful as it is, and grow the way it's growing, if my [current] role were the norm?" he asks. "Ultimately, what the country needs are corporate leaders who are giving their all, trading it all off."

But the needs of his wife and children, ages 14, 12 and eight, spoke louder. It still pains him to recall how his son David, then 12, told him two years ago: "Dad, you keep saying it's going to get better and you're going to be home more, but it never changes. Well, you're running out of time. Pretty soon, I'm going to change, and I'm not going to care much after a while." Only half-joking, his family made him run a gauntlet when he left on trips, lining up at the door and holding him back.

"Anyone who thinks men don't have the same issues as women in these situations isn't in touch with reality," he says. Also, after years of adapting to his and the kids' needs, his wife won a seat on the Lexington, Mass., school board. It was only fair, Mr. DiGiammarino felt, to support her by helping out at home.

His family is much happier with his expanded role as father, coach and community volunteer. At work, he sees his slowdown as temporary and is finding new ways to contribute. "There are still days when I'm ready to be off again, starting great things. But then I look at the children and tell myself, 'Be careful. . . . Make sure you're going to be able to live up to your desire to balance your life.' "

Eugene King, 42, a lead bus mechanic for the city of Oakland, Calif., has to reach deep inside himself some days to summon the energy it takes to be an involved father. After commuting 80 miles a day and working long hours, it's tiring spending every remaining waking moment with his daughters, ages two and six. Most days he's too worn out to miss the fishing he loves and the friends he no longer has time to see.

But Mr. King is creating for himself and his daughters something he missed as a child: The opportunity "to love and be loved" every day at home in a rich, stable, father-child relationship. Mr. King's own father moved out of the house when Mr. King was six and, though they remained very close, he remembers wishing his dad would move back in. Now, he says, "I love hearing" the "I-love-yous" that his girls offer daily.

They greet him at the door each evening, pull off his oil-stained work boots and settle on the couch to talk. While his wife takes a break (she is at home caring for the children during the day), he helps six-year-old Jene with homework.

He tries to stay in close touch with Jene's teacher through calls and conferences. For Mr. King, who couldn't afford the computer-science degree he wanted and had to start work as a janitor, the education of his children is a top priority.

Later, father and daughters share playtime before he falls into bed for his usual six hours' sleep. Even on his one day off a week, Mr. King rises early to clean the garage with Jene or do bills or yard work. "I wish I had a little more room to breathe," he admits. But he quickly adds: "Your children don't ask to be here. Until they're grown, it's your responsibility to make them as happy as they can be, to make sure they don't need anything that you are humanly able to provide."

Robert Boehringer runs a quality-management consulting business from his home and loves caring for his kids, ages six, four and one. But he doesn't love all the stuff that comes with it. On bad days, he says, "I feel like I'm crossing into [a woman's] world. I do laundry, I do cooking, I do cleaning . . . typical household chores that aren't the male domain. If this were 25 years ago, I wouldn't be doing any of this. I'd be able to sit in front of the TV or play golf with my friends."

Nevertheless, Mr. Boehringer, 39, values the sense of potency and fulfillment he gains from his deep bond with his family. In sharing duties with his wife, an active school and community volunteer, he says he wants to have "a much more significant impact on child-rearing" than men of his father's generation. Though his own entrepreneur-father was a strong and loving parent, his long absences for work left "a void in my upbringing," he says.

He uses his freedom as owner of N-Compass Consulting in Stamford, Conn., to shape his business travel around family needs. When he's home, he helps get the kids up and fed, works 10 A.M. to 4 P.M., plays with the kids again from 4 P.M. to 8 P.M. and returns to work. Meanwhile, he helped start a dads' club at his son's school. Sometimes, he breaks from work at mid-morning to take his son skating. His various roles, he adds, have become so integrated that "I can't imagine not being here and being part of raising my kids."

—April 22, 1998

Latest Backlash Against Dual Earners Ignores Some Realities

The unsigned letter practically sizzled as it rolled off my fax machine.

"What have you been smoking out there on the Left Coast?" fumed the writer, angered by a column on how parents balance work and child-rearing. The letter blasted me, a working mother, as one of a class of uncaring narcissists who neglect their kids for the ego high they get from work.

Judging by the temperature of my fax (near meltdown) and recent media coverage, once-obscure work-family concerns are heating up. The headlines, like "The Myth of Quality Time: How We're Cheating Our Kids" in *Newsweek* and "Lies Parents Tell Themselves About Why They Work" in *U.S. News & World Report*, for example, are enough to give working parents a guilt rash.

The Time Bind, Arlie Hochschild's new book asserting that parents are choosing work as a refuge from family life, is helping fuel the uproar.

I think all the attention to the family side of the work-family equation is good. The work-family debate has long been too biased toward enabling people with families to get to work and stay there. It's time for the pendulum to swing the other way, and Dr. Hochschild has given it a thoughtful and needed push.

The outcry, however, amounts to a backlash. The message, as many interpret it: Dual-earner parents are greedy and neglectful; if they cared about their kids they'd cut spending so one parent could stay home.

I have nothing against traditional families. Many do a fabulous job raising kids. But I see some real distortions at work. First, the focal point of much of the media coverage is a stereotype that reflects only a small minority of the work force, based on the interviews, calls and letters that are the basis for this column and my talk-radio show: The work-obsessed professional careerist who could choose to be a good parent but fails to do so.

Second, a vast middle tier of working parents, I estimate 30%, are already making choices in favor of more family time. They are part of what historian-author Neil Howe calls a continuing "parenthood revival," and they have long believed the quality-time argument is bunk.

Many still show up in statistics reflecting rapid growth in dual-earner couples, but they make their living far from the corporate fast track and often split parenting evenly. Their home-focused lifestyles are better reflected in the 7% annual growth in home-based self-employment, the accelerating "voluntary simplicity" movement and the fatherhood movement.

Consider V.K. Blumenthal, a mother of two and sales manager who refuses to work more than part time. She has changed jobs and industries three times to keep her part-time hours, "going backward" in status to her current job as a marketing manager for a small financial company. To preserve family time, the former TV director spends workdays in a tiny windowless room, cold-calling prospects.

To these parents, the notion that there's only one good way to blend work and family disregards the complexity of choices parents make over the long course of raising a child.

"Sure, I could quit and move to a trailer park in Omaha," says a New York City communications manager who has passed up higher-status jobs and lives near work to preserve family time. "But I want to bring my kids up here in this culturally charged environment. My personal belief is that my kids are happier here. And I don't want to walk around feeling guilty about it."

Finally, another large segment of working parents hasn't any choice about how to blend work and family; they either work full time or go broke.

Merry Ellen Korpan, a university administrative worker, would love to work part time. But her job is at least 8:30 to 5; her family needs her benefits (her husband gets none in his job) and the 60% of household income she contributes to paying their apartment rent and debt accumulated when her husband was unemployed.

She feels "an underlying frustration that I should be at home with the kids. But I can't be. People talk about mothers who work to buy another Mercedes. Well, excuse me, but I'm driving a Ford. I'm not working so we can have fabulous vacations."

Chip Johanni, an insurance-company manager who works 50-hour weeks, would love to spend three-day weekends with his two children. But while his employer has offered compressed work weeks in the past, his manager said no when Mr. Johanni asked. Bosses see no reason to give workers four 10-hour days when they're already working five 10-hour days, he says.

Haranguing parents like these about making better choices reflects a dangerous naivete about the workplace and risks taking the heat off employers at a critical time for families. Many employers are growing less family-friendly, as layoffs wreck flexibility policies and larger-than-life workloads make reduced hours a prescription for failure on the job.

A careful reader of Dr. Hochschild's book knows even the family-friendly workplace conditions she studied had vaporized by the time she finished, wiped out by layoffs and management's loss of interest.

Until all parents have more authentic choices in the workplace, fixating on Ozzie and Harriet as role models isn't going to do most kids much good—even if we send them to a trailer park in Omaha.

—May 14, 1997

Woman's Resignation from Top Pepsi Post Rekindles Debates

The voice-mail message crackled with emotion as the caller, a New York marketing consultant, reacted to the news that Brenda Barnes, one of corporate America's highest-ranking women, was quitting to spend time with her family.

"This has set the rest of us back a long time," the woman lamented. "It verifies all the worst stereotypes about women in the workplace."

Throughout the week after Ms. Barnes resigned as head of Pepsi-Co's North American beverage business, emotional reactions rolled into my office. The comments ranged from the skeptical executive who insisted she had political reasons for resigning (such as resentment over the course of her husband's recently ended career at Pepsi) to the at-home mom who saw a new trend. Our collective angst about work and family is running so high that career decisions by executive women have become a Rorschach test. Ms. Barnes had no desire to be a symbol, stressing that other women shouldn't be judged by her choice. She declined to be interviewed for this column.

Nevertheless, her unprecedented candor about the toll executive life had taken—years of hectic travel, living apart from her husband, missing her three kids' birthdays—reopened old work-family wounds among millions, making her a lightning rod for all kinds of feelings.

Some career moms who have experienced workplace discrimination were angry. Ms. Barnes "was too honest" about her reasons for quitting, says the marketing consultant. "The workplace isn't the place for frankness. If it were, your boss would be able to say during a review, 'I'm not promoting you because I don't like you.'" Women on her level should "exert a little creative spin" on their plans, she adds.

Sole breadwinners felt vindicated. To foundation executive John

Mecklenburg, who with his wife sacrificed for years so she could stay home with their sons, Ms. Barnes proved "that you can't have it all, be supermom and super-executive, too. Men can't have it all either."

Others attacked the values reflected in the debate as upside-down. At-home mom Heidi Brennan found Pepsi executives' regretful assertion that they "had been grooming [Ms. Barnes] for bigger things" laughable. "Hey, [raising kids] is a big thing," she says. Similarly, a broadcast consultant mused: "What state is our society in, that deciding to take care of your kids is headline news?"

Some must-work mothers were flooded with yearning. The day the news broke, says one single mother who works in a tire plant, her daughter begged her to quit. "If I could stay home, I would love it," she says. Instead, she daydreams: "If I win the lottery I'll go back to work one more time, just to get on the loudspeaker and tell those guys what I really think of them."

Meanwhile, many Gen-Xers wondered what all the fuss was about. Jennifer Prosek, 28, co-owner of a 13-employee marketing firm, fully expects blending work and family to force tough choices. "I think she made it all right for women to make that choice and feel positive about it," she says.

As emotions ran high, so did predictions that more mothers would quit work. This, however, has proved in the past decade to be the most oft-predicted trend that never materialized. Instead, mothers' movement into the work force has proved remarkably durable. The Bureau of Labor Statistics says the proportion of mothers of kids under 18 in the work force rose to 70% in 1996 from 67% in 1993.

Many mothers satisfied with their work-family balance predicted Ms. Barnes will soon return to the workplace in a more balanced role. "I love my children, but I couldn't be home with them all the time," says Denise Watkins, an information scientist.

Another looming stereotype, that women can't take the heat at high levels, also crumbles under scrutiny. Calling a 22-year high-achiever like Brenda Barnes a slacker is like calling Sylvester Stallone a wimp because he stopped bodybuilding. Anyone with her record has nothing to prove. Instead, her candor reflects a new-found confidence among high-ranking women, that they no longer must hide their conflicts.

Therein lies the real news here: For the first time, Brenda Barnes has drawn the work-family spotlight to the executive suite, and the personal costs it illuminates aren't pretty. "The truth is, no one wants to say it or print it, but a lot of these jobs are crap and a lot of these demands are just awful" for men and women alike, says John Sullivan, a former accounting-firm partner who runs his own business. "One day, you come in after your latest trip on the red-eye, beat to crap, and you say, 'I don't want this stuff anymore.' And you say, 'The hell with it.' "

Increasingly, executive life is an island apart from the mainstream trend toward integrating work and family. An *Inc.* magazine study of 700 entrepreneurs and big-company executives finds that while both groups work equally hard, entrepreneurs integrate personal and work life, while corporate executives divide them. I wouldn't be surprised if after she regains her balance with her family, Brenda Barnes returns to the workplace. She may find some potent but more balanced leadership role, perhaps overseeing some of those Gen-Xers who take work-life choices in stride. Then, she could help forge a new executive model—one that doesn't require people to sacrifice their lives on the altar of power.

—October 8, 1997

Part   Three

RAISING
KIDS

One of the biggest mistakes I made as a working parent was to assume that once my children reached school age, the toughest stage in combining work and family was over.

Carol Lay

The years from age five on are at least as challenging for working parents as the preschool years, and often more so. School-age children spend only about one-fifth of their total waking hours each year in school. The rest is up to parents.

Older kids have complicated needs laden with values-related questions only parents can answer. Delegating child-care duties for older children is far harder than for younger ones. Older kids' extracurricular activities are voracious gobblers of parental time, requiring the services of a cheerleader, chauffeur and chaperone (not to mention a banker to cover those ever-rising extracurricular fees). A parent also needs to be on-call all hours as counselor, advisor and friend, not just when it is convenient for you, but *when your child feels like talking.*

The columns in this section focus on some of those challenges, from arranging after-school and summer care to coping with homework and household chores.

Saying Goodbye, and Many Thanks, to a Trusted Caregiver

As a working parent, I've had my share of bad child care, enough to know I'd prefer Chinese water torture.

I've also had child care so good that it enriched my whole family. At those times, I feel like Allison Anders, the director who insisted on adding her child-care providers to the credits of her Universal Pictures film, *Grace of My Heart.* She says, "I couldn't have done this work without them."

I'm saying goodbye this fall to the best child-care provider I've ever had. Chris Chenoweth, 45 years old, took my son James into her family child-care home for about seven hours a day, from age two until he started first grade last month and outgrew the need for preschool care. With child care in the news, the story of my family's relationship with Ms. Chenoweth (whom we call Chris) illustrates the vast potential, and the overwhelming demands, of family child care—a flexible mode of care that is one of our society's best hopes for navigating welfare reform and the 24-hour workplace without hurting kids.

I chose family child care for James in 1993, after a cross-country move had left him anxious and unsettled. Good family child care, where a caregiver takes a few children into her home, can offer the best of two worlds: the enduring bond with one adult provided by a nanny, and the stimulation of contact with other kids offered by child-care centers.

But family child-care homes range wildly in quality, from warehouses of neglect to loving surrogate families. Chris, a 10-year veteran, fit the Families and Work Institute's profile of a good provider: She is licensed, has sought out training, operates in a businesslike way and views child care as a profession. Chris' husband and their own children, 11 and 16, take part, too, welcoming other families and forming friendships with many.

Noticing right away that my son resisted touch by anyone but his parents, Chris patiently built his trust by offering lots of comfort and reassurance. Soon, she also spotted in him a pattern of developmental snags that a raft of pediatricians had failed to interpret: tics, motor-skills delays and trouble comprehending words, hinting at neurological problems.

As I battled my own confusion and denial, Chris documented the concerns on videotape. Then she comforted me in my journey through that dark emotional place parents go when they first fear for their child's future. "He's so bright, Sue," she said. "You've caught it early."

Armed with Chris' videotape and supporting memo, my husband and I wended our way through a maze of doctors and special-education officials, securing remedial classes and occupational therapy for James. In the next two years he made remarkable progress, his skills soaring and the tics vanishing. His success in kindergarten, his teachers say, arose largely from the early assistance Chris helped us get.

My sometimes-shaky parenting skills didn't escape Chris' keen eye. Noting my tendency to ask too little of James—scrambling to get his shoes or tolerating his spine-wrenching leaps into my arms— she insisted, "You have to set limits, to tell him when he demands too much." It was hard to hear. She was right.

The skills Chris taught her charges—to express feelings in words, negotiate, compromise—echoed through our neighborhood. A neighbor told me how, when her child exploded in tears of frustration with a friend, James took her aside, put his arm around her shoulder and counseled her, "I'm sure we can work this out"— words I'd heard Chris say dozens of times. Her nurturing skills spilled over, in James' delight at younger children ("Mom, look, it's a baby!").

Over the years, I wondered how Chris—holder of a business degree, an astute manager, an adventuress who once wandered Europe for months in a beat-up van—could sustain the confining, mostly invisible work of child care. She acknowledges that the second-class status of her profession gets to her.

One parent complained indignantly that Chris' services (now $35 a day for children over two and a half) cost more than her car payments. Another couple once forgot to pick up their child, leaving Chris to explain the lapse to the little girl.

To ride out a career crisis, she networked with other providers and trained at Windflower Enterprises, a Colorado Springs, Colo., family child-care consulting and advocacy firm. "I developed a vision of family child care," Chris says.

"If I can teach children who can go out in the world thinking they are worthwhile people, respecting other people and themselves, identifying and talking about what they're feeling, getting along with other people and getting what they need in the world, then I've contributed a little to the world," she says. "It's so simple. And it's right here in my backyard." Now she trains other providers on evenings and weekends.

As I reflect on our years with Chris, I realize that this column and others I labor over will be read, discarded and ultimately used to line the bird cages of America. But when the front door of Chris' modest home swings shut for the last time behind my son, she will have sent into the world a legacy far more enduring: A child permanently enriched, and parents better equipped, for the challenges they face.

It may be simple. But it is no small thing.

—October 29, 1997

Deciding How Soon to Prepare Your Child to Stay Home Alone

K ay Jackson, an engineer at Eli Lilly, arrived home from work last month to every parent's nightmare.

After her nanny quit without notice, Ms. Jackson had to leave her sons, ages nine and 11, home alone after school and put her toddler in day care. But the boys, who usually run to meet her at the door, were nowhere in sight.

"I thought someone had kidnapped them," she says. "I had 10 minutes of total panic" before the boys finally came running out of the woods behind her house, where they had been playing.

For many people, the words "home alone" evoke images of thoughtless parents or Macaulay Culkin fending off burglars. But the reality is that many caring, level-headed parents leave their children in "self-care," as child-care experts call it. Some are forced to do so by child-care breakdowns or a lack of after-school programs. Others choose self-care because, in measured quantities, it fosters self-reliance and self-esteem.

An Urban Institute study shows 4.6 million, or 22%, of five- to 14-year-olds, including three million kids under 12, stay home alone part of each week; some experts say the actual numbers are higher, partly because parents are reluctant to admit they leave kids alone. Eli Lilly found in a survey of 14,500 employees that 50% of parents of 10- to 13-year-olds and 6% of parents of five- to nine-year-olds leave them home alone.

Few parents make lightly a decision to leave a child alone. Many experts say children can stay alone for short periods of an hour or two after the age of nine or 10, assuming they are mature enough and have safe surroundings and neighborhood backup. But first, parents need to ensure that kids have the skills and confidence necessary to care for themselves.

A recent seminar on self-care for Lilly families, offered by Work/

Family Directions, a Boston-based consultant, provides a window into that decision-making process. Sixteen parents and their 17 nine- to 12-year-olds gathered on a Saturday at Lilly's Indianapolis head-quarters for help from child-care experts in making a decision on self-care and preparing their kids for it.

In an adults-only session, Carol Katterjohn, a regulatory associate at Lilly, says she is struggling with fears about the issue of self-care. A switch to a job-share setup has left her unable to afford after-school care for both her sons, ages six and 10, so she is preparing her 10-year-old to stay alone. But she can't shake a disturbing memory—of three teenagers in a nearby town who were murdered after school at the home of one of them. The tragedy left her "so paranoid," she says. She agonizes over striking a balance between freedom and lim-its for her son. She is setting rules: No visitors, no going out. Yet she fears making their home "like a jail."

Ben and Robin Akers offer a reassuring success story. In the year their children, Tad, 10, and Kelly, 11, have been home alone for an hour each day, they have grown closer and gained valuable practice at being responsible, says Mr. Akers, a mechanical engineer. To guard against "external influences" in the neighborhood, the Akers set firm rules, allowing no visitors and assigning chores and home-work. He urges other parents not to worry about isolating their kids. "The bottom line is, [strict rules] keep them alive," he says.

Like Ms. Katterjohn, Liz Peck, a Lilly chemist, is torn. She under-stands her fourth-grader's desire to quit day care; the child, Alex, 10, wants some quiet time at home after school. But "I'm reluctant to let her grow up," Ms. Peck says. Her office is a half-hour from home; with Alex in day care, she enjoys peace of mind.

Kay Jackson listens closely. She feels her boys are ready to care for themselves, but she realizes "I need to establish clear rules," she says.

She gets a chance to do that when the parents rejoin their kids, who have had their own discussion and coaching session, to play a Work/Family Directions game that teaches safety skills. Seated cross-legged on the floor with Chris, 11, and Matt, 9, she reads from a game card: What would you do if you arrived home and found the door of the house open? "Go inside!" Matt replies.

"Go inside? No!' Ms. Jackson says firmly. Together, they work through the steps: Leave, find a helpful adult, call the police, call a parent.

Nearby, Ms. Katterjohn is reassured when her son Kyle answers several safety questions well. In an opposite corner of the conference room, Ms. Peck and Alex, a dark-haired child bubbling with confidence, are still on the fence. The game has uncovered gaps in Alex's skills; she needs to memorize her father's office phone number, among other things. "We've agreed that I can come home after school three days a week, right, Mom?" Alex asks. No, her mother replies, "we're talking about that as a possibility."

You could argue that such family-support sessions don't belong within the walls of corporate America. But that amounts to sticking your head in a demographic sandpile. By 2001, 69% of families will be headed by single parents or dual earners, up from 64% now, says Wefa Group's consumer-markets unit. Clearly, millions more children will be coming home to empty houses.

Lilly, at least, which has a long waiting list for future seminars like this one, has concluded the trend warrants a corporate response—and thoughtful support for families.

—March 20, 1996

Costly Camps Put Many Parents in Bind for Summer Day Care

Many working parents in Patty Miller's area of the Midwest this summer are arranging a rich mix of activities for their kids: art, science and computer camps and theater and environmental-studies programs.

But for Ms. Miller's 12-year-old daughter, summer offers little more than a demand that she grow up too soon. She'll be staying home, caring for her 10- and 11-year-old siblings, because Ms. Miller, an administrative staffer at a nonprofit concern, can't afford the summer programs in her town. "I feel like I'm letting my kids down," says Ms. Miller, a single mother who makes $12,000 a year.

She hates leaving them alone and knows it's risky and hard on them, "but I don't know what else to do. There's nothing out there I can afford." The $150-a-week tab for sending her children to camp would eat up most of her pay.

Amid the summer rush by working parents to plan activities for school-age kids, a nagging problem is getting quietly but inexorably worse: The gap between haves and have-nots, worrisome enough during the school year, widens into a chasm when schools close in June.

High-end summer camps in special-interest areas ranging from space travel to Shakespeare are booming, says a 16-state survey by Child Care Aware, a nonprofit Rochester, Minn., child-care improvement and referral concern. But lower-cost programs that suit less-affluent parents' budgets and work hours are scarce.

One result: Staffers I interviewed at six nonprofit child-care resource-and-referral agencies across the country see signs that the number of children left home alone is rising. The agencies are getting more calls from parents asking when they can legally leave kids alone. (State laws vary; while some specify an age, usually 10 to 12, others set no limit.)

Child-care affordability problems "are particularly acute in the summer," says Barbara Reisman of the nonprofit Child Care Action

Campaign, New York. Day-care-weary children ages nine and up often resist going to day-care centers or having a sitter; the recreational programs they like average $100 a week and range from $50 to $700, Child Care Aware says. "I went to an Ivy League college, and I'm paying for four weeks of camp what my parents paid for a year of college" in the early '70s, says a New Jersey mother, whose son is spending a month on a Vermont lake for $2,200.

Some inexpensive programs are being cut. Palm Beach County, Fla., officials eliminated summer school this year for 14,000 children through eighth grade. And government child-care subsidies, for parents like Ms. Miller, often don't apply to summer programs not licensed by the state.

Good, affordable, full-day programs are packed. In Charlotte, N.C., parents bearing sleeping bags start lining up at 3 P.M. the day before signups begin to get a slot in Mecklenburg County's $74-a-month camp. "We could easily double the enrollment" but lack funds and facilities, a spokeswoman says.

There isn't any data over time on kids in self-care during the summer; the latest national sampling, in 1990 by the Urban Institute, found 19% of children ages six through 12 are left alone at least part of the time in summer, usually for short periods; self-care was the primary arrangement for 2%. But the population of kids six through 13 has increased 8.4% since then, and a growing percentage come from single-parent or dual-earner families.

Self-care can be risky; in Detroit, officials report a 25% summer rise in residential fires caused by children left alone. Beyond that, it seldom yields the idyllic, Tom Sawyer-like experience of fishing and hanging out enjoyed by kids in the past; today, many parents forbid kids left home alone to even leave the house.

The Child Care Resource Center in Tulsa, Okla., has been getting urgent calls from parents each June for help finding child care. "They say, 'We were going to do self-care and it's just not working,' " says the center's Sharon Bentley. She says parents spend a lot of time on the telephone with kids who are frightened or bored and want to leave the house.

It's a wasted opportunity, too. Summer learning directly affects school performance, says Joan Bergstrom, a professor at Wheelock College, Boston, and author on educational issues. The 11- to 13-

year-old age range is crucial for developing qualities, such as self-reliance and resourcefulness, that foster success in adulthood, she says.

"It's really important to feel good about yourself and get competent in something around 11, 12 or 13."

Once again, a few employers are proving a source of creative solutions. The American Business Collaboration, a 156-employer group, is helping finance more than 100 community summer camps, including 81 programs on an Olympics theme.

In New York City, a partnership of 10 employers organized by Child Care Inc., a resource-and-referral group, is planning to expand community programs for kids.

In Livingston County, Mich., where 10,000 more summer child-care slots are needed, Citizens Insurance Co. of America helps fund community recreation programs.

"We know we're not going to get more funding from the government for these programs," says Linda Herbert of the county's Community Coordinated Child Care Council. "We're really looking to employers," collaborating with community agencies, for help.

—June 19, 1996

Finding Smart Ways to Help
Your Kids with Their Homework

In a previous life as a manager, I commuted home most evenings feeling reasonably competent to run an office and help people get their work done. But by 10 P.M., my state of mind typically had deteriorated from Master of the Universe to muddlehead. The catalyst: homework.

Specifically, my teenage stepdaughter's trigonometry. I couldn't seem to find a way to help her avoid late-night math marathons, or the frustration of tackling too many pages of tough problems too late.

Homework is demanding for any parent; it's more complex these days and there's more of it. It can raise high hurdles for working parents, who often must cram homework into the end of the day and may have more trouble communicating with teachers.

Some homework tips are basic: Make space and supplies available and teach kids skills such as keeping track of assignments, breaking big tasks into steps and doing the hardest jobs first, suggests Kate Kelly, author of *The Complete Idiot's Guide to Parenting a Teenager.*

Beyond that, some parents say they have figured out how to successfully apply some subtler management skills, learned at work, to helping their kids at home.

As parents know, workplace tactics usually fail when applied at home. The context and purposes are too different. One workplace trump card, for instance—the paycheck—is a nonstarter at home. Sylvia Rimm, an author on parenting and director of the Family Achievement Center, Cleveland, says one teen whose parents paid him for homework went on "strike," refusing to do more without a "raise." Token rewards should be used sparingly.

But since homework is partly a tool to help kids learn to approach all work with skill and confidence, some of the more savvy techniques of the modern workplace can come in handy, parents say. Here are a few:

Time management. Helping a child "take ownership" of time can work well. Though an excellent student, Sharon Lobel's son, age 10, sometimes turned in homework late. Follow-up (a Management 101 maxim known at home as nagging) wasn't working, says Dr. Lobel, a management professor.

She took a problem-solving approach. She calculated the hours available each day after school, then told her son: "We've got this problem with homework. Let's figure out a way so it will get done on time."

She asked him to come up with a schedule, including time to organize his binder and desk and time for study, basketball, dinner and fun. While his schedule wasn't one she'd have chosen (he clustered all two hours of free time right after school) it works. At six o'clock he knows he must do homework, she says. And he has begun turning in projects early.

Using the right incentives: Just as good bosses scope out what motivates workers, successful parents know what incentives work with their kids. Jim Pierobon's 12-year-old daughter loves to impress friends with her chess skills. So father and daughter spend time playing chess when she does homework well, says the marketing executive.

Understanding kids' diverse approaches to work is helpful: Sandy Devine, a systems-consulting executive, says her grasp of the personality types identified by the Myers-Brigg test her company uses helped her fathom her eight- and 10-year-olds' contrasting homework styles. While one is a "J" or "judging" type with a planned, orderly approach, the other is a "P" or "perceiving" type, who enjoys spontaneity and needs more breaks and incentives to finish homework.

Positive coaching: Janice Kaplan, mother of boys ages 11 and 13 and an editor and producer, draws on the coaching skills she uses at work to help her sons. Instead of criticizing mistakes, she first finds something to praise.

The benefits flow both ways. Mike Cavanagh, an executive editor, spent four hours a night for many years helping his three children, now ages 17 to 24, with homework. Learning to pace his demands to his kids' development taught him to be more patient at work, he says.

Making it fun: Though tired after work, attorney Diane Ambler finds working with her son "energizing." While once helping her son, then eight years old, build a rocket from a 7-Up bottle for a science project, she spent hours helping shave down its balsa fins with a nail file and pressurize its waterfilled fuselage with a bicycle pump. Finally, mother and son stepped into their yard late one evening for liftoff. But instead of soaring, the rocket exploded, spraying water everywhere. While getting soaked "wasn't what I had in mind," Ms. Ambler says, "we laughed and laughed." Her son went on to complete the project and drew a high mark.

In my own case, I've made some progress since trying to help my stepdaughter (who conquered trig on her own and has gone on to bigger things). I get a kick out of helping my younger daughter, age 10, become a self-starter. I enjoy giving my son, seven, the instant feedback, praise and hugs he needs.

Of course, his problems still run more along the lines of "add 7 + 3" than "define the cosine of a given angle." But regardless of how well I keep pace with my kids' assignments over the years, my experience with my stepdaughter taught me a more important lesson: The time we spend together on homework will be remembered long after the grades they get have been forgotten.

—January 28, 1998

Busy Parents Let Kids Off the Hook When Assigning Chores

A t the end of a long workday, I was trying to teach my eight-year-old daughter how to open a can of dog food when she dropped the can opener on the kitchen counter in frustration. "I can't make this thing work," she said.

At a loss for words to guide her, I picked up the gadget and tried to figure out how to break down the task into simple steps so I could teach them to her. But as I was thinking, my daughter slipped away; I heard the door slam and saw her race past the window dribbling a soccer ball. I started to call her back. Then I checked the clock. It was late. I was tired. It would be easier to feed the dog myself, I rationalized. So I did.

Many dual-earner parents are making similar choices. Trends in such families suggest kids increasingly are "withdrawing from domestic responsibilities," say professors Linda Waite of the University of Chicago and Frances Goldscheider of Brown University in a study. The pattern is strongest in families with two college-educated parents, where children were estimated to do 11% of household chores, compared with 20% in families with less-educated parents. Ironically, that's largely because men, particularly in highly educated couples, are doing more, Drs. Waite and Goldscheider found, based on data on married women nationwide, from a federally funded study of 10,000 women by Ohio State University over 15 years.

Instead of relieving women, husbands are doing housework that would otherwise be done by kids; for every eight chores done by husbands, children do seven fewer. "The picture of family life that modern, egalitarian parents often present is one in which both parents are picking up after and waiting on their children," the researchers say. With the exception of single-parent families, where kids do more, children are likely to do less housework as younger, more educated parents take the front lines. One likely result: A new generation with "extremely low levels of competence in domestic skills," they say.

The research spotlights an aspect of my family life that I hadn't examined. As a kid I did lots of housework, and conventional wisdom finds value in that. The American Academy of Pediatrics' latest tome on child-rearing declares doing household chores "an important part of learning that life requires work, not just play."

But as a parent, I let my son and daughter sluff off, and my own informal survey of 10 dual-earner parents of school-age kids shows more than half aren't teaching their children many household skills.

Many, of course, hire help or shun housework themselves. "My son does no housework [because] I am a slob," says a San Francisco attorney, adding that she and her husband clean so seldom that "we don't have dust bunnies, we have dust elephants. When my kids play with mops and brooms, I know they've gotten it from the babysitter."

Most parents said they value more their kids' activities outside the home. A retailing executive says her teenager is "so busy becoming a young woman and doing things in the community and being a top honor student, that I don't care if she can clean a toilet bowl."

Others value the self-esteem, organizational skills and sense of mastery children can learn from such tasks as making meals and ordering their environment, but they are so busy overseeing kids' schoolwork, music lessons and sports they don't have time to teach them. "There's just so much to do that I don't want to fight about it," says a New York brokerage manager. "It's the way our competitive society is evolving. Mothers in the '50s weren't all that worried about how their kids were going to go out there and survive in the competitive world. And I'm not all that worried about whether my son is a slob."

Are we missing anything here? The middle ground, perhaps. There's no way I want my kids to be chained to housework. But as Drs. Goldscheider and Waite point out, knowing how to sew, clean a house quickly or fix an appealing meal can be a means of sharing and giving for men and women alike.

We're also bypassing a chance to lighten working women's loads. After years of doing 75% of her family's housework while working full time, Rebecca Sher, a Needham, Mass., photographer, enrolled in night classes, putting her "right over the edge," she says. So she called a family meeting and laid out chores for her kids, 13, 11 and six. Now, she posts their duties on computer printouts; even the six-year-old does laundry. "There are some unmatched socks," Ms. Sher says, but the kids are learning good work habits and her housework share is down to about 40%.

A subtler loss may be the opportunity to teach kids a certain sense of humility, suggests Trudy DeSilets, a senior marketing manager and mother. She recalls a scene from the film *Gandhi*, wherein the nonviolent leader, also a lawyer, insists his patrician wife clean latrines, just as he does. "It's one way to learn that each man's labor is as important as another's," Gandhi says. "In fact, while you're doing it, cleaning the toilet seems far more important than the law."

Some kids may be missing "that sense of service to others," Ms. DeSilets muses. "I would change that if I could. But I'm not sure how."

I'm not sure either. But I'm planning a modern-day adaptation: I'm going to take another shot at teaching my daughter to feed the dog. First, though, I'm buying an electric can opener.

—April 17, 1996

Family Togetherness Is an Issue
That Goes Beyond Dinner Chats

The topic, family dinners, sparks guilt in many working parents. "It's a subject that makes me go berserk," says my friend, an administrator for a New York financial-services concern. When she grew up, her family ate together every evening. Now, with her husband working long hours as an attorney, nightly dinners with their two school-age children are next to impossible.

"It's a source of agony to me," she says. "I constantly have this image in my mind that looks like my dinner table with my folks. I read all this stuff about how teens are better connected when families have dinner together. But when I say to my husband, 'Why can't we?' he says, 'Name one family who does.' And I can't think of any."

Family dinners have gotten a lot of good press lately. Study after study shows a correlation between thriving kids and families that dine together. Research by the University of Minnesota and the University of North Carolina found parents' presence in the home at key times, especially at dinner, was associated with a reduced incidence of drug use, sex, and violence and emotional distress among teens. A similar finding in another study led one pediatrician, quoted in a Florida newspaper, to proclaim that the waning of such family rituals as shared dinnertime means "we have lost those values" we once held dear.

Making family dinners a focal point for such sweeping judgments is too pat for me. I have fond memories of the dinners my family ate together, but my dearest recollections aren't of dinner; they're of family trips, long front-porch talks and working together on our farm. In my husband's close-knit family of 10 siblings, dinners were so clamorous that his brother, then three years old and unable to make himself heard, once climbed onto the table and walked across it to get the mashed potatoes.

My husband and I still eat together with our kids as often as possible, and 13 of the 16 other working parents I surveyed said they take pains to have regular family dinners. Talking over dinner helps kids learn reasoning and verbal skills, says Mary Ann Vlahac, a Connecticut market researcher and single parent of a 14-year-old. Her son debates politics over dinner with her and his 70-year-old great-aunt, who lives with them. One recent evening, he defended President Clinton from his great-aunt's criticism. He has won honors for the reasoning and language skills he displays in essay-writing.

Jack Valancy, a Cleveland Heights, Ohio, consultant, and his wife, a pediatric social worker, see dinners with their 13-year-old son as a time to support each other and reinforce values. Their son recently related over dinner how disgusted he was that his school jazz band had been disbanded because some kids were misbehaving.

Mr. Valancy and his wife listened as he criticized the adults involved. Then, they reminded him, "We know you feel angry about this. But you can't call teachers bad names." They counseled him to accept what happened and to find another place to play his clarinet, Mr. Valancy says. The teen soon calmed down and then joined another jazz combo. Without their dinner-table talk, his son might have remained troubled about the incident, Mr. Valancy says.

But as meaningful as dinnertime can be, there's a risk in mistaking correlation for causality. A deeper look at the research suggests family dinners are actually one motif, or recurring element, in the larger drama of healthy family life. Factors far more powerful and harder to measure actually predict well-being in kids.

In the two-university study of 12,000 adolescents mentioned earlier, researchers found parental presence at key times such as dinner is "consistently less significant" than overall "parental connectedness"—feelings of warmth, love and caring from parents—in protecting teens from risky behavior.

Another study, a 15-year look at Generation X by researchers at the University of Nebraska and Pennsylvania State University, focused on how often parents had talks with their children, showed affection for them or helped with personal problems or homework, and on how close children felt to their parents. The study found the best predictor of kids' well-being was the quality of their parents' marriage.

Amid all the social trends working against family dinners today—the longer workday, the late-afternoon clustering of kids' extracurricular events and so on—many families are taking alternate paths to closeness. Barbara Blair, a college public-relations specialist, says her husband, an investment banker, often doesn't get home until after 7:15 P.M. Her kids, ages 11 and 13, have sports and dance activities that interfere with dinner.

So her family comes together in other ways. They gather weeknights in the kitchen from 8 P.M. to 10 P.M., where Ms. Blair and her husband oversee homework, answering questions and offering guidance. "There's constant interaction going on among all four of us" during that time, Ms. Blair says. Sundays, they attend church and hold a family meeting in the evening, where they discuss scriptural teachings, relate them to events in their lives and tell stories that hold meaning for them. Many weekends, they hike together.

"What's really important," Ms. Blair says, "is that families build regular family time together to share ideas and concerns." That means regularly calling a halt to society's frenetic pace long enough for families to provide emotional support, affection, parental guidance and fun.

—July 29, 1998

Parents of Teens Find Some Peace of Mind in Working at Home

Candace Cohen, owner of a busy insurance company, was talking on the phone with a client when the walls of her office began to vibrate.

An earthquake, perhaps, or an alien invasion?

It was Pearl Jam, thundering from the basement bedroom of her 15-year-old son, one flight down from Ms. Cohen's home office. To halt the uproar, she stomped her foot on the floor. "When he hears me banging, he knows I'm going to come down and strangle him and his friends" unless they quiet down, she says.

Working at home, a lifestyle long ballyhooed for parents of preschoolers, is fast winning favor among parents of teens, too. Despite challenges like Ms. Cohen's, parents of adolescents are helping drive 7% to 10% annual growth in work-at-home households.

Ray Boggs of IDC/LINK, a New York market-research concern, says 14.7% of telecommuters and other corporate employees with home offices have 13- to 15-year-olds, compared with 11.5% of all U.S. households.

The coming of summer accelerates the trend. Studies show much of teens' risky behavior takes place at home while parents are at work. Given the scarcity of supervised programs for teens, many working parents worry about perils, from their "being abducted or getting into drugs, to getting hit in traffic," says a San Francisco mother of a 13-year-old who is asking her boss to work from home part-time from now on.

"There's just too much that can happen" to teens home alone, says Shirley Longshore of Philadelphia, a mother of children ages 12, 15, 19 and 26. She is changing jobs this summer to an employer that will allow her to telecommute. She and her husband, John, who also has worked from home in the past, "don't want to take that chance."

Adolescents' problems are often so complex and laden with

values issues that parents feel compelled to address them themselves. "The teen years are times when you really can't delegate" parenting, says Kate Kelly, author of *The Complete Idiot's Guide to Parenting a Teenager*, and a mother of three.

If you aren't around at the moment a teen feels like talking, he or she may never air issues at all, Ms. Kelly says. One Westchester County, N.Y., human-resource consultant didn't realize her middle-schooler was being verbally abused by other kids on the school bus until it had gone on for days, mainly because she wasn't home after school to see the effects. She now works from home.

Work-at-home parents also say they share more of teens' joys. When her 11- or 13-year-old makes a team or wins an award, "I hear it hot off the press" after school, says Debbie Depp, owner of Fenemore Group, a Southborough, Mass., management consultant. "Their lives are lived in 'Kodak moments.' "

The lifestyle poses unique challenges. The immediate effects aren't always what parents hope. When Maxine Casalbore, a Carmel, N.Y., insurance broker, first moved her company into an office attached to her house, her teenager fled to her friend's house. "I wish you were back out," Ms. Casalbore says her daughter told her. "It was so much easier for me to do whatever I wanted to do."

The profound self-absorption of many adolescents can make it hard for a parent to draw work-home boundaries. Telephones become a bone of contention; "Teens are always sure every call is for them," says one mother.

Ms. Longshore says one of her teens answered the phone, "Yo!" or "Talk to me!"—usually when one of her most important clients called. She banned teens from answering the phone and later got a separate line.

Teenagers can be as oblivious as toddlers to parents' pleas for silence. Ms. Depp's kids sometimes walk into her office and start talking during a client phone call, heedless of her frantic hand-signaled pleas for quiet. "Waiting isn't on their list of options," she says.

Teens' emotional needs are often so intense they derail a parent's work. Mr. Longshore says he has set aside planned projects to help his teens with peer relationships or other problems. After empathizing with their angst, he often is too drained to go back to work.

Despite the drawbacks, a work-at-home parent can broaden a

teen's perspective on work, Ms. Kelly says. Over time, Ms. Casalbore's daughter started wandering into her mother's office to use the computer or watch her work. Now in college, she holds a job in Ms. Casalbore's company doing spread sheets and brochures—a career option Ms. Casalbore suspects she wouldn't have considered without exposure to her home office.

Misunderstandings among clients and customers are other obstacles that can usually be overcome. After Ms. Cohen's teenage son answered a client call, the client was miffed: Should he avoid calling her, he asked, because he might get her son instead? After making sure her son hadn't been rude, Ms. Cohen explained her reason for working at home and told the client, "If you can't deal with my life, maybe I'm not the right person for you." Though she feared losing the client, the exchange provided a foundation for a stronger relationship. She went on to "save him a ton of money" on insurance, she adds, and "now, he doesn't mind at all if he gets my son on the phone."

—June 18, 1997

Moms and Dads Are the Scariest Monsters on Any Screen

W e all have our obsessions, and mine is work; I'd like to think my kids aren't affected. I thought I had them fooled.

Imagine my surprise to find my workaholic ways portrayed one evening on their favorite cartoon show—and to hear them laughing. There I was: a work-crazed mother obsessing aloud about her business travel schedule, blind to the comical but increasingly desperate bids for attention by her three-year-old daughter. The character, Charlotte on Nickelodeon's *Rugrats,* was even wearing one of my old power suits.

Frazzled, overworked or neglectful working parents are an emerging stereotype in family TV and movies, and the message is mostly negative. Charlotte is so much a parody of a self-absorbed yuppie mother that she's funny. But other images are painful, portraying stressed-out or emotionally absent parents as a real and predictable part of children's lives. Consider:

- A recent episode of *Are You Afraid of the Dark?* a Nickelodeon drama: A frazzled single mother arriving home from work brushes off her teenage son's pleas to listen to his dilemma and collapses on the couch, lamenting that her boss is forcing her to work all night.

  "They're killing you, Mom. Tell them no!" her son says.

  "I can't," she replies, then falls asleep, leaving him to solve his problems alone.
- *We're Back,* a 1993 Spielberg film: A little girl's work-crazed father and socialite mother are so neglectful that she flees their Manhattan apartment to work in an evil sorcerer's circus.
- *North,* 1994: A young boy is so disgusted with his workaholic parents that he sets out in search of better ones.

- *Hook,* the 1991 Peter Pan fantasy: A distracted father becomes a hero by giving up his obsession with work.
- *Lassie,* the 1994 family film: A stepmother is so frantic trying to combine parenting with her bank job that she crashes into her stepson while offering him breakfast, sending him running into the street. Mercifully, the family soon quits the city to become sheep farmers.

TV and film writers have never been enamored of corporate America—nor of parents, for that matter. In the past, parents had often been portrayed in children's media as well-meaning but ineffectual or, in cartoons, simply absent. But there is new edge and specificity to the latest stereotypes. "Hollywood for the past couple of years has been consistently questioning adults who are so consumed with their work that they neglect their primary obligation to children, mirroring deep-seated concerns that have grown in American society since the 1970s," says Annette Insdorf, chairwoman of Columbia University's film division.

Writers say they are simply portraying reality. "Our writers base stories on the way life is. It's not like we're making it up," says Adrienne Lopez-Dudley, executive in charge of production at Nickelodeon. "Most kids have either experienced something similar or have a friend next door who is experiencing it."

In many ways, the diversity is welcome. I'd rather have my kids spend an evening with the earthy types who populate TV now, such as the single mother in ABC's comedy *Grace Under Fire* with her worries about latchkey kids and a Neanderthal boss, than with Jim Anderson (*Father Knows Best*) or Ward Cleaver—neither of whom had any visible means of self-support. (Did you know Jim sold insurance, and The Beave's dad was a producer?)

We also might do well to check out how our kids see us. When the Families and Work Institute asked parents what their kids would say if asked how they would change their relationships, parents said, "They want me to spend more time with them." But kids said: "We want you to come home less stressed-out."

But such stereotyping carries some risks, not only for individual kids but for the future work force. Stereotypes of neglectful parents could hurt children who already feel vulnerable, making them "identify with the character who is being shuffled off" by a parent, says T. Berry Brazelton, the Harvard Medical School pediatrician.

And without countervailing examples, kids are likely to absorb as truth the negative messages—that bosses are monsters, mainstream jobs are all-consuming, and somebody always loses out when adults try to combine parenting and work. When researchers showed children cartoons portraying wild animals with fictional traits, as well as natural-history videos, the children were most influenced by whichever portrayal they saw first, regardless of the medium. "If kids don't have another source of information, they accept what they see on TV as reality," says R. Ben Peyton, a Michigan State University professor and an author of the study. The burden weighs on parents to counteract the message. Kathy Hazzard, a human-resources manager for John Hancock Financial Services, talks about her job to her children, 10 and 12, explaining how it benefits the family and others, and involves them in her work when possible. She also mediates their reactions to media stereotypes. After the movie *Home Alone*, she reassured her children that "we could never forget them," as the movie parents had.

But the stereotypes may have some value in reminding us of what's important. Arlene Klasky, co-creator of *Rugrats* with Paul Germain and Gabor Csupo, recently took her cellular phone to her son's soccer practice and started making "a million calls." Suddenly, the realization struck: "Oh my God. I'm turning into Charlotte!"

—October 26, 1994

Part Four

THE HIGHWIRE WALK

Carol Lay

Amid all the seismic changes rocking the work-and-family landscape—gender-role evolution, technology growth, the expanding workday—one driving force unites them all: The breakdown of boundaries.

Men's life choices are no longer bounded by societal dictates that they be sole family breadwinners, or breadwinners at all.

Women's life choices are no longer bounded by societal dictates that they abandon all other pursuits for child-rearing.

The workplace is no longer bounded by the walls of the office or factory, national boundaries or even global hemispheres. It expands into the kitchen, the car, the hotel room, the airplane, wherever technology allows.

The workday is no longer bounded by the time clock or 9-to-5 routines. It extends across time zones, spanning night and day among workers united by the increasingly global economy.

All those broken boundaries are creating great opportunities—and great anxieties—for people combining work and family. Amid an expanding array of choices about how to organize home and job, many workers also experience an overpowering sense of confusion and isolation in the tradeoffs they inevitably must make.

People often describe this decision-making process as a kind of inner highwire walk, the theme that unites the columns in this section. Among other things, the columns cover the hazards of overwork, including my own bout with burnout; the dangers of forgetting your spouse and friends amid a welter of other demands, and the risks to family relationships posed by overuse of technology. Also in these stories, working parents at all levels of the work force, from a White House policy aide to an Oakland, Calif., bus mechanic, tell how and why they made difficult tradeoffs in favor of family life.

People Are Working Harder—
and Taking More Heat for It

Being married to a workaholic can be hard work.

Consider the experience of a Chicago sociologist:

She was reading a novel in bed one evening while her husband, a physicist, worked late on his computer in the next room. She turned and saw him crawling into bed with his laptop.

"It was unbelievable!" she says. Angrily, she protested: "Listen, you have gone too far this time!" Though he was "thrilled at being able to get into bed with a computer and his wife—a ménage à trois with the two loves of his life," the sociologist says, she insisted the machine go.

Overwork is surfacing as a point of conflict in more relationships. Many people are working harder, and personal relationships are often the first casualties. Yankelovich Partners says half the 1,000 workers it surveyed have much more to do at work than two or three years ago; 42% of those surveyed report spending less time with their spouses in the same period.

Bonnie Michaels of Managing Work & Family, an Evanston, Ill., consulting firm, says that among 150 couples she sees each year in workshops and focus groups, those troubled by one partner's long work hours have doubled in five years.

Also, because both spouses tend to hold jobs, one is more likely to be savvy about the other's bad work habits. Bryan Robinson, a therapist and University of North Carolina professor who is studying the impact on the family of workaholism, says spouses complaining to him about overworked mates have doubled in the past 10 years.

"More spouses are bold enough to brush aside rationalizations for overwork and say, 'Yes, but there's more to life than that,' " says Harvey L. Rich, a Washington, D.C., psychoanalyst.

Of course, not everyone who works a lot is a workaholic; the term defines those who are so neurotically obsessed with work that they lose touch with their feelings. But more people are acting like workaholics as job demands mount.

The overworkers, deep in denial, can respond to complaints with a laundry list of sanctioned excuses: I'm supporting the family; I'm scoring points at work; my boss demands it. They are often the last to notice that relationships are suffering.

Jeffrey Ullman, founder and former CEO of a nationwide video-dating service, is writing a book with his wife on how overwork affects relationships; he says workaholics deny any adverse impact. Asked about their work habits, "They say, 'No, I don't have a problem.' Meanwhile, the spouse is sitting there saying, 'Who do you think you're kidding?' " he says. Children are harmed, too, he adds.

Strained relations with children are what sparks some spouses to action. One New York securities lawyer has faced such a sharp increase lately in the billable hours demanded by his workaholic supervisor that he rarely sees his two small children, says his wife, a brokerage-house manager. When the kids showed no interest in sitting next to him at a rare family dinner together, he nearly wept. She has begun insisting he spend more time with the family on weekends.

Many partners find the cure for overwork has to be as extreme as the habit. Insisting that her fiance's 16-hour workdays leave too little time for her, Lisah Chen is pressing him to take an extended overseas vacation through Asia and Europe with her this summer, sans computer and cell phone. Leaving the country, concedes her fiance, Tom Tirone, owner of an investment-analysis firm in Champaign, Ill., might just be the only way to get him to slow down. "When you're up to your ankles in mud in Ulan Bator [in Mongolia], you're not going to do any work," he says. He vows not to call the office.

Some resort to skillful subterfuge. After 10 years of supporting the marathon work hours of her successful entrepreneur husband, Marlene Amon secretly signed him up to coach their six-year-old son's basketball team. "When the league called him and said, 'You're signed up as coach,' he was shocked," Ms. Amon says. "Now, he loves it."

She also has started insisting he take time for dinner dates with her and golf games for his health.

As Azriela Jaffe's work hours as a career coach, consultant and author have spilled into the weekend, her husband, concerned for her spiritual life, often urges her to stop working at least all day Saturday to observe the Jewish sabbath. The Lancaster, Pa., entrepreneur often complies, something she would do less often without his urging, she says.

If both partners are open to change, a loved one's protests can spark serendipity. Philip Song, a Long Beach, Calif., entrepreneur, says he "was working like a dog" in his corporate real-estate firm when his wife began questioning the personal cost. She says they would lie in bed at the end of a grueling day and discuss the pressures facing him. She asked, "Is the money you're making worth it?" Her concern moved Mr. Song to focus on life beyond money and work. He switched to network marketing and works less than half as much, spending time with his wife daily and still making "a healthy six-figure income," he says. "I decided, 'I can either moan and groan about this, or I can do something about it. So I did something, and I am so proud.' "

—February 26, 1997

Marriages Go Begging for Care
as Focus Turns to Kids and Jobs

The idea of fortifying marriage gets a lot of lip service these days. From Congress to state capitols around the country, pro-marriage rhetoric is flying on such issues as tightening divorce laws, eliminating the marriage tax and reducing poverty.

I can't help but notice, however, an opposite pattern in the workplace and time-use trends I track, one that suggests marriage is taking it in the ear. In their Day Timers, travel planners and time cards, people are making marriage an also-ran in their daily priorities, trailing kids, jobs, household and family-care duties.

I'm an example myself. I decided to write this column after reflecting, while sitting across from my husband over breakfast one morning in a caffeine-induced fit of raised awareness, on how I neglect him in my effort to do right by kids and job. If I apply the adjective "long-suffering" to him one more time in my appreciative talks with friends and coworkers, somebody just might nominate him for sainthood.

Consider the trends:

Married people are spending less time together.
A study last March in the journal *Social Forces* focused on two sets of data on young couples of equal age, one collected in 1980 and the second in 1992. Authors Stacy Rogers and Paul Amato, professors at the University of Nebraska, found the 1992 couples interacted significantly less, ate fewer meals together and went out together less often. They also fought more and had more marital problems. Similarly, Yankelovich Partners found in a 1996 poll that 42% of working parents are spending less time with spouses, and one-third see more tension in their marriages.

One in five workers are on nontraditional shifts.
Such a schedule, says Harriet Presser, a University of Maryland

professor and an authority on shiftwork, significantly increases the chances of divorce. Also, Steve Mardon of Circadian Technologies, Boston shiftwork consultants, says one-quarter of dual-earner couples work different shifts.

Commuter marriages are rising.

Windham International, New York relocation consultants, says 13% of married employees left their spouses behind for overseas job assignments in 1996, up from 7% in 1995. Though comparable data for U.S. transfers don't exist, Tom Peiffer, a veteran consultant with Runzheimer International, believes U.S. commuter marriages have been rising for three to five years.

Though the setup isn't always bad, "it's really difficult for most people to continue a commuter relationship over the long term," says Linda Stroh, professor at Loyola University Chicago and co-author of a study of commuting couples.

Kids in many households are doing less housework and leaving more chores for parents.

A study on household chores by the University of Chicago and Brown University suggests adults now have less quality time.

Despite the stresses, the divorce rate isn't rising. The National Center for Health Statistics says it fell 19% to 4.3 divorces per 1,000 people in 1996, from 5.3 in 1981, outpacing a 17% decline in the marriage rate.

My mail and the dozens of interviews I conduct with working couples each month suggest many are developing a set of hardy, hang-in-there marital skills with a '90s edge. A patient commitment to shared values is one example. Darin Minter, an executive assistant, and her husband Steve, a carpenter, spend nearly all their off-the-job time with their four-year-old son Chase.

Friends tell them they should spend more time alone as a couple, Ms. Minter says. But while "our relationship has taken a back seat, it hasn't suffered," she says. "It's a shared choice. We could use more quality time as a husband and wife, but we realize there's a higher calling, and it's our child."

Some couples consciously strive under stress to appreciate each other's sacrifices and efforts. Robert Peiser, CEO of Western Pacific

Airlines and a corporate turnaround expert, has maintained a commuter marriage for seven years. During his job stints in five cities, including one as CFO of Trans World Airlines, his family has stayed in Bloomfield Hills, Mich.

He and his wife are sustained, he says, partly by a shared appreciation for each other's effort and sacrifices. His wife, who values steady friends and home life, appreciates the effort he makes to commute, as well as what he achieves professionally. He is grateful for her tolerance of the setup, as well as the "incredible amount of time" she invests in their four children. And they share a commitment to stability for their kids.

Others hone an ability to make midcourse corrections. Chris Reilly, controller for a financial-services company, says she felt a "huge sense of loneliness" recently after a long spell of spending too little time with her husband, also a financial executive. After weighing priorities, they took a five-day vacation away from their three children, giving their relationship a high-octane refueling. Though both place the highest priority on family life, they realize their children depend, too, on their having a strong relationship.

With the holidays upon us, I, for one, plan to spend some time pondering such subtle stories. While they provide only a glimpse of what it takes to keep marriages together, the skills they illustrate will in the long run, I suspect, do far more to fortify marriage than any action by Congress ever will.

—December 24, 1997

No, You're Not Too Tough
to Suffer a Bout of Burnout

Though I've written about burnout as a workplace issue, I secretly believed it was a malady suffered by others.

Studies have said as much as 25% of the work force is at risk of burnout. Nevertheless, I thought of the term as a pop-culture label for fatigue, or a scapegoat for bad work habits. With a flexible job I enjoy, I thought I was immune.

That's what I thought. And with that attitude I ran my life—straight into the ground.

In experiencing a bout with what I now respectfully call work-family burnout, I learned some things. Burnout is progressive; it sneaks up on you and, unchecked, gradually destroys your ability to see and solve problems. It's most likely to strike those who are doing something they perceive as important, and it undermines their ability to achieve it. At worst, burnout blacks out the most healing dimensions of life: self-awareness and closeness with others. Some notes on my experience, in hopes it might be helpful to others:

March: Spring brings a burst of energy, and I throw myself into a variety of roles, covering a spate of news, working on a new job project, managing my son's T-ball team, driving my daughter to soccer and volunteering at my kids' school (Colin Powell would be proud).

The phone rings nonstop, mail pours in, the fax bumps and grinds through the night. Enthused about everything I'm doing, I rise earlier and work later.

Early April: I begin misfiring at work. I send my usually receptive editor a column proposal and am startled to learn she finds it hare-brained. I spend days interviewing experts for a story only to realize I can't use the information. Brain rot sets in. I call my boss to tell her about a new project; she listens patiently, then says, "You told me about that last week"; I have no recollection.

Mid-April: To compensate for time poorly spent, I work longer and later. Sitting in my office, I doze off during phone calls. On the floor playing with my son one evening, re-enacting the movie *Twister* with an imaginary tornado whipping through a play village, I fall asleep sitting up. By the time I awaken, the entire "village" is destroyed. I wonder what else I've been sleeping through.

Late April: Cherished family relationships start to suffer, as the irritability and impatience symptomatic of burnout set in. As I approach my son's room one night, he slams the door. "Mom, you yell too much," he calls from behind the door.

I haven't walked my dog in weeks, but I fail to notice that the calm and perspective afforded by exercise are slipping away. My spiritual life atrophies; a phone message from my church, asking where I've been, sits on my desk.

Early May: My grim mood spills over to my daughter, who grows tense about school. Though I'm vaguely aware something is wrong, I can't see a way out.

I am startled to see out my window one evening dozens of artificial flowers sticking out of the ground. My son has "planted" them, creating a facsimile of the garden I haven't found time for. The fakes remind me I want a real garden, but I can't imagine when I might plant one.

Late May: After a month of minor illnesses, I raise a white flag and see my doctor. Hearing my pathetic litany of ailments, he eyes me askance and asks, "Don't you write about balancing work and family?" Get a grip, he orders: I'm burning out. (Though neither psychiatrists nor physicians include burnout in their listings of clinical ailments, I later learn, many use the term frequently in practice.) A false alarm—an X-ray showing what are later diagnosed as harmless lung abnormalities—provides another reality check. As my nine-year-old daughter, who has accompanied me, stares perplexed at the X-ray on my doctor's wall, I look at her and wonder, "What if this is all the time I have? Have I lived my life in the way that is best for her?"

Early June: Back in my office, I call the man who coined the term burnout. Herbert Freudenberger, 70, a Holocaust survivor, author and New York psychoanalyst who has been practicing for 40 years, experienced burnout in the 1960s, working in clinics providing free care to street people, and named it in the 1970s. The term has been overused and abused, he acknowledges. Nevertheless, he sees real burnout (a process brought about by excess demands on one's energy and coping mechanisms) as widespread, worsened by mass firings and disenchantment in the workplace. Also, jugglers like me are trying to do too much.

Over the years, Dr. Freudenberger says, he has learned to hold burnout at bay. He stopped conducting seminars and agreeing to certain media appearances. His acid test for any activity: If you had one more year to live, would you do it?

Then, "I draw a line," he says.

By Dr. Freudenberger's measure, I have a way to go in pruning my life. Humbled, I realize my kids will probably look back one day and laugh at me as an artifact of the baby boom age: someone trying to do it all, a cultural relic that will be as scorned in the future as multicolored shag rugs are now. Chalk it up to self-awareness.

For now, at least, I'm going to work right away on another remedy Dr. Freudenberger prescribes: closeness with others. If you'll excuse me, I'm off for a long weekend at the beach with my family.

—June 25, 1997

Growing Web Use Alters
the Dynamics of Life at Home

M y beloved husband of 17 years is a straight and steady guy, a true-blue sort whom I trust enormously.

But I have to admit: When he disappears into his home office at odd hours to log onto the Internet, I sometimes wonder what the heck he's doing. Where is he roaming on that electronic frontier? Is he working on professional projects? Or is he just chatting? Is he finding any e-mail contacts more interesting than our family?

Though I know where he's *sitting*, I don't really know where he *is*.

Soaring home Internet use is further blurring the already-hazy boundaries between work and family. Tom Miller of Find/SVP, an Ithaca, N.Y., research concern, says at-home Internet use has more than doubled since last year to 14.7 million households, driven in growing part by women.

While most adults first used home computers primarily as work tools, the rich menu of opportunities the Internet brings into the home is changing all that. Now, many adults tap computers as an avenue to both work and play, spending a growing proportion of Internet time on personal e-mail or just surfing the Web.

The Internet can be a powerful tool for strengthening families. Dozens of people have told me how it helps them rebuild ties with distant relatives, stay in touch with family members from business trips and communicate with college kids. Quentin Steele, a Roseville, Calif., professional speaker, says he and his wife sustain "a steady stream of messages" with adult siblings and a daughter who is a freshman at Brigham Young University. In just the past six months, "e-mail has taken a prominent role in our family's life," he says.

On the other hand, the large amounts of time many users spend on the Internet, coupled with the secrecy, freedom and easy intimacy of e-mail, cause tension for many couples, says Azriela Jaffe, a

Lancaster, Pa., consultant and career adviser who interviewed 130 couples for her new book, *Honey, I Want to Start My Own Business.* Many find the Internet so enticing that it "subtly degrades the privacy" of home life, she says.

At worst, an e-mail affair can threaten a shaky relationship. An Internet poll by *Self-Help and Psychology*, an on-line magazine, has drawn more than 100 responses by participants who said they had e-mail affairs.

In my own unscientific survey, I asked 14 couples in which at least one partner is a heavy Internet user how it's affecting them and found: Six said the Internet was a focal point for tension in their relationships, three described it as a source of fun and growth and five said it had a neutral effect.

Several said they often resent losing their spouses to the work opportunities posed by the Web. "When my husband was home before, he was home," says a Washington writer. "But now, he can get up in the middle of a Sunday afternoon and be gone" for hours, lost in e-mail and a Web-page design he is doing. She tried e-mailing him herself, the writer says, but he seemed uninterested.

For other spouses, Internet access widens an existing gulf. A Boston-area lawyer says she wondered when her husband bought a program with nationwide addresses and phone numbers whether he was searching for an old lover she resents. Thus she was upset when she awakened at midnight and found him in their computer room with the door closed. "There was no reason to have the door shut," she says. Though the computer screen was blank by the time she entered, she never asked, and he never explained, what he had been doing, leaving her with a "feeling of jealousy."

Still other spouses said the Internet robs them of time once spent together in homier pursuits. In the past, says a Connecticut counselor, she and her husband would sit together on the couch and "relax and read the newspaper. We might have a conversation about something one of us read," she says. "But now, it's hopeless. He's so involved with the computer in the evening that I just don't say anything to him."

On the positive side, Nikki Stern, communications head and Web-page designer for Hillier Group Architects, Philadelphia, says that while she sometimes has to nudge her husband to get off the computer when his on-line sessions last past midnight, they both enjoy sharing new Web design or data discoveries.

And when a former boyfriend took the trouble to look up Ms. Stern on the Internet and send her a romantic e-mail, it provided a little spark for her marriage. When she showed her husband the boyfriend's missive "waxing poetic about our times together . . . he was a tad impressed," she says. She e-mailed the old flame about her happy marriage and he soon stopped writing. "It worked out real well," she says.

In my house, the bottom line on the Internet is positive. We use e-mail to stay in touch with our adult kids; my husband taps such conveniences as on-line airline reservations. And after looking over his shoulder one evening, I finally found out what he is really looking for on the Web: his own version of the surfer's Perfect Wave—a simulated drive in his own virtual-reality Porsche.

—November 20, 1996

Too Many Gadgets Turn Working Parents into "Virtual Parents"

Working parents note: From the folks who brought you virtual reality and the virtual office, now comes a new kind of altered state: virtual parenting.

No one is pushing virtual-reality headgear as a substitute for parents—yet. But if Martians landed tomorrow and sampled a few high-tech ad campaigns, they might think we were close.

Many marketers are promoting cellular phones, faxes, computers and pagers to working parents as a way of bridging separations from their kids. A recent promotion by AT&T and Residence Inns suggests that business travelers with young children use video and audiotapes, voice mail, videophones and e-mail to stay connected, including kissing the kids goodnight by phone. A joint promotion by three companies aimed at business travelers urges faxing homework back and forth or arranging family conference calls—"a virtual family reunion." Kinko's, the business-services chain, promotes videoconferencing, and Motorola pushes pagers for families.

These ideas can work well, of course. Family use of all kinds of high-tech gear is booming, and the trend is meeting a real need for working parents, who often wish they could be in two places at once. When Mark Vanderbilt, a network systems engineer, was planning a scientific expedition to Antarctica, he taught his wife and three children to send and receive live video feeds over the Internet.

Philip Mirvis, a consultant and University of Michigan management professor, e-mails his nine- and 10-year-olds when he travels or works late. And flight attendant Marianne Bradley-Kopec of St. Petersburg, Fla., made a video of herself singing lullabies for her baby; her sitter used it to calm him, she says.

But at the risk of sounding cranky, I think some marketers are pushing a good thing too far. One joint brochure by AT&T and others suggests to parents that if they must miss a child's Little League game, they call the field for a play-by-play account by cellular phone.

("All it's going to do is bother everybody!" says Susan Ginsberg, a New York educational consultant who advised MCI on another family-oriented campaign.)

More advice from adland: Business travelers can dine with their kids by speakerphone or "tuck them in" by cordless phone. (If anyone suggested to my kids that they cuddle up with a cordless phone, they'd probably throw it across the room.)

Separately, a management newsletter recommends faxing your child when you have to break a promise to be home, or giving a young child a beeper to make him feel more secure when left alone.

The man who apparently coined the term "virtual parenting"— Gil Gordon, a Monmouth Junction, N.J., management consultant— sees a risk in such excesses. Mr. Gordon, a telecommuting expert, was among the first to warn against burnout among high-tech workers who overuse their gadgets. He uses faxes and e-mail with his own kids, ages 12 and 16. But again he sees a hazard in overusing technology, with working parents' using it "instead of being there."

High-tech gear fails families when they try to use it:

1. As a substitute for warm human contact. A New York banker raised the ire of family members by calling them only from his car phone when stuck in traffic. His family knew he was reaching out only during time he couldn't spend doing anything else, says Wayne Myers, a psychiatrist and professor at Cornell Medical School.

2. As a Band-Aid for too much absence. At one East Coast company that pressures employees to stay at work late every evening, working parents try to compensate by secretly sending e-mail home, says Deborah Swiss, a Boston author and gender-equity consultant. In that setup, she adds, no one wins—the kids, their distracted parents or the employer.

3. As a stand-in for adults. Sharon Maltagliati, an Ellicott City, Md., entrepreneur, tested a computerized calling system with 50 families to check on children home alone after school.

But so many parents failed to provide adequate backup, in the form of adults who would step in when needed, that she dropped it. "People were using it like a babysitting service," she says.

As a working parent who grew up on *Star Trek*, it's easy for me to harbor unrealistic wishes about technology. During years of missing my young children while traveling on business, I looked forward to sharing long talks from the road by phone. So when my daughter reached first grade, I called her one night from a hotel room 2,900 miles away and eagerly questioned her about her day. A pause ensued. "Mom, when are you coming home?" she finally asked. After mulling my answer, she reminded me that her favorite TV show was on and hung up. (Sometimes, I guess, you just have to be there.)

The trick for working parents is to find the middle ground— where technology enriches our ties with children, rather than underscoring separations. People already are drawing those lines on work matters. When AT&T tested an ad campaign for a fax machine that could be used to get work done on the beach, consumers told researchers they didn't want to work on the beach, an AT&T executive told a recent conference.

We might do well, it seems to me, to be just as thoughtful about using technology in family life.

—November 29, 1995

For Many, Work Seems Like
a Retreat Compared with Home

Have people become so attached to work they don't want to do anything else?

While the question will strike you as nuts if you make a living in a job that doesn't suit you, like gutting dead chickens or cold-calling telemarketing prospects, it's a theme in my mail from readers with more pleasant jobs.

"I struggle constantly with the urge to service my clients [vs.] wanting to be with my kids," writes a Massachusetts investor-relations adviser. A New York public-relations executive confesses that for years, "I was consumed by work," too detached from family life. A caller to my radio show, a Los Angeles entrepreneur, says he loved building his business so much he used it to avoid working on his marital problems.

The same question is the theme of a new book that's likely to get a lot of attention. In *The Time Bind: When Work Becomes Home and Home Becomes Work* (Metropolitan Books, 316 pages) due in bookstores next month, sociologist Arlie Hochschild sees a cultural reversal under way in which the workplace is for some people becoming a retreat and surrogate home, while the home is being invaded by the time pressures and deadlines of work.

Based on a study at a company with family-friendly policies, Dr. Hochschild finds workers are too attached to their jobs to take advantage of the policies and spend more time at home. Instead, consciously or unconsciously, they choose longer hours at work because they feel more valued, get more recognition or have friends there. Some workers, she also acknowledged, fear the consequences of appearing uncommitted to their jobs.

Home, in turn, is becoming more like work for many, Dr. Hochschild says. As workers sink more time and energy into their jobs, their home lives are compressed into fewer hours and ultimately consumed by the pressure and rushed behavior native to the workplace. The result, says the author of the 1989 bestseller *The Second Shift*: the emergence of a new "third shift," after one's job and second shift of housework, made up of the time needed to understand and repair damage done to loved ones by too much stress and pressure. The book enriches existing research on the notion that home life can actually lose out to work. In a 1996 book, *Home and Work*, Christena Nippert-Eng created a term "the greedy workplace" to describe an increasingly common kind of employer, one that demands so much energy and commitment that it limits workers' choices about managing work and family. Other research suggests people lack the will to make tough choices about family obligations. A survey of 100 CEOs by Christian & Timbers found that while 85% say they want to spend more time with family, only 7% believe they actually will.

I don't think the cultural reversal Dr. Hochschild sees is universal. The workplace she describes will seem like another planet to workers at less benevolent employers; some of the families she focuses on are especially troubled. But her take on the coping mechanisms we use to kid ourselves into accepting the shortage of fun, romance and leisurely family time in our lives is worth considering:

- We embrace "emotional asceticism," she says, minimizing the care we or our families need. Getting along without fun, understanding and support is a coping method computer consultant Teresita Dabrieo knows well. In the midst of a breakup with a previous husband a few years ago, Ms. Dabrieo took refuge in the work she loved, thinking, "Hey, if I throw myself even more into my work, I can avoid the fallout."

  But after building and selling two successful businesses in Washington, D.C., she realized she was partly to blame for the marriage's failure. So she started over, buying a lakeside home in Pella, Iowa, where she preserves time for a rewarding personal life.
- In her successful second marriage, she spends hours daily walking and talking with her husband. And in her business, helping start-up consulting firms, she stresses life balance.
- We pay other people to meet too many of our family needs, delegating caregiving to nannies, housekeepers and so on. This

tendency is so strong among executives and top managers that Jessica DeGroot, a Philadelphia work-life consultant, laments: "Is the world we are shaping one where everyone works and leaves the family side of 'work and family' to hired hands?"

- A third coping mechanism is developing a "potential self"— fantasizing you'll revel in a rich personal and family life sometime in the future. This one hits home with me. I work at home and try to put my family first. But I work so much that I often make my kids wait, promising we'll take that bike ride Saturday or spend lots of time together on our vacation. Meanwhile, they sometimes drift at loose ends.

As I talked on the phone recently, my nine-year-old daughter thrust a paper in my face with a multiple-choice question: "How much longer," it asked, would she have to wait to get my undivided attention? The choices: Minutes, hours, months, years, centuries. It's no fun to have a spotlight cast on our trusty mechanisms for denial. It's even less fun to discover yourself lurking in the shadows there. But if you believe, as Plato wrote, that the unexamined life isn't worth living, Dr. Hochschild's criticisms bear at least a few moments' thought.

—April 16, 1997

Good Time-Managers Try Not to Manage All of Their Time

The time-management industry is booming as millions try to regain a sense of balance and control in their lives.

Relatively new to the field is get-it-together guru Stephen Covey, a bald 63-year-old with a 200-watt smile and $100 million in annual revenue at his Provo, Utah, "leadership center." Dr. Covey is many things to many people: management guru, leadership trainer and mentor to CEOs and presidents (Clinton, that is). Lately, he's used one of his "Seven Habits of Highly Effective People" to start a time-management specialty, with 1,500 companies buying his "First Things First" seminars for employees.

You may think of time management as working harder, smarter, faster. The Covey pitch has a different focus: Create a mission, balance personal and work roles, build relationships and focus on activities with long-term payoffs. He encourages people to spend less time on unimportant activities, no matter how urgent they may seem, and instead attend to deeply felt lifelong values, such as relationships or other personal pursuits.

To see what all the fuss is about, I enrolled in the one-day course, which Covey trainer Bryan Kroff offered at Sun Microsystems. Since I write about life-balance issues, I should breeze right through this. Right?

I am in for a shock. In the course of the day, I learn that I live mostly in Dr. Covey's "Quadrant I," the time-management domain of hapless deadline addicts who neglect important life roles in favor of the adrenaline rush that comes from procrastinating until you're looking career oblivion in the face. This addiction to urgency costs me not only peace of mind but quality of work. And unless I change course, a lot of people won't have very nice things to say about me when I'm 86.

But more on that later.

You may have heard coworkers mutter, "I'm in Quadrant IV

today." That refers to Dr. Covey's four-quadrant grid classifying tasks as urgent and important (Quadrant I); not urgent but important (Quadrant II); urgent and not important (Quadrant III), and not urgent and not important (the "Well, whatever!" category, Quadrant IV). Got that?

It all seems a little canned. But Dr. Covey isn't a man to be taken lightly; recalling a story about how he once delivered a speech to 900 people lying flat on his back on a table because he didn't want a back injury to interfere with his commitment to appear, I plunge ahead.

Soon, I am engaged. A quiz on my use of time shows 60% is spent in Quadrant I. That's not all bad; corporate America often rewards such behavior. But over time, making a habit of scrambling to finish things fosters stress, panic and anger, then burnout and bad work. Worse, I spend a hefty 17% of my time in Quadrant III taking care of tasks that are unimportant in a larger sense. Mr. Kroff says most people need to spend less time in Quadrants III and IV and more in Quadrant II, attending to projects that have lifelong importance. To identify Quadrant II goals, we are told to write a mission statement.

At first, I fumble. To help, we are told to imagine how others will describe us on our 86th birthday. Though Mr. Kroff turns on some calming New Age music, a horror show unfolds in my mind: Stooped into a permanent computer-gazer's slouch, I peer through my bifocals at a parade of family and neglected friends, neighbors and charity workers recounting my failings.

Mercifully, Mr. Kroff's voice pierces my thoughts: "Remember, these are things you HOPE people would say about you if you had fulfilled all your roles as you'd like." I dream up a set of tributes that would fill Mother Teresa with envy, and produce 26 words on such long-term goals as serving others through my work and community activities and raising children who will make the world a better place.

I'm impressed by Dr. Covey's emphasis on the quality of relationships, a litmus test of life balance. While I have been congratulating myself lately on tackling a big new project without falling behind, I realize I have been sacrificing effectiveness for efficiency, a cardinal Covey sin. I shoehorn so much into each day that I find myself saying things to my kids like, "OK, we have 20 minutes to play Barbies before bathtime!" Could this be why my son has taken to shouting, "Stop the clock!" when he gets up to get some juice? Such micro-scheduling, Mr. Kroff reminds us, is demeaning to people.

My briefcase bulging with six pounds of Covey stuff, I trek home feeling it's far too much to absorb in a day. Under the banner of time management, these seminars serve purposes met in simpler times by such rituals as attending church regularly, celebrating the harvest, helping neighbors or pondering the sunset: Getting us to slow down and reconnect with long-term values.

But the course does alter the way I see things and schedule my weeks. Shaking off the urge to stall, I file this column a week early. (My editors are stunned.) I set Quadrant II goals: Staying in closer touch with a beloved family friend battling cancer, cultivating deeper daily communication with my kids.

Will it stick? Borrowing Dr. Covey's own eighth habit for personal success—dressing up common sense as profundity—I conclude that time will tell.

—October 9, 1996

Five Friends Get the Lift
They Need from a Girls Night Out

Many of the people I talk to in writing this column say they have stripped down their lives to the bare essentials—work and only the most pressing family and personal responsibilities—just to get everything done.

That's undeniably efficient. But it robs us of a powerful source of renewal: Aimless time spent with friends, for perspective and support.

I had dinner recently with five New York professionals who, in a remarkable friendship, have met every two months for 13 years since they graduated from New York University with M.B.A.s. All landed good jobs at well-known companies. Over the years, their friendship has overcome deep lifestyle differences of the kind that usually divide people. Three married and became parents, two remained single. Three moved to the suburbs, two stayed in New York City. Two started their own businesses.

Through all the changes, the group—"Girls Night Out," or GNO, as they call themselves—has been united by shared values: Delight in financial independence, commitment to their work and insistence on a rewarding, healthy life off the job.

Ronald Reagan had just settled in at the White House when the allure of business careers drew the five young women to NYU's Wall Street campus. Ruth Elman had been a professional dancer, Andrea Rothberg a teacher, Joanne Spigner a department-store buyer, Rebecca Riorden a paralegal and Joan Ellis a museum fund-raiser.

Sparks flew from the beginning, when the five teamed up at NYU in a class competition to market a hypothetical soft drink. The women pulled many all-nighters to come in second place. (When the winners tried during the competition to skimp on market research and asked the women to share their findings, Ms. Rothberg told them to drop dead.)

From the start, GNO members explain over Chinese food, they

encouraged each other to aim high. After graduation, when Ms. Elman hesitated to interview at a big real-estate firm, GNO urged her
on. She landed a job that began a 13-year rise through the ranks,
to equity vice president at the firm. Later, Ms. Ellis, a securities analyst, hesitated to ask for a raise. GNO insisted she was worth it and
should try. She got what she asked for.

They shored each other up through the trials of corporate re-
structurings. Ms. Rothberg was devastated when her brokerage-
house bosses, who had praised her work earlier, laid her off. "You're
just not working out," they said. But GNO "rallied all around me,"
she says. "They told me it wasn't me, that it was a stupid situation,
that [the bosses] were ridiculous, insane." Heartened, Ms. Rothberg
quickly landed a new post as a product-marketing manager at another brokerage firm. (The GNOers were later proven right, when a
former boss called Ms. Rothberg to apologize. Her performance
had been excellent, he said, but she was chosen for layoff because
"you had an MBA, you were young and bright and we knew you'd
land on your feet.")

As workloads grew, members focused increasingly on sustaining
their lives off the job, reflecting the evolving values of the work
force as a whole. By the late '80s, infant seats appeared under the
table at GNO gatherings as Ms. Rothberg, Ms. Elman and Ms.
Spigner became parents. Ms. Ellis and Ms. Riorden also have avid
nonwork interests; Ms. Ellis studies Aikido, a martial art, and cares
for an aged aunt. Ms. Riorden, a budgets and planning manager,
plays softball and has close ties with five nephews and nieces. In fact,
Ms. Ellis says she and Ms. Riorden "set better boundaries [on work]
than the mothers."

Ms. Rothberg, the marketing manager, is trying to set better
boundaries, too. When she announces she has taken some time
lately to read and volunteer at her temple, she endures some teas-
ing. "Andrea packs her life more than anyone I know," Ms. Ellis says.
Stories of Ms. Rothberg preparing elaborate fried-artichoke dishes
after 80-hour work weeks, or frosting dozens of cupcakes, are retold.

When asked about the change, Ms. Rothberg, turning serious, explains that she and her husband were both working so hard that she
feared the things that matter most to her "were going to get lost."

GNO also encouraged Ms. Spigner and Ms. Elman when they left corporate jobs to start their own businesses. Some coworkers mis-interpreted their motives as spending more time with their kids. While both women value that, their real goal, reinforced by GNO, was to reap greater career rewards. "We left to do meaningful work on our own terms," says Ms. Spigner, who had risen to managing director at a financial-services company.

The talk turns to men. GNOers tell of Wall Streeters under heavy stress; one dropped dead in his soup at age 42, another yearns for time with his children. Many men they know envy the support GNO-ers enjoy. One told Ms. Rothberg, "I wish I had a group like that, but when I mention it to the guys, they think I'm out of my mind."

Fortune cookies arrive, and the group is asked what they will be doing in 20 years. "No idea," they agree, but they'll still be meeting. And what are their hopes for the children in their lives? A thick armor of self-esteem, the women respond; better ways to cope with the mounting competitiveness of the workplace—and friends like GNO. "I hope my sons," says Ms. Spigner, mother of two boys, "have a group like this."

—May 29, 1996

Keeping Your Career
a Manageable Part of Your Life

L ong ago, I thought juggling work and family was like anything else in life: It would all work out if I tried hard enough.
Several years and two babies later, I felt as though I had
been hit from opposite directions by two speeding trains. My
kids had experienced all sorts of day-care traumas, I had a bad case
of burnout, and my career track, through no fault of my employer,
looked like a dying man's cardiogram.

Could I have used a few more skills in managing work and family?
You bet. Would I have listened if someone had tried to teach them to
me in advance? Maybe, maybe not. But the idea that self-management
skills—all the rage in career planning—can be taught in a formal way
to ease work-family conflict was powerful enough to draw 20 business-
school professors and corporate work-family managers to Merck
headquarters at Whitehouse Station, N.J., recently to discuss it. The
group, named the Wharton-Merck Work-Life Roundtable for its orga-
nizers, University of Pennsylvania's Wharton School and Merck, includes Xerox, Johnson & Johnson and Marriott International, among
other employers, and Northwestern University, the University of Virginia, Seattle University and other schools.

To identify "work-life balancing skills" shared by successful people, roundtable members did case studies of 36 professionals and
managers. Some common abilities they discovered: clarifying and
acting on your values; building trusting relationships at work; asking
for what you need from bosses and family members and (heretical
though it may seem) learning to accept from yourself "less than
100% some of the time"—a corollary to "working smarter," says
Stewart Friedman, director of the Wharton Life Interests Project
and a roundtable organizer. Wharton and Merck plan to publish a
guide on the skills next year.

The focus on self-management is long overdue. While corporate
work-family programs such as child-care aid and flexible scheduling

are important, a huge majority of Americans work for companies that offer no such supports. High-pressure jobs increasingly force people to pull out all the stops to manage personal and family responsibilities, yet few feel free to talk about it at work. Encouraging organizations to elevate successful examples to a level worthy of "forced time and attention," Dr. Friedman says, can break the silence and get people thinking about life balance earlier in their careers.

Indeed, learning from the stories of the Wharton-Merck research participants could help many of us make the kinds of mid-course corrections in life that forestall career derailment, burnout—or waking up on our deathbeds realizing we blew it.

For most of us, a few days in the life of Wendy L. Lewis, for example, a 39-year-old single mother of three who is human-resources manager for the Chicago Cubs and studies weekends for an M.B.A., would feel like swinging a leaded bat before stepping up to the plate. Ms. Lewis trains like an athlete for her 19-hour days, watching her diet and often rising at 4 A.M. to work out.

She has learned how much her body can take. She tried sleeping only four hours a night, only to start dozing at the wheel of her car in broad daylight, she says. The lesson? "We have to take care of ourselves. We can manage the heck out of our time, but our bodies will only give up so much," she says. Another learned skill: Ms. Lewis doesn't shrink from talking about her role-juggling with anyone affected by it. Though she sometimes uses vacation time or takes work home to meet commitments, she frequently discusses her schedule with her boss so he knows "I'm going to get the job done," she says. At home, she talks "constantly" with her daughters about their feelings and needs.

Another necessity: Delegate, delegate, delegate. Ms. Lewis' 18-year-old twins have learned to pay household bills and plan meals. At work, she recently gave a staffer the task of interviewing job candidates.

And in perhaps the toughest challenge, she reaches out to others. After suffering "a lot of guilt" because she can't always pick up her youngest daughter, 10, from afterschool care, she asked another mother to drive her home a few days a week. To Ms. Lewis' relief, the mother was happy to help.

In other cases, work-family successes were constructed on a foundation of past failure. One manager said he bowed early in his career to pressure to take an overseas assignment without his wife and children. Though he came home for a long weekend every few months, the separation "was just too much" for his family, he says. A painful divorce followed. Chastened, the manager, now remarried, finds ways to devote more energy to his second wife and family.

Why should employers care? Perry Christensen, Merck's director of human resource strategy and planning, paraphrases noted author and consultant Peter Senge of MIT: "You can't build an effective company on a foundation of broken homes and strained personal relationships." Self-management skills are the building blocks of good management, says Mr. Christensen, a co-organizer of the roundtable. Just as cross-training or a stint abroad can increase an employee's value, the ability to savor a rich personal and family life also affords "depth, perspective and skill."

—April 12, 1995

In Real Life, Hard Choices
Upset Any Balancing Act

Multitasking may be all the rage, but applying it to family life can produce pretty trivial advice.

"Learn to do two things at once!" shouts an article stuffed with "How-I-Do-It-All" tips. Among them: Pay bills in the bathroom while watching your toddler in the tub; do errands while spending quality time with your spouse; call in catalog orders while feeding the baby in the middle of the night.

Such tips may make it easier to get two lifetimes' work done in one. But conspicuously absent from the pop-culture rhetoric is any discussion of making tough choices—when a job demands too much, when the urgent needs of an employer and a family member can't be reconciled or when you find yourself unable, ever, to leave the office behind.

"Even the words we use about work-life conflict—'juggling,' 'balancing,' 'managing'—all imply that if you just do it all skillfully enough, everything will be OK," says Faith Wohl, director of the federal Office of Workplace Initiatives. "There's an implicit arrogance about the idea that you can manage your way through some of the crises that people encounter—crises that affect their soul, their spirit and their being. Integration is a better word," she adds.

We looked last week at some examples of work-life balancing skills used by successful people, as identified by the Wharton-Merck Roundtable, a group of academics and corporate managers, including Ms. Wohl, organized by Merck and the University of Pennsylvania's Wharton School. This week, we look at two examples from the group's research, showing how people's lives change when work-family conflict pushes them beyond juggling into a realm the roundtable calls "life lessons." Both reflect a truth that should guide employer policy on issues from child care to career planning: The drive to integrate work and family is often a lifelong process, and it is powerful enough to reshape careers in unforeseen ways.

Trudy DeSilets has spent much of her career searching for an employer who would allow her to satisfy personal and professional values. The first step, after her child was born 16 years ago, was learning when to bail out of a repressive corporate environment. Though she was performing well in a fast-track sales job, travel demands left her exhausted. When she asked to job-share, her bosses turned her down.

By the time her daughter was three, she hit burnout. "I felt like I couldn't do anything right. I wasn't doing my job right. I wasn't doing my mothering right. I wasn't being a wife right," she says. "One day I just broke down and cried. I said, 'I've got to quit my job,' " a wrenching decision because "I loved what I did."

But Ms. DeSilets soon learned she could thrive outside a big company. She started a successful marketing firm, enabling her "to work at 2 A.M. if I wanted and still deliver the goods to the client," she says. She also got her M.B.A. But work and personal values collided again during a stint for another employer, where she was required to work through a religious holiday with "no recognition of the fact" that it was important to her and her family, Ms. DeSilets says. She soon resigned.

By the time she joined retailer Eddie Bauer 1½ years ago, Ms. De-Silets, 45, knew how to spot a corporate culture that matched her values. As Bauer's manager of marketing systems, she says, she has found an environment that is rigorous in strategy and flexible with employees. She can start her day at 6:45 A.M. so she can leave for afternoon activities with her daughter.

No such flexibility marks the workplace of options trader Steve Bloom, 38. Efforts to blend a consuming career with fatherhood got off to a rocky start when his first child was born just before the 1987 stock-market crash. "My wife said, 'I really need you here now,' " yet market turmoil forced him to work 100-hour weeks, he says. Caught between two once-in-a-lifetime events, Mr. Bloom did his best. But "my wife had to be more understanding than humanly possible," he says.

As his family grew by two more children, Mr. Bloom found his work so demanding that he "was constantly making an effort to turn it off" and be psychologically present at home. He managed more than many traders to be present, getting home by 6 P.M. and cutting a business trip short to attend his son's birthday party. But the psychological demands of his work intensified when he switched to the 24-hour-a-day currency markets.

When the compromises weighed too heavily, Mr. Bloom took a break. He quit the firm where he was founding principal and, for two years, has attended mostly to family, renovating a house and traveling. While the family time has been "terrific," he says, he's "getting itchy. For the first 10 years I probably overweighted the professional life. For the last two years, I've overweighted the family side," he says. "I'm still searching to find that balance." He says he has defined a crucial value: A work environment where family concerns are recognized.

There is, many would say, no right or wrong way to integrate work and family. There are only more or less costly ways in terms of career, relationships or health. Roundtable members hope their research on self-management will help students, managers and workers anticipate their own life dilemmas and be more sensitive to those of others, says Stewart Friedman, an organizer and Wharton professor. "What we hope to do," he says, "is to get people asking the right questions."

—April 19, 1995

Forget Juggling and Forget Walls; Now, It's Integration

The work-home split—the belief that you have to be different people on the job and at home and erect thick mental walls between them—is narrowing.

People like Rusty Grim are speeding the trend. The former river guide moves back and forth between work and personal life many times a day. As art director at Oliver Russell & Associates, a Boise ad and interactive-media concern, he breaks to take a walk with his wife and toddler, banter with coworkers' kids playing near his desk, take his daughter to swimming class or work out at the gym. He has finished projects at his office holding his baby in a Snugli.

At home, he works via e-mail or phone, or returns to the office after his daughter's bedtime. For him, work and home "are all part of the same thing. I can't turn either on or off," he says. "It all has to be part of the rolling-forward experience."

The name for this is "integration," and it's the hottest work-life buzzword since "juggling." A behavior ascribed to people (mostly women) with multiple but disparate roles, "juggling" denoted a circus-like act that allowed little sustained focus and was destined to fall apart. It has fallen out of favor in recent years as a solution to anything.

The newer idea, integration, encompasses both men and women. It means drawing the worlds of work and home closer through technology, workplace flexibility and other means, so people can move seamlessly between the realms. The assumption is they will accomplish more and lead richer lives on both fronts.

People who work from home or their cars have been integrating their lives for some time. Now, the idea is seeping into corporate life and acquiring cachet among consultants and researchers, not only as an individual work-family strategy, but as a societal avenue to a broader shoring up of family and community life.

Most people, of course, haven't had a chance to try this idealistic strategy. Many hands-on jobs in the service and manufacturing sectors prevent it; so do rigid or workaholic corporate cultures or long commutes. Also, some people have a psychological need to draw a deep separation between work and home. Nevertheless, forecasters at Battelle, a Columbus, Ohio, research concern, call the convergence of work and home life one of the top 10 trends of the next decade. A few chief executives are making integration a workplace norm. Russ Stoddard, president of Oliver Russell, Mr. Grim's employer, sets no work-home boundaries for employees. He asks them to focus on serving clients and meeting goals; when and how they work is up to them. While "it's hectic as hell around here," he says, "you can't find a better model for attracting and keeping people."

Tina Williford, a vice president, loan operations, at First Tennessee National, Memphis, says she gets 50% more done both at work and at home since she and her boss agreed on a plan for her to integrate her life. She limited her work at the office to seven hours a day but is available a total of 12 hours via pager, phone and PC.

She moves between work and home roles dozens of times a day. Instead of eating out with the family three times a week, she is home by late afternoon every day to prepare dinner, often taking work calls at the stove. She also works during lulls in her school volunteer stints.

A voice-mail message she left for her boss included the remark, "Yes, Honey, it is a blue truck," an aside to her toddler. "The joke at the company is, 'There's no telling what you're going to hear on Tina's voice mail,' " she says. Her bosses are happy, her kids love the setup and she is less frazzled.

Integration poses mental and emotional challenges. Too often, home life suffers when work spills over. In a letter to me, an Ohio wife laments that "dinner is often interrupted by phone calls and faxes" from her husband's job. Yet, "I am continually berated for making a big deal out of all this," she writes.

The damage to relationships in such cases is a big deal; avoiding it requires sensitivity.

Among the ways Donna Kauffman, a computer specialist at Lancaster Laboratories, Lancaster, Pa., integrates her life is by taking work to her son's sports practices. But she takes pains to watch when her son wants her to. "It's read this, look up, read this, look up," she says. Her new flexibility allows her to stay home long enough in the mornings to see her kids off to school.

Successful integration requires mental disciplines, too: Schedule personal time thoughtfully and assign it as much importance as work. Communicate skillfully to let everyone involved know your plans. Make clear, agreed-upon work objectives a personal mantra.

Despite the demands, I see benefits in giving more workers a chance to try integration. It's a great employee-retention tool. And the dozens of employees I know who have freedom to integrate are valuable to their communities, providing an adult presence at school-bus stops, volunteering at schools and charities and looking in on aged relatives. All of them say their experience proves that a satisfying personal life makes them better workers. Mr. Grim comes up with some of his best ideas, he says, on workday walks with his family. To serve clients with relevant products, he adds, "you have to have a life yourself."

—February 18, 1998

Do We Work More Or Not?
Either Way, We Feel Frazzled

Harvard economist Juliet Schor declared in 1991 that Americans are working an average 163 more hours a year than in the 1960s. Her book *The Overworked American* was embraced by the media, striking a chord with stressed-out workers.

In 1997, University of Maryland's John Robinson and Penn State's Geoffrey Godbey declared Americans were working 2.8 hours LESS a week (or 140 hours a year assuming 50 weeks of work) compared with the 1960s. Their book, *Time for Life*, was embraced by the media, with one newsmagazine delivering stressed-out workers a verbal slap upside the head with a headline, "Get over it."

What's going on? Are Americans working more or less?

The dispute has experts duking it out anew over an old issue, the best way to measure Americans' work effort. It also sheds new light on our pursuit of the Holy Grail of the '90s: more time.

First, a look at the conflicting studies. How can researchers reach such different conclusions, studying roughly the same time period, about how much Americans work?

Basically, they're measuring different things. Dr. Schor, contending Americans are working more weeks each year, gauges annual rather than weekly work hours. She corrects for growth in unemployed and under-employed workers, pushing work hours higher. She relies mostly on a monthly government survey of 50,000 households, the Current Population Survey, that asks people to estimate time spent at work.

Dr. Robinson and Dr. Godbey measure weekly work hours, counting only time actually spent working (not schmoozing or goofing off at work). They draw on three smaller studies at 10-year intervals in which 1,200 to 5,400 people filled out detailed "time diaries" accounting for every minute of the day. Each camp criticizes the other's yardsticks on points too complex to analyze here.

Whom to believe? You should probably join the Robinson-Godbey camp if you think only time spent actually working should be counted as "work" (the more important measure to empiricists, including employers) and if you favor precision over breadth (the small diary studies are unmatched in accuracy). The Schor camp is probably for you if you think all time spent at work should be counted as "work" (the more important measure to those concerned with work's effect on family and community life) and if you favor breadth over precision (the Current Population Survey is unmatched in scope and continuity).

Like Dr. Schor, other economists see a trend toward increased work time. The Bureau of Labor Statistics says employed women are working 233 more hours a year than in 1976, men 100 more hours. That helps acccount for Americans' feeling so pressed for time, says Dr. Schor, whose new book, *The Overspent American,* is to be published in January.

But even the 163 additional hours of annual work time she sees Americans putting in isn't enough, in my opinion, to explain the profound sense of time pressure Americans report in surveys. On that question, the Robinson-Godbey team has come up with another, equally interesting explanation. Like Dr. Schor, they say Americans' "sense of the necessary," their desire for goods, services and experiences, has expanded too fast.

But by training a microscope on our workdays, Dr. Robinson and Dr. Godbey also document a trend toward integrating work and personal life that is changing the way people experience time. Where the two were separate domains, we increasingly blend them into "a seamless web," Dr. Godbey says.

Vacations are shorter, and "leisure" has become part of the actual workday, with 25 of Americans' 40 hours of weekly spare time (excluding all personal and family chores) coming during the week in such short bursts we can't immerse ourselves in calming, refreshing pursuits. Also, work spills into personal life—aided by technology and a sense of rising demands—with workers "at home working, in an office working, at the beach working."

The result: In our rush, we forget how to fully experience each moment.

As we become a nation of integrators of personal and work

pursuits, it would make sense for employers to let their staffers shape their own work hours and workplaces. Then, employees could do their work when and where they are most efficient.

There's a message for individuals, too: If we integrate too much, too fast, we may blur boundaries so badly that the moment loses integrity. For many, savoring the here and now means separating work and personal realms, with no support from our fast-paced culture.

Marketing manager Brendan Carr is pulled many ways by his job and life with his wife and three children. But he draws broad borders around his workday, arriving at 7 A.M. to make the most of the quiet early hours, working intensely for 10 hours, then leaving.

"I don't sneak out the door. I walk out saying, 'Good night, good night, good night.' "

Home time is similarly self-contained. "Flying by the seat of your pants doesn't work," he says. "You've got to plan and manage your time. Otherwise, it's just gone."

Until more people draw better boundaries, "just gone" will continue to describe our national perception of time.

—July 30, 1997

Some Top Executives Are Finding a Balance Between Job and Home

Whenever a major article runs in this newspaper or elsewhere about women who have broken the glass ceiling, I hear two reactions: First, applause. And second, a question: Why did they have to give up so much?

Family life is often a casualty among men and women in the executive suite. Former Labor Secretary Robert Reich, who last January joined a string of top government and corporate officials who have quit to spend more time with family, declared in a *New York Times* op-ed piece that if you love your job and your family, "there's no way of getting work and family into better balance. You're inevitably shortchanging one or the other, or both."

If that's true, we're all in trouble. So I set out to find men and women near the top, or moving rapidly toward it, who are sustaining a passionate commitment to family. Among those I found, many (particularly the men) wouldn't be interviewed because they feared exposing the personal choices they have made. Those who did agree work in company cultures that are comparatively supportive to family. They also enjoy relative normalcy at home.

Nevertheless, their stories, summarized in this column and next week's, say a lot about what it takes to lead more than a one-dimensional life at the top: stamina, clarity about values and a determination to buck conventional corporate behavior.

Nailing down core values: As complex as Anne Mulcahy's life is—holding down a Xerox vice presidency, mothering two sons, ages nine and 13, sustaining a marriage and commuting 1½ hours a day—it all orbits around one core principle: "Our kids are absolutely the center of our lives," she says of herself and her husband Joe Mulcahy, a Xerox general manager, "and we never mess with that. That IS what we're about."

Ms. Mulcahy, 44 years old, is rising fast; last month, the former sales manager was named Xerox's chief staff officer, one of its top

10 executives and the first woman to report to CEO Paul Allaire. Subordinates say she has unusual ability to focus on core business issues, a knack that helped drive her 21-year rise through sales, general management, marketing and staff-management jobs. She also has a knack for spotting her kids' needs and organizing her work around them. She makes time for school field trips, and dentist and doctor visits. She has turned down transfers and other opportunities for the sake of her family. "You always have to be in control of your boundaries," she says. "The minute you let any company, any manager, try to set them for you, you've lost it."

She instead works to fashion what she calls a good relationship with the company and a reasonable career path, without compromising family. In seeking that delicate equilibrium, "Xerox has always reached to meet me halfway," she says.

That clarity didn't come easy. A failed first marriage years ago gave Ms. Mulcahy "a lot of motivation" to avoid risking personal life for career, she says. In her first pregnancy, too, she "tried to make it invisible," taking only six weeks' maternity leave—a stance she now says was a mistake. "When you don't make [work-family conflict] visible, you're doing a disservice to what is required to make it work."

She took a longer leave after her second baby and now takes plenty of vacation and personal time. When she has to leave the office for family needs, she tells people what she's doing. Men and women will both continue to suffer, she adds, if work-family conflicts remain "disguised so that nobody understands."

Her candor has earned her a following. She drew a laugh during a speech to Xerox women when she admitted feeling "out of control" blending work and family. "To hear somebody at her level say that, to realize 'I'm not the only one,' was a powerful experience," says a woman who was present.

Ms. Mulcahy's is not a "you-can-have-it-all" story, a myth she says deserves final burial. "I am no more than two-dimensional," she says. "I do work and I do family. When it comes to writing down hobbies on résumés, I make them up." She envies people who have time for community service. And her life isn't "a pretty, clean picture; there are tons of messiness and stress."

Nevertheless, her discipline has won her substantial time with her kids. "I'm not a believer in quality time over quantity time," she says.

She and her husband, whom she calls an essential source of support, give their nanny a normal workday and make sure one parent is present at all their kids' important events.

In the process, Ms. Mulcahy has learned to tolerate the whiplash that can set in when plunging from the status of the executive suite into the down-and-dirty demands of parenting. When she shows up at school, her boys chide her: "Mom, do you have to come looking like you just came from work? Can't you go home and change into jeans?"

Nevertheless, her presence, she believes, is filling up "an emotional bank" her sons will draw on indefinitely. When her older son was having some school difficulties, she spent months supervising his homework, then worrying that she might be pressuring him too much. The payoff: His excitement and pride when he made the honor roll. "It was a moment when you could sit back and say, 'Wow, it's working!' "

—April 23, 1997

Bill Galston Tells the President:
My Son Needs Me More

People quit jobs all the time to spend more time with family. But they aren't usually men in policy-making roles at the White House.

Bill Galston was at the peak of his career when he resigned recently as a domestic-policy adviser to President Clinton to return to teaching at the University of Maryland. He wanted to "strike a new balance" between work and life with his family, particularly his 10-year-old son, he says.

Few people have paid such a high career price for family time. A look at his decision provides a glimpse of life on the razor's edge of work-family conflict, when two commitments—one to a job, the other to a child—simply can't be reconciled.

Mr. Galston, an ex-Marine, professor and adviser to the Progressive Policy Institute, a Democratic think tank, had worked on losing presidential campaigns for John Anderson, Walter Mondale and Al Gore before he was tapped to join the administration. After more than a decade of getting trounced at the polls, the slight, bespectacled scholar—at 49 already older than many Clinton aides—was bringing into government ideas he had nurtured for years behind the scenes.

At the White House, his influence was evident in the president's call last January for a national campaign against teen pregnancy, an idea Mr. Galston had worked on as a private scholar. He planned the national service program, worked on education-reform and Head Start legislation and consulted with administration officials on matters from affirmative action to consumers' mood.

"He had an excellent reputation here, and he loved his job," says Gene Sperling, an economic policy adviser who shared an office with Mr. Galston.

Also at stake was no ordinary father-son relationship. In a speech last fall before the National Fatherhood Initiative, an advocacy group, Mr. Galston said of his son Ezra: "Fatherhood for me has been the most deeply transformative experience in my life. Nothing else is a close second. It is a prism through which I see the world."

Mr. Galston tried many of the usual ways to integrate his child with his workaholic schedule. Though he worked 12-hour days, he often brought Ezra to his White House office on the evenings his wife, a law professor, taught classes.

"He'd flop down on the floor of my office, do his homework and we talked," Mr. Galston says. When he was called into meetings, his efforts to be two places at once "got to be a joke" among staffers as he raced back and forth to check on his son, a White House aide says.

When Mr. Sperling complimented him on his "Herculean efforts" to juggle everything, Mr. Galston looked at him and said, "It may show a lot of effort, but it's still no way for a 10-year-old to be treated."

Many afternoons, he missed Ezra's Little League games; the child started rising at 6 A.M. because it was "one of the few periods I could be counted on to be around the house," Mr. Galston says. Many evenings, he came home "so wrung out that even though I was technically physically present at 8:30, I wasn't present in any other meaningful sense." After seeing Ezra to bed, he sometimes headed back to work at 10 P.M.

He made the rounds of meetings and conferences, often speaking on the welfare of children. A frequent theme was one he laid out in "Putting Children First," a 1991 monograph written at the Progressive Policy Institute with Elaine Kamarck (now an aide to Vice President Gore): The acid test of any societal change is how kids are served, and "somehow our nation has gotten socially and culturally poorer" in that regard, he says. His speeches and writings on revitalizing the nation's civic life drew bipartisan praise.

All the while, Mr. Galston sensed that his own house was in disorder, that "the sand was running through the hourglass" of his son's childhood, he says.

Then came Ezra's letter. Headed "Baseball's Not Fun," the note to his father began: "Baseball's not fun when there's no one there to applaud you." There followed a litany of achievements that Mr.

Galston had missed: hitting a triple and a double, stealing home and catching the final pop-up of the game. If his father was there to watch, "baseball would be fun," the letter said.

"It's not the kind of letter that a father is apt to forget," Mr. Galston says. Clearly, "what seemed like a minimally tolerable balance from my standpoint was not acceptable from his." Worse than his son's anger, he acknowledges, was his own private fear that the child might simply resign himself to his absence.

"These days, kids 12 and 13 are teenagers, looking to their peers much more than their parents," he says. He feared that if he "let those two years go by without re-engaging fully in my family . . . there would be a significant price." To a coworker surprised by his resignation, he said, "I told the president, 'You can replace me and my son can't.' "

It's easy to dismiss Mr. Galston's dilemma as an accident of timing. Families' needs ebb and flow, and his job of a lifetime got caught in a high tide. It makes sense, too, that a man who calls finding better ways to integrate parenthood and work "one of the most important agendas before our society in the next 20 years" would change jobs to improve his own work-family balance.

But if Mr. Galston and others are right—if we as a society are beginning to agree that the declining welfare of kids is a problem and that we need to put children first—we may see more decisions like his.

—June 21, 1995

Software Ace Turns His Life
Upside Down, and Is Happier for It

At age 41, software whiz Rocky Rhodes could write his own ticket.

As a co-founder and chief engineer of Silicon Graphics, he could pick among cutting-edge R&D projects at his company. He had a chance in 1994 to help Silicon Valley legend Jim Clark, Silicon Graphics' primary founder, start up another Wall Street darling, Netscape Communications.

Instead, Mr. Rhodes charted a course that felt "like jumping off a cliff," he says, by cutting back to a part-time schedule at Silicon Graphics. Few people at Silicon Graphics (or in Silicon Valley, for that matter) work part time, and no one at Mr. Rhodes' level. The move has baffled acquaintances and left him adrift at the margins of the company he helped found, casting about for projects that fit his oddball hours.

Why would anyone make such a choice? The answer lies in a faded yellow Post-It note, stuck to the refrigerator in his Los Altos, Calif., home—a note that turned his life upside down. But more on that later.

Mr. Rhodes (whose real name is Charles) hardly seemed a decade ago like a man who could pass up a career challenge. After co-founding Silicon Graphics in 1982, he toiled seven-day weeks for years, creating three-dimensional graphics software for the company's groundbreaking workstations.

He loved his work so much that he sometimes awoke at night with an idea and ran into the lab to execute it. His wife Diane, an Apple Computer product manager, was equally immersed in her work, and shared his passion for sports as well (both are triathletes).

But with the 1987 birth of Dustin, the first of their three children, everything changed. Ms. Rhodes quit her job; for Mr. Rhodes, life became "a constant battle, a struggle against the ability of my work life to totally consume me and, on the other side, this blossoming family life that I felt was more important."

Taking a hard look at their lives, he and Ms. Rhodes scribbled on the Post-It note four priorities they agreed were most important— God, family, exercise and work, in that order—and stuck it to the refrigerator. Dismayed, Mr. Rhodes realized that based on how he spent his time, "my working priorities were upside down." At first, he tried tinkering with his schedule. He baffled coworkers by taking three weeks' paternity leave, a rarity in 1987. He trimmed night and weekend work and gradually opted out of the new-product development cycle for an advisory role. After his third child, Gabriel, was born in 1992, he tried unsuccessfully to work at home (the kids kept interrupting), then took the summer off, going "cold turkey," he says.

He veered between family and fast track for a while, plunging on his return into a deadline project helping coworkers perfect a digital video-editing system. After working until 3 A.M. in a Las Vegas hotel room, the team finished in time to unveil it at a big convention.

But working 100-hour weeks again left Mr. Rhodes wanting "a final solution" to the tension between work and family. Taking another look at the Post-It note, he told himself, "That's what I believe. But looking at the way I lead my life and spend my energy, it wouldn't be obvious to an outside observer." In 1994, he talked with Mr. Clark about starting another company but Mr. Rhodes took a pass.

Encouraged by two books, William Bridges' *Job Shift*, on the death of the traditional full-time job, and Bob Buford's *Halftime*, on redefining goals at midlife, he switched to part-time work in 1995. At first, he wandered around the company wondering, "How do I fit in?" He worried the setup "wasn't fair to the company." But he persevered and found a satisfying niche, working on new features for the next generation of machines.

Acquaintances in Silicon Valley are puzzled. Mr. Clark wonders if Mr. Rhodes has gone "through some sort of mutation" since their 18-hour days together starting Silicon Graphics. A running buddy asked, "When are you going to really retire?"

Though he could afford to, Mr. Rhodes loves the flexibility of part-time employment and the camaraderie of the lab; on a recent walk through Silicon Graphics' Mountain View, Calif., campus, other engineers stopped him for advice. "I'm not the kind of person who could sit back and retire," he says.

Hearing he is only working part-time, others try to entice him into new ventures. Mr. Clark says he may offer Mr. Rhodes a role in yet another start-up he plans.

But advocates of finding better ways to integrate work and family would love Mr. Rhodes' example. Although not everyone can afford to work only part time, the all-or-nothing demands of today's jobs must be restructured to ease stress on families, these advocates say, and high-profile groundbreakers are needed before big changes can occur.

Mr. Rhodes wouldn't mind a stampede of imitators, but he is more interested at the moment in "getting all the bugs out" of his own schedule, he says. His new situation still creates tensions as he tries to allocate his time among job, volunteer work for a children's museum and his church, and his kids—launching model rockets with Dustin, eight; helping five-year-old Bianca with phonics and watching Ninja Turtles shows with Gabriel, three.

"I don't know if working half-time will catch on," he says. "But it would be nice if more people gave more thought to things they hold dear."

—January 31, 1996

High-Powered Fathers Savor Their Decisions to Scale Back Careers

It used to be that whenever a high-ranking executive announced he was quitting his job for family reasons, it was assumed, often correctly, that the explanation was a coverup for a firing.

That's not as safe an assumption as it used to be. As affluent baby boomers hit midlife and workloads grow, a small but noteworthy number of high-level men are scaling back careers to savor the humbler rewards of fatherhood. This Father's Day, here are thoughts from three such men on what it's like to live with that decision.

Jeffrey Stiefler: In resigning as president of American Express last September primarily to spend more time with family, Mr. Stiefler, father of four, gave up one of the most prestigious jobs in America. His move was the subject of a Page One article in this newspaper. Today, Mr. Stiefler, 49 years old, is still running hard as an adviser with venture bankers McCown De Leeuw & Co., chairing two portfolio companies. But unlike his former job, he is free from day-to-day operations and works from an office near his Greenwich, Conn., home, ending his commute to Manhattan. He is absent from home only 60% as much, he says, allowing him to dine with his kids, know their teachers and friends and "feel much more engaged in their lives."

He hasn't yet reached "equilibrium" between work and family, he says. His youngest sons, ages four, seven and nine, at first expected him to be home all the time. "The fact that I'm not has created a gap" for them, he says, a problem they have spent time talking about. (His oldest son, a teenager, lives with his ex-wife in Minnesota.)

Nor has he cut as polished a figure as a father as he did as an executive. Dropping his sons off at school recently, he accidentally slammed the door in the face of the youngest.

To make amends, he swept the child up to sit on his shoulders but banged his head on the ceiling. Among several mothers watching, half were laughing and half "felt a need to protect my son from my extraordinary ineptness," Mr. Stiefler says.

But personally, he feels "as productive and content as I've ever felt," he says. "What's absent for me is the conflict that I'd felt for years, the feeling that I couldn't be successful at work and at home, that a lot of other people could figure out how to do it but I couldn't. That conflict is gone, and that's an enormous positive."

William Galston: At the peak of his career, Mr. Galston resigned as a domestic-policy adviser to President Clinton to join the faculty of the University of Maryland and to renew his relationship with his 10-year-old son Ezra—a move toward a more balanced life that was described in this column last June.

In the year since, reconnecting with Ezra hasn't been easy or quick, says Mr. Galston, 50. At first, his son worried that "I was giving up something terribly important to me, for him . . . It scared him a little." Ezra's fear eased as it became clear that "I have never had a moment's regret," Mr. Galston says.

There wasn't any "magical transformation" of their relationship, but rather a "change of direction that over time makes a big difference," he adds. Though he still works long hours as a professor and director of the university's Institute for Philosophy and Public Policy, he finds it easier to leave work at the office, and adapt to Ezra's "kid rhythms."

Father and son regularly eat breakfast together, review homework, attend Little League baseball games and play basketball, Mr. Galston says—a humbling experience. Ezra "jumps better and runs faster and has a lot more energy. He also spends a lot more time studying fancy [basketball] moves on TV," he says. "My role? I stand there flat-footed, like a father should."

Has it been hard to leave the White House? "To tell you the truth, not really," he says.

He is still active in public life, making speeches and writing articles. And President Clinton has made many of the moves he would have recommended—confirming "my gut judgment that I was indispensable in one place and only one place," he says—at home.

Glenn McLeod: A senior manager for the Bank of Montreal, Mr. McLeod cut back to a compressed four-day work week, trimming his hours to 45 a week from 50. After traveling heavily on business while his two sons were young, he wished for the "unique richness I knew they would add to my life, if I would let them in."

His decision, made 3½ years ago, has had time to mature, and it has caused profound change. By taking Wednesdays off, Mr. McLeod, 43, was able to lead his sons' Boy Scout troop and build strong relationships with the boys, now 17 and 20, giving him new self-confidence as a father. He made new friends volunteering as stage manager for a dance company, and spent more time with his wife.

In a paradox, he has found that stepping back from his job has increased the rewards he gleans from it. Shifting gears has made him more curious, purposeful and disciplined in time use, and his community activities improved "my ability to interact with people," he says. In a related step, he made a lateral move out of line management into consulting. "I get called on to do creative thinking, and I'm having a lot more fun," he says. Though the change hurt his short-term chances for promotion, he says, "I feel a lot richer in life, and a tremendous increase in energy, to tackle whatever comes along."

—June 12, 1996

These Top Bosses May Signal
Move to More Family Time

A *Wall Street Journal* poll a few years ago of CEOs from the biggest U.S. companies showed a notable absence of work-family pressures. Among the 76 executives surveyed, child-rearing concerns and hardships fell almost invariably on spouses at home.

Studies at other levels of the workplace, however, suggest an entirely different demographic tide is lapping at the threshold of the executive suite.

Balancing work and family was a leading source of workplace pressure for 74% of men and 78% of women surveyed recently by the American Society of Chartered Life Underwriters and Chartered Financial Consultants, and the Ethics Officer Association. Some of these workers are dual earners or single parents. Many are '90s dads who want to be close to their kids.

A few of these determined integrators of work and family are breaking into top management. This column continues a look at executives who remain deeply involved in family life despite job pressures. I'm not prescribing role models; work-family choices are personal, and what works for one person may be wrong for another. But these people are forerunners, I think, of a kind of executive we'll see more of in the future.

A '90s division of labor: As head of new-product development for the nation's biggest disability insurer, Jay Menario, 37 years old, vice president, Unum Life Insurance Co. of America, feels pressured to "stay on top of the pile," he says. Yet "as devoted as I am to Unum's success, it isn't going to come at the expense of my children."

To meet both sets of demands, Mr. Menario and his wife, Diane, a manager for Bank of Boston, become shift workers at home. She takes the early shift with their sons, nine and 13, making breakfast, taking them to school and getting to work by 8:30 A.M. Mr. Menario hits his office by 6:30 or 7 A.M., then takes over with the boys at 5 P.M., running them to hockey or Little League and cooking dinner while she finishes work at 5:30 or 6 P.M. The Menarios' babysitter of 13 years, working from her own home, fills in gaps.

Mr. Menario integrates job and family whenever he can. When his older son, an avid hockey player, practices, Mr. Menario sometimes sifts through office mail in the stands. Sundays, he puts in several hours at home answering e-mail before the boys get up.

He makes tough choices on both fronts. When a Unum executive fell ill and asked Mr. Menario to make a speech for him in a distant city, he wanted to agree. But he had blocked out that evening months earlier: His son was in a school play and he knew if he missed it, "he'll be crushed and I'll feel like a heel," he says. He stayed home. (Both Menarios say their employers are very supportive.) At home, Mr. Menario resists pleas for a dog and substitutes jogging for the golfing he loves because it takes less time. He has narrowed his circle of close friends to three.

"I want people to not only say, 'He's a hell of a good employee for Unum,' but also, 'He's a damn good father and a good friend,' " Mr. Menario says. "You can do all three, but you've got to decide what [else] you're going to cut out."

Clearing boundaries: If you didn't know better, you might think Julie Cosser was two people. One is senior vice president, merchandising, at Eddie Bauer, overseeing seven divisions and 300 employees for the retailer. The other is an art docent and PTA volunteer at her daughter's school, acting at a recent fund-raiser as "tattoo lady," an image of Tweety Bird inked on her arm.

You might call it leaping broad chasms in a single bound. It takes skills prized in today's work-everywhere-all-the-time workplace: Draw clear work-family boundaries allowing time for home. Once you're home, make a clean break and plunge in up to your elbows—in Ms. Cosser's case, literally.

Many of her favorite moments at home have her up to her elbows in something—in soapsuds after dinner, talking with her husband and daughters, ages eight and four, while they clean up; in paint, guiding her daughter's class through projects on Matisse or O'Keeffe; or in dirt, gardening with her family. When she walks through the door, "I'm right down on the floor" with the kids, she says. "You have to be able to separate" work and family.

At work, she has learned to jettison nonessential tasks. She recently met with senior managers and told them to "figure out what meetings you don't need to be in" and cross them off. She encourages employees to let low-priority items slide off their to-do lists. And she has learned to tolerate piles on her own desk. "When you're inherently driven," she admits, "that's not a comfortable thing to do." She and her husband also bought a house minutes from their offices.

Ms. Cosser, 37, draws on the perspective she gained during the time she spent at home two years ago, after the menswear chain she left her job to start had failed. Her delight at extended time with her kids motivated her to trim night and weekend work when she returned to Bauer and to slip out of meetings early now and then— an attitude she says her boss, CEO Rick Fersch, readily supports. "I came to find that spending time at home was something pretty incredible," she says, "and if I wasn't careful I was going to miss it."

—April 30, 1997

More Executives
Cite Need for Family Time
as Reason for Quitting

The trickle of top business and political figures who say they are resigning to spend more time with family has widened to a stream.

New York Times Co. Chief Financial Officer Diane Baker and U.S. Rep. Bill Paxon both cited family reasons recently in announcing plans to resign. They join a string of high-level executives who have quit at least partly because of family, from PepsiCo's Brenda Barnes to Microsoft's Patty Stonesifer. A newspaper database search for people who quit to spend time with family produces 296 stories, from coaches to White House aides.

Of course, people often lie about why they resign. "Spending time with family" has often been used as a pretext for a falling-out with the boss or a looming job setback. But the family rationale isn't as phony as it used to be. The reasons are no mystery. Many top jobs have become excruciatingly demanding. The Bureau of Labor Statistics says the proportion of professionals and managers working extremely long hours—49 or more a week—has risen by as much as 37% since 1985. As baby boomers undertake soul-searching at midlife, many executives among them are concluding the price is too high.

In following up with high-level quitters, I've found most actually have scored lasting gains in family time. A few have even used the family excuse as code for seeking deeper meaning in life, and have used family as a starting point for overhauling all their priorities:

John Sites Jr.: When he quit one of Wall Street's top-paid jobs at Bear Stearns in 1995, some observers thought Mr. Sites had lost a power struggle. He said simply that he wanted more time with family. Three years later, he's still opting for a downsized professional life as a partner at Daystar Partners, a bond firm near his Connecticut home.

And he is spending more time with his family. Though he works 8:30 A.M. to 5:30 P.M., he is free of his former 2½-hour commute and the administrative burdens of his former job. Also, his work no longer keeps him chained to global market trends. He often goes home for lunch or picks up his kids, ages five and seven, at school. "They used to see me mostly in the dark. They knew me by my silhouette" at bedtime, he says. Now, they are part of his day-to-day life.

For Mr. Sites, resigning "to spend more time with family" was, in a broader sense, a way to reorder his priorities in life. He now carves out several hours a week for charitable and religious pursuits. "Changing your lifestyle frees you up to do what you want to do, as opposed to what you have to do."

Patty Stonesifer: When she quit as head of Microsoft's interactive-media division in 1996, she cited more time with her two teenage children as one goal. For Ms. Stonesifer, like Mr. Sites, family time was just a starting point for a life overhaul that included changing her work.

Her three-day-a-week job as head of the Gates Library Foundation, which provides Internet access to libraries in low-income communities, has rekindled her passion, she says. She loves "empowering people who want to make a change in their own lives." She also delights in a sharp increase in time with her teenagers.

She is still extremely busy, and strives to savor each moment and to find time for the "whole range of things I love." In pulling off such a change, she says, "you have to be extremely diligent about what it is that you really want."

Susan Molinari: This once-bright political star resigned her U.S. House seat in 1997 to be with her daughter, age two, and work as a TV anchor on *CBS News Saturday Morning.* She has indeed gained several days a week with her child, and more control over her time, she said in an interview on my radio show. Last month, her husband, Rep. Paxon, announced his own retirement plans, also citing family reasons. The news was met with skepticism. Mr. Paxon was a few weeks into a tough battle for the House majority leader's

job. In any event, both Ms. Molinari, scion of a Staten Island political family, and Mr. Paxon, son of a judge and a Republican party
activist, insist they aren't planning to run for office.

"Susan and I understand uniquely what it's like to raise a child in
politics, and to be children in politics . . . You spend your life under
the reflected glare of politics. It's there every minute, every time
you open the paper . . . You live with that as a child," says Mr. Paxon,
who often cares for their daughter while Ms. Molinari works. "We
want to have more children, so I don't see a political elective office
in the future."

Reed Hundt: The jury's still out on this one. Mr. Hundt left the
Federal Communications Commission chairmanship last November, saying he wanted to write a book and spend time with his wife
and kids, ages 15, 12 and nine. Even his son was skeptical, however,
that his hard-charging dad would hang around home for long. The
close friend of Vice President Al Gore still dodges questions about
his long-term future. So far, he is writing the book, working from
home and spending more time with family. He also is a resident at
Aspen Institute and is doing some consulting while co-teaching a
business course at Yale University. At least one person is delighted:
On his 50th birthday last week, his daughter, nine, gave him a card
that read, "Dear Dad, I love you because you quit the FCC."

—March 11, 1998

Executives Reflect on Past Choices Made for Family and Jobs

Peter Lynch, former Fidelity Magellan Fund manager, seven years ago uttered the quote heard around the world: "Nobody on his deathbed ever said, 'I wish I'd spent more time at the office.' " Ever since his take on that well-worn office idiom, anticipating one's dying sentiments has become a popular pastime.

Increasingly, people are evaluating their personal life-balance equations earlier in life—certainly long before the deathbed and even sooner than midlife.

I asked experienced executives and businesspeople over 50 years old, many of them successful parents as well, this question: Looking back, if you could change one thing about the way you balanced your career, personal, family and community activities over the years, what would it be?

Overall, those who responded seemed at peace with their life choices. Here is what they said:

Laurel Cutler, vice chairman, Foote Cone & Belding: "I wish I had known sooner that if you miss a child's play or performance or sporting event, you will have forgotten a year later the work emergency that caused you to miss it. But the child won't have forgotten that you weren't there. I learned it, but not in time for my own kids. I was a very good boss in this respect, though. By the time I had a number of young parents working for me, I would tell them, 'It's more important to be there for your child.' "

Ilene Dolins, senior vice president and a founding partner, relocation consultants Windham International, and an at-home mother for 15 years: "The most creative thing I've ever done is being a parent. I'm very proud of the way my children have turned out. At home, however, there were times I felt very frustrated and felt I could have been very successful in the business world. If I look back, I would have had child care more than once a week and I would have always worked some, part time." Blending paid work with full-time parenting would have eased the transition to M.B.A. school, she added.

Muriel Siebert, 65, president of Muriel Siebert & Co., the first woman member of the New York Stock Exchange and former New York banking superintendent: "I ran for [the Senate] 15 years ago [and lost]. If I have a frustration, it's that I should have run again, because I really have a very deep feeling for people. I've had a career that you can almost say could only happen in America, and maybe I could have spread the message better. Those of us who are fortunate enough to have been succcessful, have an obligation."

J. Michael Cook, 55, CEO, Deloitte & Touche: "I wish that over the years I had had more control over my time and more opportunities to be involved in family things. I wish I'd understood the importance of that Thursday afternoon soccer game. But it was a given [in the '60s] that you dedicated yourself to your job. Flexibility was unheard-of. One thing we've tried to do culturally [at Deloitte] is to say to people, 'Though client demands drive our days, we also have the flexibility of having multiple clients and the freedom to make our own schedules and to decide how and where to spend our time. Take advantage of that flexibility.' "

James Orr, 54, CEO, Unum Corp.: "Though I've been incredibly active in the community, I'd spend a lot more time on education reform. We need to raise the education standards in this country. We aren't properly preparing a segment of our young people, those who don't go on to college, to work in a civil society or in a business environment or to compete in a global economy." Also, he said he would like to have done some teaching, something he may still do at some point in the future. "We all remember a defining moment when a teacher made a difference in unlocking our imagination and thirst for learning."

Faith Wohl, 61, president, Child Care Action Campaign, former head of the federal Office of Workplace Initiatives and previously, one of DuPont's first women senior managers: "I should have gone to field day," a sixth-grade event one of her adult children recently reminded her she had missed. However, in the 1960s, that wasn't a choice.

"Businesses had no patience with the needs of working parents, and work hours were sacred. It's hard for young people today to know that was true. The flexibility to have family life become a part of the working day has evolved only over the past 35 years. Also, I should have learned to relax. My children play as hard as they work. I never learned to do that."

Randall Tobias, 54, chairman and CEO, Eli Lilly: "I can remember some blurry choices when my children were younger, when I may not have attended a play or a soccer game because I had some conflicting business commitment. It's ironic that 25 years later I can remember I didn't go to that event, but I can't remember what business thing I did and in some cases I have to stop to remember where I was even working.

"We have a clearer perspective when we get a little maturity. . . . When it comes time for someone to write my obituary, I don't want to be defined solely by the boxes I happened to occupy on organization charts. As important as that is to me, I want to be defined as the father of my children, as someone who made my community a better place."

—December 31, 1997

Part Five

AT WORK

Carol Lay

In the heyday of the Organization Man back in the 1950s and 1960s, work was work and home was home and never the twain did meet. A cardinal rule taught new hires on the job was, "Leave your personal concerns at home."

That day is gone. As pioneering work-family advocate Faith Wohl often says, workers' mental images of their children and aged parents often hover right beside them at their desks and workstations throughout the day, an invisible but powerful influence on productivity and morale.

The columns in this section describe the workplace issues that arise as a result. They address workers' struggles with face-time demands, relocation, travel and bosses who disapprove of their juggling act. Others discuss when and how to speak up about family matters at work and how to advocate for workplace change.

Finally, this section contains columns on one of the most fundamental changes in individual workstyles since the Industrial Revolution: The trend toward working at home or in your car. The challenges for workers and the potential benefits for home and community life are described. And on a lighter note, some pioneers in this high-tech way of working lay out the rules of conduct (or lack thereof) on the new workplace frontier.

Some Workers Find Bosses Don't Share Their Family Values

Before I had kids, I once criticized a colleague on a previous job for staying home because his two children were sick.

Annoyed that work was piling up in the news bureau we co-managed, I asked him, "Can't you just put your kids in one of those hospital programs?" (Hospitals then were experimenting with offering temporary day care for mildly ill children of working parents.) He shot me a disgusted look and stomped out of my office.

I was puzzled at his response to what I thought was sensible advice. I didn't know then what every working parent knows: The idea of dropping your sick child off in a strange hospital with sicker kids is repugnant.

Family matters are surfacing more often in the workplace, not only because of changing demographics, but because of changing values. Increasingly, employees feel it's OK to talk about family issues that affect work. In a study of 2,958 workers by the Families and Work Institute, New York, "open communication" in the workplace outranked all other factors as a reason for taking a job, netting a "very important" ranking from 65% of those surveyed.

Clearly, the new openness beats lying, which is what most people did in the past. It's tough to be nostalgic for an era when workers had to pretend to be ill to stay home with a sick child, or make up phony excuses for turning down a transfer.

But as the Great Wall between work and family crumbles, many people are having trouble finding common ground. Too often, work-family decisions become a battlefield for clashing values, diverting attention from the work at hand. My coworker and I had some problems to solve: Could he delegate more duties during absences? Were there ways he could get more work done at home? But our distraction over family matters kept us from solving the real work issues.

The conflicts have varied roots. Some managers are too inexperienced, as I was, to fathom work-family stress. Other, older managers are part of a post-World War II generation whose rigid gender roles left little room for ambiguity. In a complex twist, people who have made the most difficult personal or family sacrifices for career sometimes get the most hung up on how others handle work-family conflict.

When Cheryl Melinchak, a human-resources manager, turned down a transfer that would force her to uproot her baby from a good day-care setting, her boss on a previous job criticized her sharply. "I don't accept this stuff about, 'I can't move my family,' " he told her.

He offered a rationale that to him seemed logical but to Ms. Melinchak was bizarre: "I relocated 10 times. My son had to go through counseling, but he's fine now."

Ms. Melinchak says she "just looked at him and said, 'Are you listening? That's exactly the point. I don't want my daughter to go through counseling because of me.' " Angry, her boss gave her little help advancing after that, leaving her stalled for two years before she won a different promotion.

Clashing values can snarl management. Top managers at one manufacturing company were "dumbfounded" as growing numbers of employees turned down the frequent transfers offered by the company to groom them for advancement, says Maury Hanigan of Hanigan Consulting Group, New York. The values shift left management stumped over how to develop bench strength.

How to cope? Employees need to communicate, communicate, communicate. If family affects your job in a way your boss can't understand, explain why it's so important, says Mortimer Feinberg, author, psychologist and chairman of BFS Psychological Associates, New York. That may require some honest talk about why you can't miss a special event in a child's life or transfer when an elder is ill. If the family obstacle is temporary, make that clear, preferably in a documented performance review, Ms. Hanigan advises.

Employers need to view employee career planning as a long-term affair, tracking people over time to avoid casting temporary family snags as permanent barriers to advancement, Ms. Hanigan says. Managers also need to avoid the trap I fell into—giving ill-informed advice on family issues. Johnson & Johnson and other companies train managers to sensitize them to varying viewpoints. Others are writing policies to sidestep values conflicts. John Hancock Financial Services, Hewlett-Packard and others encourage managers to consider employees' flexible-schedule requests without regard for the reason, relieving them of deciding whether one worker's planned MBA is more important than another's ailing mother.

The great leveler—shared human experience—usually fosters understanding over time. Chris Kjeldsen, J&J's vice president, community and workplace programs, tells of a J&J executive-committee member who paid little attention to work-family issues until his daughter prepared to return to work after giving birth to his grandchild. Then, "the whole child-care issue suddenly rang true," Mr. Kjeldsen says.

In my case, a year after I criticized my coworker, I had a baby myself. A few months later, I missed work because she was sick. As I explained my absence, the same coworker grinned and asked: "Can't you just put your kid in one of those hospital programs?"

"No way!" I gasped. Then, remembering my own advice to him two years earlier, I briefly considered crawling under my desk as he exited my office, laughing.

—July 12, 1995

All Work and No Play
Can Make Jack a Dull Manager

Past research has shown that letting your life tilt out of balance—working so hard that you fail to "get a life"—can damage personal and family relationships.

But can it also make you fail on the job?

Two new studies suggest life imbalance—a dissatisfied sense that one's life is out of synch with work, personal and family priorities—is a factor in job performance, especially in new jobs where pressures are heaviest. Based on polls and interviews with 1,000 managers, Edward Betof of MC Associates, a change-management consulting unit of Manchester Partners International, Philadelphia, calls a "lack of balance between work and personal life" one of the top six reasons new managers fail, along with problems like confusion over expectations and learning the job too slowly.

When managers "place high value on what's going on at home and how they're spending their life outside work, and they can't get those areas under control to their satisfaction—that begins to have a very significant effect" on performance, Dr. Betof says. Distraction, irritability and a loss of commitment to the job can result, causing managers to fail or quit, he says.

Separately, in a study of 3,222 relocated employees and their spouses, Right Management Consultants, also of Philadelphia, and the University of Tennessee found a high correlation between family stress following a move and a transferee's job problems, including confusion about duties and failure to adjust quickly to new coworkers and procedures.

Richard Pinola, Right's CEO, rates family problems as one of the top five reasons relocations fail.

Why is the issue surfacing now? Because of a growth in dual-income and single-parent households and a '90s shift in values that puts personal and family pursuits above employer loyalty—all against a backdrop of intensifying job demands. "The message from the top is, 'Results, results, results, dollars, dollars, dollars and work, work, work, work, work,' " says Dee Soder, an adviser to senior executives.

The conflicts show up regularly in the protected confines of focus groups, says Charles Rodgers, a principal at Work/Family Directions, Boston. "People say they're not doing their jobs as well as they should because of their desire to balance their lives," he says. "Very few feel they can satisfy both job and family needs and do well on both counts."

The pressures are greatest in new or newly re-engineered jobs. David, a manager for a telecommunications company (who asked that his full name not be used because he still works in the same community), felt his family life slipping away as his company went through re-engineering. As he worked longer hours and took on new duties, he lost touch with his wife and children. "I couldn't leave the stress in the office. I would come home and I didn't want my kids to bother me. My life got completely out of balance," he says.

Though David had been known for creativity, he became distracted. "The juices weren't flowing," he says. Family concerns weighed on him; in meetings, his mind wandered to worries about whether he would face "a negative atmosphere when I go home tonight."

Unconsciously, he began trying to relieve stress. "I was just going through the motions, thinking, 'I just want to get this project off my desk.' I was so overwhelmed," he says. When his job was eliminated, he was almost relieved. Though his performance wasn't a factor, he believes his work had declined in quality. Now, David has drawn close to his family again while starting his own business, and he believes he is doing some of his most creative work ever as a marketing consultant. "My mind is clear again of the family worries that kept me awake at night," he says.

Other managers lose their ability to relate to coworkers, says Bonnie Michaels of Managing Work & Family, Evanston, Ill. She recalls one manager who, assigned to set up a new R&D unit for a consumer-products concern, worked such long hours that she lost her sense of humor and her ability to communicate without criticizing. The result: Everyone in her unit was uptight and nervous.

How to cope? Anticipate new-job stress and plan for it, Dr. Betof and others say. Ms. Soder advises some clients to take a weekend at a hotel with a spouse or a day alone with the kids before starting a new job, to shore up relationships and fortify the "perspective" needed to sustain top performance.

When Keith Foxx was promoted to national marketing manager for his company, he and his wife, Nancy, discussed anticipated stresses, including a transfer and overseas travel. Though she was eager to get a job after their move, Ms. Foxx delayed working for a year to get settled with their preschooler while Mr. Foxx pulled out all the stops at work. Her flexibility, Mr. Foxx says, eased family stress that otherwise "would have held me back."

Now that he is well-established, Mr. Foxx is reciprocating, doing more child care and housework while Ms. Foxx starts a job as a sales representative. He also made another lateral job change at work that required less travel. "I need to pay her back for the last year, for the things she's done for me," he says.

Though striking a balance isn't easy, Mr. Foxx believes it makes him a better manager. He can quickly spot family stress among his employees, and reassure them. "Don't worry," he recently told a subordinate concerned about child care. "I've been there."

—January 24, 1996

Work-Family Issues Go
Way Beyond Missed Ball Games

C onflicts between work and personal life aren't just a family
matter any more.

A New York attorney was working late after her boss, insisting she finish an urgent project, had gone home. As the
offices around her emptied, she grew increasingly resentful. She
had been planning for weeks to attend an event that evening. Near
midnight, she finished work, but missed most of the event. Eventually, the incident and others like it drove her to quit.

What did she miss? A party thrown by her closest friends, an occa-
sion her boss deemed unimportant, but that to her was essential to
sustaining a life off the job. "I'm a single woman and I'd like to meet
someone. But when you work long hours, it's difficult." Her boss
had "absolutely no respect for that," says the attorney, who asked
not to be named for fear of tainting her relationship with her new
employer. "I want a more balanced life."

Work-life conflict is hitting employees of all kinds, and it's having
a deeper impact on the workplace than most employers think. One
of the most extensive corporate studies so far, an 18-month effort at
Baxter Healthcare, shows work-life conflict is a sweeping concern,
afflicting men and women, single and married people, and low-
income and high-income workers alike.

The study shows 30% of employees at Baxter, known for its family-
friendly programs, struggled with work-life conflict at least weekly;
42% had looked for another job because of it. Contrary to the common belief that women with families are most pressed by demands
from home, men, singles and dual earners without kids were among
the groups most likely to have considered changing jobs because of
work-life conflicts.

By probing the nature of work-life conflict in 125 focus groups
and interviews and surveys with hundreds of employees, researchers
found the most painful experience for employees, especially hourly

workers, was not being treated with respect or afforded dignity as "whole people" with lives off the job—being ordered to work overtime on short notice or to change schedules abruptly, or being arbitrarily denied time off. Salaried employees said their efforts to find balance in life were frustrated by expectations for weekend and evening work and nonstop voice-mail availability.

Such conflicts in some units affected employees' behavior on the job, making them unwilling to put in extra effort, volunteer for overtime or talk positively with customers. "Why should you bend over backward if they're not committing to you?" one employee in the study said. The opposite was also true, with employees who felt supported saying they would go the extra mile on the job, says Marci Koblenz of MK Consultants, an Evanston, Ill., human-resource firm that conducted the study with Alice Campbell, director of work and life at Baxter, Deerfield, Ill.

A separate study at two other employers highlights one reason life-balance is such a broad concern. Mary Young of Boston University's Human Resources Policy Institute found long hours and a lack of clear work-time standards fed dissatisfaction among all workers, parents and nonparents alike. Post-layoffs, "the old idea of 'a day's work' has little meaning," Dr. Young says.

I see similar signals in my mail; the CFO of a marketing concern writes, "Just because I'm single and childless doesn't mean I have the will or the desire to work a 12-hour day, six days a week."

Many companies are recognizing employees' frustrations in a nominal way, giving work-family programs a broader "work-life" label and rolling out perks like at-your-desk massages and pet-care subsidies.

But frothy perks do little to erase the unease of workers who feel their lives are fundamentally out of balance. At a past employer, says Tarrytown, N.Y., writer Caitlin Kelly, a policy of feting employees on their birthdays didn't ease their frustration over their huge workloads. Ms. Kelly especially resented the expectation that she work through lunch. Five days after her birthday party, she quit. "I'm not five years old," she says. "I need a lunch hour, not a birthday cake."

To foster commitment, the Baxter study identifies a hierarchy of work-life needs, similar to Maslow's, that must be met. Denial of the most basic needs cause the most pain (stress, low morale, marital conflict); these must be satisfied before higher needs come into play. The most basic work-life need, the study says, is respect; second is balance between time on and off the job; third is flexibility, and last are work-life programs, like seminars and referrals.

"If a work-life program isn't grounded in basic respect for employees, it's built on sand," says Brad Googins of Boston College, an authority on work-life issues. Baxter executives are making balance a more mainstream concern, including it in standards for evaluating managers and adding work-life questions to its employee surveys.

The study helps fill a gap in work-life research. Management theoreticians have insisted an effective company can't be built on a foundation of strained personal relationships. We know now, from listening to employees of all kinds, that workers whose drive for balance is frustrated will respond in ways that undercut management goals. That's a finding worth thinking about.

—May 28, 1997

What You Should Say About Family Duties in a Job Interview

Anne Weisberg thought she had landed the Big Job she wanted when the Big Chill settled in instead.

A Harvard Law School graduate with a high-octane resume, Ms. Weisberg was lunching with partners in a law firm where she had completed three rounds of interviews and met nearly everyone. She knew "they were very interested" in her, she says.

Until, that is, she mentioned her family. "I work really hard, and I know I can do a good job. But I need to get home at the end of the day because I have a one-year-old, and my grandmother lives with me," she told the partners.

The response: "Their eyes glazed over," and she never heard from the firm again, she says. Her follow-up calls were brushed off. "I got the sense they were just praying I'd get another job," says Ms. Weisberg, who soon was hired and worked successfully at another firm.

What do you say about family in a job interview? The issue poses a dilemma for job seekers and employers alike. Unless you explore an employer's expectations for face time and night and weekend work, you might end up working for the wrong company. Yet if you raise the issue in the first place, you may never get in the door. Employers, too, need to know how well an applicant can manage overlapping work and family responsibilities. But antidiscrimination law makes it either unwise or illegal for an employer to ask questions about family.

These tensions create some pretty weird interview situations. Some bosses resort to amateur theatrics to get the issue on the table. When a New York public-relations executive interviewed for a job, the interviewer, who knew the executive had two young children, made a point of boasting about her marathon work hours, claiming she hadn't seen her own two children on a weekend for months. Later, the executive asked the interviewer's assistant, "Does this woman ever see her children?" The assistant replied, "No, she has the morning nanny, the afternoon nanny and the overtime nanny."

If the interviewer was trying to discourage anyone with family duties from hiring on, it worked, says the executive, who left in tears. "I decided my life isn't 100% for sale," she adds.

Another interviewer told the executive, "Look, I know you have children, and this isn't a job for a woman with small children. It wouldn't stop me from hiring you, but we work seven days a week with lots of travel." Though she says she appreciated his candor, his reluctance "to hire someone with my personal specifications . . . was a downer."

Under federal antidiscrimination laws, an employer who questions or makes remarks to a woman about her family, marriage, childbearing plans or pregnancy, then hires someone else (or hires the woman but fires her later), may find the words used in a lawsuit alleging sex or pregnancy bias. The Americans with Disabilities Act makes it illegal even to ask applicants about family members with disabilities, such as an ailing parent or a disabled child.

But some employers ask the questions anyway. "Who's about to sue anyone for that?" the public-relations executive says—a move that could poison the network of friends, contacts and headhunters who help advance your career.

Other employers are so gun-shy that they fail to explore with applicants such issues as face time and overtime—matters that concern most people with a life outside work, whether they have family responsibilities or not. Instead of making assumptions, bosses must examine "whether the individual can perform the essential functions of the job," says Michael Lotito, a managing partner with Jackson, Lewis, Schnitzler & Krupman.

Applicants need to think of family concerns not as a need for accommodation, but as cause for a businesslike inquiry into working conditions. "You have to sell them before you can do anything else," says Marilyn Moats Kennedy, a Wilmette, Ill., career adviser. Then, ask neutral questions that focus on what a typical workday is like, whether everyone is on the same schedule, and so on. If you can afford to risk a job opportunity, bring up specific family duties yourself—but not until you know an employer is interested.

If interviewers ask prejudicial questions, Ellen Bravo of 9to5, National Association of Working Women, suggests mounting a good offense. If asked what kind of child care you have, say, "I assume your concern is, 'Am I a reliable employee?' and I can assure you that I absolutely am. It means a lot to me to perform my duties, and I take every measure to make sure I can get to work," she says.

To lay the groundwork for a good working relationship, pregnant applicants should volunteer their plans in a matter-of-fact way, says Ms. Weisberg, now a Scarsdale, N.Y., work-family consultant and author.

Before Susan Miller, a former Avon Products executive, joined Bloomingdale's, she told executives there she was four months pregnant and assured them she would manage her work without jeopardizing the company's interests or her health. Her openness has set the tone for her tenure there. As vice president, shopping services, she sometimes leaves work for activities with her two kids and asks not to be invited to every evening promotion.

For Ms. Miller, any other stance would command too high a price. "I know when I'm 75 and sitting in a rocking chair on some porch," she says, "I'm not going to get my kicks out of remembering what happened on Shopping Night in 1996."

—April 10, 1996

How to Look Like a Workaholic
While Still Having a Life

In one of my darker moments in a previous life as a bureau chief for this newspaper, I started asking reporters to be at their desks by a set time early each morning.

It seemed like a good idea. But in a newsroom where people often worked until 10 P.M., traveled on short notice and put in seven-day weeks, my demand worked about as well as the 1993 Mets. I was hoping to raise productivity, but what I got was worn-out reporters—and a lot of empty desks after everybody put in an appearance, scattered a few papers around, then left again for bagels, coffee or a nap on the conference room sofa.

Managers' obsession with "face time"—assuming that output depends on hours spent at one's desk under the watchful eye of the boss—is the No. 1 enemy of employees trying to juggle personal and family needs with jobs. Rigid face-time demands wreak havoc with people's private lives, from child-care and school schedules to carpool plans, doctors' appointments and exercise needs. Face time doesn't work very well as a management tool either, unless you happen to run an assembly line. It values visibility over results, rewarding people who spend a long time doing work that others might do quickly.

Nevertheless, face time is enjoying a revival at some companies, where it is again politically correct, post-downsizing, to demand that people put in unnaturally long hours at their desks, regardless of the effect on productivity. "With all the 'do more with less' sloganeering going on, it is seen as heretical at some companies to leave" before 8 P.M., says Gil Gordon, a Monmouth Junction, N.J., management consultant.

The holidays seem like a good time to question this trend—and for me to atone for my own face-time sins. This column is dedicated to the face-time underground: the legions who daily find clever ways around bosses' face-time demands and live to tell about it. Here, from interviews with dozens of face-time veterans, are eight tips on making the boss think you're putting in long hours at your desk—when you're not.

The Well-Timed Appearance. At a Midwestern law firm where the managing partner often jogged through the halls yelling, "Work longer, harder, faster!" young lawyers developed an antidote, says Beth McCarty, a Chicago consultant familiar with the firm. They came to the office on Saturdays but sat at their desks paying bills and making personal calls. Then they lunched in the firm's cafeteria, where their presence was invariably noted by partners. One young lawyer who made more of these appearances than others was rapidly promoted to partner, Ms. McCarty says.

The Well-Timed Disappearance. This corollary to No. 1 requires timing your absences for periods when the boss is least likely to be worried about face time. A rising star at one management consulting firm disappeared at 3 P.M. every day to work out. But he was always back at his desk between 5 P.M. and 8 P.M., "night after night, working so hard," says Marcia Brumit Kropf, a vice president at Catalyst, New York. "Nobody even noticed that he wasn't there in the afternoon."

The Stripped-Down Escape. A former city employee in Houston grew so bored with her 8-to-5 job that she sometimes dumped the contents of her purse into a paper bag in the afternoon and told coworkers she was taking some trash out the back door to the dumpster. Leaving her purse at her desk, she slipped into her car and sped away.

The False Trail. This strategy entails planting signs of your presence—coats, briefcases, cigarette butts—around the office even if you're not working. Writer John Buskin discovered the benefits after a Saturday stint in his office at a previous employer, spent mostly playing video games. He left the remains of his lunch "peeking out of the trash near the office coffee pot," he says. His former boss came up to him the following Monday, marveling, "Were you here over the weekend?" says Mr. Buskin, now editorial director for a publishing concern.

The Computer Smokescreen. At an oil company's Houston offices, an information-systems engineer programmed his computer to change the material on the screen every few minutes when he wasn't there, says another engineer who worked nearby. When the boss stopped by, the screen always looked as though the engineer had been there only moments earlier.

The Legal-Pad Ploy. At a former employer, Mary Hickey, now a magazine editor in New York and co-author of *The Working Mother's Guilt Guide,* planned her children's birthday parties on her office telephone while talking in hushed, serious tones and writing on a legal pad. She took copious notes from someone portraying Barney, the purple dinosaur, as well as from a clown "who did all these different voices for me while I was sitting in this staid office, furiously scribbling away," she says.

The Five-Minute Rule. This technique, as explained at a recent conference by a manager of a Big Six accounting firm, requires everyone "to wait until the most senior person leaves. Then five minutes after that, everyone else goes home."

The Accomplice. A human-resources manager at a New York financial services concern camouflages trips to the gym by leaving a steaming cup of coffee atop papers strewn over her desk. When an energy-saving lighting system threatened to blow her cover by turning off her office lights minutes after motion ceased in the room, she had her secretary come in now and then and jump around in her absence. The result: The lights stayed on, and the boss remained in the dark.

—December 28, 1994

Was That 24-Hour Flu That Kept You Home Really Just the Blahs?

I s the "mental health day"—the traditionally secret practice of taking a day off work to ease stress—coming out of the closet?

A report due out today suggests that it is. The annual absenteeism survey by CCH Inc. shows a sharp rise in stress and "personal need" as causes of unscheduled employee absences, the most costly kind for employers, and a steep drop in personal illness as a factor.

That means people are taking a lot of time off work when they're not sick. And the issue is coming out in the open, fast.

Absenteeism is a big concern for employers intent on wringing more productivity out of smaller work forces. Employer responses to the six-year-old survey by CCH, a Riverwoods, Ill., publisher, jumped 79% from last year to a record 559 this year. After rising for three years, the average absence rate stayed about flat at 2.8%. But reported causes of absence turned topsy-turvy. Illness, traditionally blamed for most absences, was cited in only 28% of cases, down from 45% in 1995.

Nearly half of the absences were caused by a complex stew of personal concerns. Stress was cited in 11% of cases, up from 6% in 1995. "Personal needs," defined as activities such as signing a mortgage, rose to 20% from 13%. And something called "entitlement mentality," the tendency to take the maximum time off allowed no matter what, rose to 15% from 9%. ("Family issues," such as childcare problems, remained nearly unchanged at 26% of absences.)

The survey shows how the dual trends of restructuring and changing demographics are altering the chemistry of the workplace. It's not clear whether workers are being more honest with bosses when they call in "sick," or whether the human-resource managers surveyed are just looking deeper at causes.

Either way, it suggests that for employers trying to cut absenteeism, traditional wellness programs that focus on physical health are no longer enough.

One reason: The rhythm of work is changing. "There is a trend toward employers working employees really, really hard for a stretch of time and employees' needing some down time" afterward, says Carol Sladek, a specialist in time-off issues for Hewitt Associates, Lincolnshire, Ill., benefit consultants. In response to the workload, more employees are coming to work with minor illnesses, Hewitt's employee surveys show.

But when the pressure's off, they feel they deserve a break. "I hear it all the time," says Diana Freeland, a corporate manager of employee-assistance programs. "People say, 'I woke up and I was so tired I just couldn't get up. So I called in and said I had food poisoning,' or a 24-hour virus," she says. "When people have to have some space, they'll carve it out for themselves one way or another."

Tina Brand, a graphic artist, can attest to that. At previous employers, she sometimes took a sick day to avert burnout. "If you work yourself to the point of exhaustion, you can come up with" great work, she says. "But if you do that too many times in a row, you'll get to the point where you don't really care." At such times, "I would call and say, 'I'm calling in sick today.' And I'd be thinking, 'I'm not telling you what part of me is sick.' "

Second, the wrenching workplace changes that are common practice these days can feed an "entitlement mentality." Absenteeism soared among 40 members of a special-project team at an energy concern after their business was sold and their project thrown into limbo, says a communications specialist for the team. Where members once took pride in their low absence rate, now "there's a sense of entitlement, a feeling that, 'Well, I killed myself for 20 months and they yank this thing right out from under me. I need a break,' " the specialist says.

Finally, demographics feed the change, as the pressures on frazzled single parents, dual earners and caregivers for elders force them to take time off just to reorder their personal lives, says M. Michael Markowich, a Huntingdon Valley, Pa., consultant who conducted the CCH survey.

Unplanned absences are damaging to employers; customers go

unserved, projects lag and temporary replacements must be hired. To reduce them, 67% more employers in the past five years have embraced paid-time-off banks, lumping vacation, sick and personal days together, for employees to manage at their discretion, he says.

Flexible use of vacation time is a trend. At U S West Inc., Ms. Brand's current employer, she can take a vacation day to ease stress. That enables her to arrange in advance for coworkers to handle her duties and give her supervisor several days' notice. She returns refreshed without disrupting her work.

Flexible scheduling goes deeper as a remedy, giving employees more day-to-day control over their time. After offering alternative work arrangements, Hewlett-Packard, First Tennessee National and other employers have seen reductions in unscheduled absenteeism.

All the methods respond to a change in employee values. The wish for more free time, Ms. Sladek says, surfaces repeatedly in surveys as employees' No. 1 desire.

—July 24, 1996

Family-Friendly Firms Often
Leave Fathers Out of the Picture

When *Working Mother* magazine judged this year's competition for the 100 best companies for mothers, its writers had to use a mover's dolly to cart the boxes of hefty applications submitted by hundreds of companies. The annual contest has been growing in leaps and bounds since its inception in 1985.

But when *Child* magazine decided to select the best firms for fathers in 1992, "it wasn't that easy" to find even 30 companies that supported men in parenting, says Freddi Greenberg, editor in chief. The magazine had to hire a consultant to search out candidates and passed up running another contest last year; nothing much had changed for fathers at work, Ms. Greenberg says.

Fathering is still largely devalued in the workplace, even in this era of the enlightened '90s male. Companies compete to woo skilled women by vying for a *Working Mother* listing, among other things. But many still assume that men will continue to work regardless of how they are treated as fathers. Even at companies that offer family-friendly programs, the prevailing attitude among managers is often that men who use them aren't serious about their careers.

One pharmaceutical company regularly set a sales conference on the third weekend in June—Father's Day. Another firm featured in its employee newsletter an engineer who worked 72 hours straight, regardless of the impact on his family, says James Levine of the Families and Work Institute. Attorneys say men also have difficulty using the 1993 family leave law; some companies have told workers it covers only new mothers, says 9to5, National Association of Working Women.

Companies "haven't been paying enough attention to the values shift that has produced a new generation of concerned working fathers," Mr. Levine told a conference on fathering last week. To many people, "'working mother' means conflict, but 'working father' is a redundancy."

There's a social movement brewing that aims to change all that. The Dallas conference was sponsored by the National Fatherhood Initiative, a new Lancaster, Pa., nonprofit organization that is laying plans to promote fatherhood as a national priority. The initiative has potent bipartisan support: Its chairman is David Blankenhorn, a New York City Democrat and former community organizer who heads the Institute for American Values, and its president is Don Eberly, a former aide to Republican Rep. Jack Kemp and head of the Commonwealth Foundation. Former Education Secretary William Bennett, pollster George Gallup and actor James Earl Jones are on its board.

Participants in this political stew argue that more active and committed fathers would ease poverty, crime and delinquency, as well as easing the burden on working mothers. They are targeting not only fathers who abandon their children, but those who are emotionally absent because of overwork or other factors. The group is part of what Neil Howe, an author on generational issues and a respected historian, calls a "parenthood revival"—a broad societal resurgence of concern for children.

Among the initiative's key goals is pressing employers to give fathers more flexibility. "Corporations can absolutely count on this becoming a bigger and bigger issue," says Mr. Howe, who just completed a book on how generational cycles affect business. Employers "have to take very seriously this parental role and realize that employees will make sacrifices for it."

There is plenty of evidence that men are pained over conflicts between parenting and work. Research by Rosalind Barnett at Radcliffe College shows that men are just as likely as women to worry about family problems at the office, echoing a raft of other studies.

But social movements are fired by emotion, and most men are stifling fathering concerns in the workplace. Wandering the hallways like a lonely prophet at the conference was one father, James Stow, who long repressed such worries—and regrets it. A former computer engineer for a defense contractor, Mr. Stow dedicated much of his life to the premise that "you show your love by providing for your family."

Though his employer gave lip service to the importance of family, "when the crunch came and projects were due, they'd say, 'We know you're working 12 hours a day, but could you work 15?' " he says. Sensing that "the sharks are always circling" one's career, Mr. Stow stifled family concerns and complied. Parenting his two sons was left largely to his wife.

Then Mr. Stow's world turned upside down. His younger boy dropped out of high school in sophomore year, "decided he didn't like the rules of the family" and went to live under a bridge. Stunned to learn the boy was abusing alcohol and drugs, Mr. Stow was "scared to death," he says. But still, he hid his anguish at work, drawing support from other parents in a treatment program his son enrolled in.

Now, several years later, his son's life is back on track—and Mr. Stow is "coming out." He has changed careers, earned a master's degree in counseling and joined the staff of the nonprofit Dallas Center for Fathering. The lesson he hopes to impart is a simple one: "There needs to be a father presence for kids in the home. The nurturing that a father can do is very different from the nurturing a mother can do." If fathers doubt that, he says, he hopes his example will help get the message across.

—November 2, 1994

A CEO Opens Up About Loss
and Finds He's a Stronger Boss

O f all the personal and family experiences typically kept quiet in the workplace, grief over the loss of a loved one is among the hardest to discuss.

Many of the estimated four million workers who are bereaved each year keep their grieving secret at work, says Naomi Naierman, president of the American Hospice Foundation, a nonprofit organization that counsels employers and individuals on grieving. Others deny their pain altogether, only to have it resurface later with disabling force.

This is the story of a CEO who did the opposite.

Throughout the illness and tragic death of his 42-year-old wife Andrea, Bill Foote of USG Corp., Chicago, a building-products maker with $2.59 billion in sales, took the unusual step of talking openly at work about his loss and his role as a single parent.

By all accounts, both Mr. Foote's leadership and the corporate culture at USG, a 96-year-old company, emerged stronger. His example illustrates a growing openness about personal and family issues among a new generation of CEOs. Striving to engage workers' "whole selves" in the drive to raise productivity, these executives believe that to reveal any less of themselves doesn't work.

The 1995 breast-cancer death of Ms. Foote, an accomplished attorney and mother of three young daughters, ended the couple's all-out, 14-month battle against her illness. She died just one month after Mr. Foote, a Harvard M.B.A. and former McKinsey consultant, achieved a goal she had enthusiastically supported: being named CEO of USG.

Grieving and immersed in single parenting, Mr. Foote halved his travel and cut his office hours to attend his daughters' games and performances. Family and friends pitched in to help. He drew a big family calendar, color-coded yellow for days he had to work late, blue for days he was traveling. In the evenings, he sat by his daughters' beds, telling stories about their mother and grandparents.

In helping his girls, now 13, 11 and 10, cope with their loss, he says simply, "I can never do enough for these kids."

Talking about his grief at work didn't come easily. A private man known for listening well, Mr. Foote resists airing deep emotions. Asking for help isn't "a guy thing," he says. He agreed to my request to discuss his experience only after a long private conversation about the goals of this column.

But to hide his grief at work, he says, would have clashed with his principles as a leader. He cites a favorite book, *Sacred Hoops* by Phil Jackson, on how the NBA coach uses spiritual principles to inspire teamwork, in explaining his management philosophy.

Mr. Foote, 46, says team-building requires trust and knowledge of how teammates will respond under pressure. That means setting ego aside, being open and honest about weaknesses as well as strengths and never ignoring painful realities in each other's lives.

On that belief, just one month after his wife's diagnosis, he told managers at a meeting his family was "facing one of the biggest challenges we're ever going to face, and I'm going to need some help."

Eighteen months later, the battle lost, he opened his first speech as CEO to 150 USG managers by talking about his loss, the help his family received from a grief counselor and the spiritual lessons he had learned:

Life is precious and fleeting, the CEO told his coworkers. Live in the moment. Simplify your days to emphasize what really matters: Kids, self, family, work. Though he loves USG, Mr. Foote said, "My No. 1 priority is my family." As he paused, struggling to contain his emotion, "you could have heard a pin drop," one executive recalls. Some crusty USG veterans wiped away tears.

The response: Strengthened commitment to Mr. Foote and a renewed sense of the corporate value placed on family, listeners say. "There wasn't a person in the room who didn't think, 'Here's a helluva strong guy,' " says one senior executive.

As managers talked afterward, he adds, "The clear message was, 'If we have to go through a few walls for this guy, we're going to do it.' "

Several managers quietly volunteered to handle extra business trips and executive duties for a time.

Today, Mr. Foote's openness continues to mark USG's culture. Employees have seen their share of turmoil: Nearly 2,000 salaried workers were laid off in the early 1990s. Still, when executives decided in 1996 to close a Virginia plant, workers got 2½ years' notice and ample outplacement help.

Mr. Foote's candor plays especially well with the forty-something middle managers charged with carrying out such cost cuts, part of a strategy that has won him some high marks on Wall Street. It also lends credibility to the team-building and diversity initiatives he is embracing.

On the home front, though he and his family continue to grieve ("a lifelong process," he says), they are rebuilding their lives. He has just remarried, to a woman who knew and cared for Andrea. He still holds down travel and "extraneous activities," such as nonfamily socializing, to preserve time with his daughters. His family is strong.

"We got through this and we're closer than ever," he says. "There's nothing we can't deal with now."

—September 10, 1997

There Are Ways to
Get Your Boss to Be More Flexible

R eaders often ask, how can I get my company to be more flexible and employee-friendly?

Change happens in different ways at different companies. While guerrilla tactics like conducting an ad hoc survey or starting a work-family network might get you fired at one company, they could make you a hero at the next.

At Baxter International several years ago, an employee dropped a copy of *Working Mother* magazine's "Best Companies for Working Mothers" list into the CEO's mail with an unsigned note, "Where's Baxter on here?" The CEO relayed the message to his human-resources chief (a task force on work-family issues was formed around the same time) and the health-care concern subsequently made the list. At Weyerhaeuser, a forest-products company, two secretaries "bought" the senior human-resources VP in a charity auction and made him listen to a four-hour pitch for expanded work-family efforts. (Already receptive—and grateful that he didn't have to wash coworkers' cars all day, as he had in previous years—he backed their proposals.)

Rather than lobbing grenades, it's always better, experts say, to stick to the handful of principles that guide most successful grassroots efforts. The changes must serve a business purpose, says Linda Marks, head of Flexgroup, an employer coalition organized by New Ways to Work, a San Francisco workplace-flexibility group. At GTE's Dallas operations, an employee group linked workers' desire for flexible scheduling with marketers' effort to sell more telecommunications gear. The result was a 120-employee telecommuting pilot so successful that it helped fuel flexible work practices throughout GTE.

And typically, advocates must adapt their goals to the corporate culture, adds Marcia Brumit Kropf, vice president at Catalyst, a nonprofit New York advocacy group for women in business. At

Hewlett-Packard's Boise, Idaho, operations, Julie England, an ener-
getic personnel rep, sparked one of the company's broadest flexibility programs by gathering data, data and more data on employees'
and managers' needs—a persuasive tactic in Hewlett's data-driven
culture.

Here are some examples of successful change tactics.

Mounting a prolonged effort:

Kim Johnson and Mary Larson were lunching in the cafeteria at
Weyerhaeuser's headquarters in Federal Way, Wash., in the mid-1980s
when Ms. Johnson looked out at the lawn and mused, "Wouldn't it
be nice to have a child-care center out there?" Suspecting others
shared their work-family worries, the two secretaries surveyed 1,100
workers (in Weyerhaeuser's relaxed culture, their bosses readily ap-
proved) and gleaned stories that "bring tears to your eyes," Ms.
Johnson says.

In response, Weyerhaeuser offered a resource-and-referral service and other family supports. The two women continued to work
on work-life issues until, in 1994, they concluded the job was too big
to do as volunteers. That's when they bought Steve Hill, senior vice
president, human resources, in a United Way auction (a bargain at
$65 for a half-day) and took him to lunch to pitch creating the post
of work-life administrator. Today, Ms. Johnson and Ms. Larson are
sharing the job, and Weyerhaeuser has expanded flextime, set up
lactation rooms for mothers and even studied opening that child-
care center, pending a cyclical recovery in its businesses.

Breaking down barriers:

Though Suzanne Tunnell didn't want any change in her usual 8-
to-5:30 schedule, she knew, as health-care promotions manager in
Bausch & Lomb's personal-products division (now the North American vision-care unit), that many of her coworkers needed stress relief. So she offered to head a 15-member team on flexible work.
First, the team held several weekly meetings to prepare a presentation to the unit's executive committee, asking permission to study
why flexibility policies on the books weren't being used. Then, team
members interviewed managers, gathered data from other divisions, and studied other companies' efforts.

With another green light from the committee, the team then hired Rodgers & Associates, part of Work/Family Directions, Boston, to run focus groups of employees at all levels as well as executive interviews. The outcome: management guidelines and a flexible-scheduling application form that address managers' and employees' worries about how to use alternative schedules fairly, without hurting the business or employees' careers. Other Bausch & Lomb divisions are already expressing interest in the new approach. "After 1½ years of work, we're elated," Ms. Tunnell says.

Spreading success stories:

When a women's network at Motorola's two-way radio division wanted to expand use of flexible scheduling several years ago, members sought out the few people who were already on flexible schedules, plus their managers, and asked them to tell in a panel discussion their stories about how their setups were arranged and how they overcame problems. More than 300 employees showed up, kicking off more panel discussions that drew more than 700 other workers. The meetings helped spark a sharp expansion of alternative scheduling.

—September 11, 1996

Parents Go to Bat for a
Little Time Off to Back Kids' Teams

I t's that time of year again, when the workday routine is broken by the crack of the bat, the thud of the soccer ball—and the groans of coworkers as parents leave early for their kids' games.

The ragged boundaries between work and family are fraying a little more this spring as 10 million kids hit soccer and baseball fields nationwide. With workloads up and corporate staffs down, "it's much more obvious when someone leaves to go to a soccer game," says Barney Olmsted, co-director of New Ways to Work, San Francisco. Coworkers are touchy on the subject, too; at a recent convention of the Child-Free Network, a 3,000-member nonparents' group, parents' leaving work to coach Little League was a major gripe.

Such conflicts demand a kind of short-term flexibility that is scarce in the American workplace. Coworkers have a legitimate beef if employees are permitted to sneak out or abandon their work to attend kids' games. One AT&T manager recalls a coworker who routinely disappeared for his kids' soccer games at inconvenient times. "That's the kind of thing that drives people nuts," the manager says.

On the other hand, many, if not most, jobs can be managed more flexibly than they are, permitting not only parents but all employees to attend to important personal needs—doctors' appointments, friends' or relatives' crises, or personal business. The potential benefit: more productive, committed workers.

Parents' feelings on the issue run deep. Consider David Onak, a self-described sports junkie who has been known to change into his own softball uniform for after-work games between the cars of a speeding commuter train. For him, leaving a half-hour early now and then to see his four-year-old son play T-ball is vital.

"The rubber hits the road right here," says Mr. Onak, a manager at Ameritech. "My view is you get the whole me. If you like me for my skills, you have to deal with me for my family." Talking openly about such values fosters teamwork among everyone in his department, he says, parents and nonparents alike.

But bosses often mismanage those passions. Failing to set guidelines usually means that only managers and professionals get to see their kids play. Marilyn Scott, a Vancouver, B.C., bookkeeper, gets angry when she sees managers "disappear in the afternoon" for games while lower-ranking workers have to fight for time off to care for a sick child.

Failing to communicate expectations openly can break down workplace disciplines. A senior lawyer at a Boston law firm was puzzled at an epidemic of 4 P.M. appointments among her partners every spring. When she figured out they were all going to soccer and baseball practices, "she started having 4 o'clock appointments too," says Deborah Swiss, a Lexington, Mass., author and consultant on gender-equity and work-family issues.

Banning participation can backfire, too. A salesman for a Dallas building-products concern wanted to coach his two sons' teams but knew his bosses "would think he wasn't committed to the business," says Waylon Ward, director of the nonprofit Dallas Center for Fathering. Upset at what he viewed as a fundamental clash of values, the salesman soon left the job.

To harness such feelings, employers need to go beyond typical flexible-scheduling options such as compressed work weeks or flextime. One remedy is to set guidelines for all temporary flexibility needs, says Paul Rupert, a flexibility specialist with Work/Family Directions, a Boston-based consultant. A boss might say, "For changes in schedule of no more than a couple hours a day once or twice a week, requests will be granted as long as the work gets done. But I like to know about them in advance."

An alternative, adds Diane Burrus, Work/Family Directions' director of training, is letting employees propose schedule changes, along with a plan to get their work done fairly and well.

Kim Summers, an administrative assistant at Deloitte & Touche, checks with her bosses in advance about days she must leave early to coach her sons' soccer, baseball or football teams. To make up lost time, she starts 1½ hours early and works through lunch most days, always swapping tasks with coworkers who cover for her after work.

Though such practices are "creating some terrible acid indigestion" among tradition-minded partners, Deloitte sees flexibility at all levels as crucial to retaining good employees, says Jim Wall, the firm's national director of human resources.

Some employers say the best solution is the most radical one: giving employees control over their hours. Studies show it encourages workers to think more broadly about the needs of the business. MIT Prof. Lotte Bailyn and other researchers found that letting workers at a Xerox administrative unit set their own schedules led to a 30% drop in absenteeism and better teamwork and customer service.

Dan Logan, president of Trinity Communications in Boston and a former Little League coach, lets his 45 employees control their hours and encourages community involvement. Though he would fire anyone who abused the freedom, he hasn't had to. "If you give people flexibility, they give back to you a lot more by coming in early, working late or even coming in on the weekend," he says. "If you want the best people, you have to give them a lot of room."

—May 17, 1995

Two People, One Job: It Can Really Work

With companies stretching fewer workers further, job sharing, it seems, has gone the way of the leisure suit.

There's been hardly any growth in policies allowing two part-timers to share one job, and few employees use the policies that do exist. Many managers groan at the mere mention of job sharing, loath to add another ingredient—compatibility with a partner—to the long list of qualities required of a good employee.

But though their ranks are thin, job sharers are anything but a dying breed. Adversity, in fact, has given rise to a hardy and entrepreneurial kind of team. Unlike the more casual job sharers of the past who usually worked one job together for just a year or two, this new breed is surviving cutbacks, winning promotions and even jumping ship for better jobs. These pairs are motivated by a desire to balance personal or family activities with the status and career opportunity of a full-time job. And their track records offer some lessons for employers: how to get more for less, foster teamwork and reclaim some of the employee commitment wasted in the layoff binge.

The best pairs bring the energy and talents of two full-time workers to one job, their bosses say. Freda London and Susan Schwartzman were sharing a sales job at Condé Nast Publications when Parenting Group, a magazine-publishing affiliate of Time Warner, recruited them earlier this year to share an account-executive position. The pair, often working together on sales and follow-up calls to clients, has landed several accounts. The women each work three days and have an impact far greater than one employee, for only slightly higher pay, says Diane Oshin, group publisher. "Employers who don't consider this are going to miss out on a lot of talent," she says.

Job sharers are winning promotions, too. When Kerri Waldner and Thea Watt, a team at a U S West unit, completed one job together, they sought a higher-level data-service planning job at another unit. The manager said he didn't want part-timers. But when they described their skills and asked if he would consider a job-share arrangement, he said, "You bet!" Ms. Watt says. They got the job.

The best job sharers are self-managed work teams in microcosm, filling in for each other and resolving any disputes on their own. Though Andrea Mims, director of management information for Barnett Banks, Jacksonville, Fla., oversees two job sharers, she says, "it's their problem if one is working harder than the other." The company profits because "two heads are always better than one. Normally, you have to pay for two heads. But in this case, I'm paying for one," she says.

Good teams elevate communication to an art form, says Linda Marks of New Ways to Work, San Francisco. In the Lawrence Livermore National Laboratories office of job sharers Sheryl Goodman and Rita Brown, a chart of pending projects is displayed, along with work under way by the five people who report to the pair. The job sharers record all daily events on a computer log. They also talk by phone daily.

The pair landed a promotion and pay raise at the Livermore, Calif., lab by preparing a joint cover letter and interviewing together, finishing each other's sentences as they talked. They have grown so interchangeable in coworkers' minds that they are often called by each other's names.

Some job seekers are even marketing themselves as a matched pair. Janice Decker, a human-resources consultant and successful fiction writer, and Wendy Riley, a former human-resources supervisor for Pacific Gas & Electric and mother of a seven year old, recently began looking for a job to share. Their joint cover letter promises "enhanced flexibility in coverage, with no job burnout," adding: "While one of us assesses client needs in Sydney, the other can deliver a workshop in San Francisco."

The two have tried to anticipate every obstacle. Unlike most job sharers, who typically each get all or most of a full benefits package, they have agreed to split one benefits package if necessary. They have rehearsed answers to likely questions, and even coordinate clothes, Ms. Decker says. Still, one employer told the pair its managers "were so stunned by us that they didn't know how to shoehorn us into their system," Ms. Decker says. Adds Ms. Riley: "We're definitely on the bleeding edge."

Applying as a team "is a gutsy move," agrees Michelle Carpenter, manager, work-family strategies, at Aetna Life & Casualty, where the Decker-Riley team nearly landed a job. But she praises the pair's "entrepreneurial initiative" as "the kind of thinking we're all trying to get employees to do inside the company."

Few managers see a job-sharing boom any time soon. Benefits costs can be an obstacle. And finding high-performing pairs "takes a perfect combination of people, akin to a marriage," says Carol Sladek, manager of work-life consulting for Hewitt Associates.

Just as many self-managed work teams fail because teammates can't or won't cooperate, job sharers often split because they don't trust each other or can't avoid competing. But companies might benefit from making the effort. "Job sharing is the concept that fits best with the current changes in the work force," allowing employees to master larger-than-life workloads without crashing, says Ms. Sladek. "But our society, and our organizations, just haven't caught up yet with the logic of the idea."

—December 7, 1994

Flight Attendants Underline
Care Woes of Overnight Workers

Alyce Desrosiers, a veteran flight attendant, had just taken off for Honolulu from Los Angeles when she noticed something amiss with her coworker.

The flight attendant seemed so distracted that Ms. Desrosiers asked what was wrong. The woman, a single mother, said she was worried about her nine-year-old son. Her sitter quit and she had found a replacement in a newspaper ad. But she left home at 5 A.M., before the sitter was to arrive, and she was concerned about whether she had shown up to get her son off to school.

If the sitter didn't show on time, there was little she could do six miles aloft over the Pacific.

The next time you board a plane, you might wonder what wild child-care problems the flight attendants are masking with their smiles. Many who started work in the 1970s, the era of hot pants and "I'm Donna, Fly Me!" ads, are now in their child-rearing years and 37% have young children. (U.S. flight attendants are 84% female.) A near-military discipline is required of them in meeting assignments and accepting rerouted flights and schedule changes. Yet few child-care providers offer flexible overnight care when the need arises. Add far-flung air travel and you have a recipe for work-family stress.

"Most people have a hard enough time putting together child care 8-to-5," says dependent-care researcher Arthur Emlen, a professor emeritus at Portland State University. Demands on flight attendants "stretch the boundaries of what we think of as possible." Similar problems engulf many round-the-clock workers caught between today's just-in-time workplace and the uncharted rhythms of family life.

Flexibility for personal pursuits is what draws many flight attendants into the profession. Though they work around the clock, they often get several days off in a row.

When family conflicts surface, many construct a sky-high house of cards to make it all work. Some call on parents to help. Flight attendant Kim Pinsker has flown her mother from Arizona to her San Carlos, Calif., home so she could get to work while her husband was traveling on business. Linda Benoit, a former flight attendant, for one year drove 3½ hours each way from her parents' home in Salinas, Calif., to work in San Francisco so her toddler could stay with them.

Spouses take up the slack, too. "What do you mean, you can't come home?" Patti Clifford's husband once lamented when she called from the airport during a weather delay. Her husband, an appraiser, missed a meeting to care for their two children.

Finding a reliable sitter to cover ever-changing hours can be daunting. Ms. Benoit once hired a sitter to stay at her house. But when she got home ahead of schedule one evening, her house was empty and dark. She sat alone, waiting, from 9 P.M. until 11 A.M. the next day, when the sitter finally appeared; she had taken the child to her boyfriend's house and made him sleep on the floor. Ms. Benoit has since quit, taking a lower-paying job as a clerk to gain control over child care.

When children get sick or child care breaks down, flight attendants scramble to swap shifts or call in sick themselves. Others get caught between a rock and a hard place. When Cathy Gasparis, a flight attendant for the USAir Shuttle, told her supervisor she needed time off because her four-year-old daughter needed emergency treatment for bronchitis, her bosses docked her 30 days' pay for missing a flight, saying it was her duty to arrange child care. Ms. Gasparis presented a doctor's note and told her supervisor she had no choice but to stay home. The response, Ms. Gasparis says: "Well, I can't stay home with my dog when my dog is sick, so why should you be allowed to stay home with your child?"

USAir Shuttle President Terry Hallcom says that while he doesn't know what the supervisor might have said, USAir tries to accommodate flight attendants with family illnesses. He says Ms. Gasparis' request was "a very last-minute thing" that supervisors didn't believe was covered by family-leave rules.

In a warning signal to the industry, a New York arbitrator recently ruled in another USAir Shuttle case that flight attendants lacking care for sick children should be treated as if they themselves were ill. The case involved Tina Miller-Silverman, who was fired after she questioned an unexpected assignment that would have kept her away from home overnight, most likely leaving her six-year-old son, who had chicken pox, home alone for several hours; she was reinstated with back pay. Mr. Hallcom says the ruling is too broad. He says supervisors weren't immediately aware of Ms. Miller-Silverman's child-care problems but were following contract rules. What's the solution? Some flight supervisors quietly bend the rules to help flight attendants through child-care crises, excusing time off as personal or sick leave. (Sometimes that means bosses cover flights themselves.) A few airlines have taken steps to help with child care; United has provided some funding for Palcare, an extended-hours child-care center near the San Francisco airport, and America West subsidizes employees' child care at a 24-hour center near the Phoenix airport and elsewhere.

But more study is needed on the cost to airlines of flight attendants' child-care problems and on the potential benefits of employer-supported referral services or flexible sitter networks, flight attendants say. The results could only help round-the-clock workers of all kinds.

—August 30, 1995

Jo Browning Built a Child-Care Agenda into a Factory's Plan

Activists are born in a lot of different ways. Some are inspired by a movement. Others learn from parents or mentors. In tire-plant worker Jo Browning of Opelika, Ala., activism was born of a private, painful search for child care.

There were few hints in her youth that Ms. Browning, the soft-spoken daughter of an Air Force medic, would one day grab the mike at a 2,500-delegate United Steelworkers convention and put down the corporate bosses of America. In high school, she never took up causes or ran for office; the closest she got to the spotlight was waving a flag in the color guard.

When she applied in 1984 for a job building tires at Uniroyal-Goodrich's sprawling plant in Opelika, an industrial town of 22,000 deep in the timber-growing Southeast, she looked scarcely strong enough to run the machinery. Seeing the 5-foot-7, 115-pound woman walk onto the factory floor, men in the plant took bets she wouldn't last. "That little skinny one ain't gonna be worth s———," she says one worker predicted.

But for 12 years, Ms. Browning proved her mettle. In that time, she married a coworker, and after their baby Whitney was born in 1991, they worked back-to-back shifts to take turns caring for her. The couple had little time together, and Ms. Browning subsisted on three hours of sleep a day. But they got by.

Enter the global economy. In 1993, competitive pressures led Uniroyal-Goodrich, a unit of Michelin North America, to convert to rotating shifts to lower costs and improve quality control, Uniroyal said.

To families like Ms. Browning's, the change meant living life on shifting sands. Instead of the stable weekday and weekend crews of the past, four factory crews began rotating among four cycles combining eight- and 12-hour shifts: One cycle of weekday shifts, a second of weeknight shifts, a third combining two weekday 3-to-11 swing shifts and two weekend day shifts, and a fourth combining two weekday swing shifts and two weekend night shifts.

The schedule capsized the fragile balance Ms. Browning and her husband had crafted. Few child-care providers wanted to rotate their hours to match plant workers'. Two of Whitney's sitters quit within 18 months. "Why doesn't [the sitter] like me any more?" she once asked.

Ms. Browning agonized that her child "had no stability in her life." Working from a list provided by a local resource center, she called 73 in-home sitters asking for weekend care and got 73 no's.

She wasn't alone. Some workers bounced their kids among three sitters. One gave up sleep while on some 12-hour shifts, caring for her children all day and working all night because she couldn't afford the 24-hour child care required to do otherwise; she napped on breaks. Another worker was advised against seeking custody of his kids in a divorce because he worked rotating shifts. Rotating shifts "destroy people's families," he says bitterly.

Angered, Ms. Browning started researching child care at the library and phoning advocacy groups. She circulated a petition and keynoted a union-hall child-care meeting.

Workers weren't rushing to tell Uniroyal-Goodrich about the child-care problems; nowhere is Americans' traditional workplace silence on family issues more pronounced than on the factory floor. But Ms. Browning was too mad to keep still. "Jo went up to the main office and talked to [management] when nobody else would," says Mary Lynn Porter, founder of the Child Care Resource Center, a local nonprofit organization.

Ms. Browning urged Uniroyal-Goodrich to survey workers on child care and learned the company had joined a 19-employer child-care alliance, administered by the resource center, and was planning a joint study. She badgered Uniroyal to speed it up, paging and voice-mailing one human-resource manager so often that "when he'd see me coming, he'd start shaking his head," she says. Next, she hand-carried the survey to each worker. Her efforts drew a 90% response from the tire plant, compared with a total-survey average of 36%.

The results were compelling, confirming child-care problems among 86% of parents. A Brentwood, Tenn., child-care concern, Child Care Systems of America, saw the study during a talk to the alliance and drew up a plan for an innovative seven-day-a-week child-care center. Ms. Browning spoke before a city planning meeting to urge zoning approval; the center, funded by parent fees, opened last fall in a sparkling three-bedroom house and is filling up fast. Other alliance projects are planned.

Ms. Browning's efforts drew coworkers' notice. "She was busting her rear end for us," says one. Last year, she was elected secretary of the 1,325-member Local 753, becoming its first top woman officer in 33 years. Swallowing her nervousness, she took the microphone last August at a Steelworkers convention, pitching help for working parents and drawing praise from union President George Becker. Not surprisingly, Ms. Browning and Local 753 President Harold Watts both resolve to make child care an issue at the bargaining table this spring.

In similar fashion throughout the country, family-care issues are bubbling onto union agendas.

—February 12, 1997

Two-Income Couples Are Making Changes at Work and at Home

Think fast. What kind of American family is most represented in the work force?

a) "Traditional" couples with one male breadwinner
b) Dual-earner couples
c) Families headed by single men or women

If you answered dual earners, you're right. After steady growth for decades, nearly half of all workers, or 48%, come from married dual-earner couples, the Bureau of Labor Statistics estimates. Though many companies are still run as if Ozzie and Harriet were the mode, only 9.4% of workers come from so-called traditional families. By 2000, two-paycheck couples will rise to a majority, or 51%, of all families, from 41% in 1980, says economist Sandra Shaber of Wefa Group.

Though the trend isn't new, major changes in the nature of dual-earner couples are accompanying the growing numbers, catching many employers off guard. Women in dual-earner households are gaining in job status and earnings as they become more experienced in the workplace, giving them more clout at work and at home. And more of the men, often the product themselves of two-income households, have more egalitarian views of gender roles.

A new kind of "collaborative couple" is emerging as a result, says Rosalind Barnett, senior scholar at Radcliffe College's Murray Research Center and co-author with Caryl Rivers, a Boston University journalism professor, of a new book on dual earners due out in May. These pairs share parenting and appear to value each other's jobs more than traditional couples.

Partners' jobs buffer each other against layoffs and career changes and breaks. Their work and home lives are intertwined; what affects one partner on the job or at home affects the other, and neither makes career decisions in a vacuum.

"It's hard to overstate the importance of this change," Dr. Barnett says. "Men's and women's work and home lives are like a spider's interconnected web; a tug that occurs at one section of the web sends vibrations all through it." In this first of three columns on dual earners, here are a few ways this web is encompassing the workplace:

Men view their careers differently than they did in the past.

Men increasingly see their careers in relation to their wives'. In a best-case scenario (assuming both have secure, well-paying jobs), the men are enjoying new freedom. Rod Schrock, a Harvard M.B.A. who heads Compaq Computer's Presario personal-computer unit, is a hard-charging manager known for working long hours. But he also is deeply involved with his toddler son, Jared, and is considering staying home for a while sometime in the future.

His wife is a director of marketing in Compaq's portables division, and "since we both have good jobs we may end up trading places every other year or so," he says. "We have this argument: Who is going to get to stay home?"

In another twist, more men are shunning traditional career paths. Executive development consultant Ed Betof has passed up promotions or enticing job offers four times, partly to avoid disrupting his wife's career. "We decided early on that her career and my career had exactly the same weight," he says. Such values can confound employers' plans. At a conference, a computer-company manager lamented that five employees, including two men in dual-earner marriages, had turned down promotions. If companies are grooming people for leadership posts they can't accept, "something is wrong," he said.

Dual-earner men hit their own glass ceiling.

In a study of 348 married male managers with children at home, Linda Stroh of Loyola University in Chicago and Jeanne Brett of Northwestern University found those with employed spouses got pay raises totaling 59% in five years, less than the 70% raises given those with wives at home. Two possible explanations: Dual-earner men worked two fewer hours per week, on average, possibly violating unwritten "face time" rules; also, they lack stay-at-home wives who aid their careers by doing all the housework and entertaining coworkers.

Resistance to relocation hits new highs.

A 1995 Atlas Van Lines survey of 147 employers found 82% had employees rejecting relocation offers in 1994, up from 68% in 1991. One reason may be that a hefty 64% of the employers offer no help for employees' spouses in finding jobs after a move. When one consumer-products company tried to relocate 300 men and women to the Midwest from the Northeast, 200 refused, mostly because of worries about spouses' jobs, says Richard Pinola, CEO of Right Management, Philadelphia human-resource consultants.

Rising demand for spousal assistance is most evident among M.B.A. recruits in their 20s, says Bev Berberich, relocation manager for S.C. Johnson Wax and president of the Employee Relocation Council, a nonprofit group. Most come from dual-earner couples and "one of the first questions out of their mouths is, 'What are you going to do for my partner?' " she says.

Women's careers benefit from supportive husbands.

Employers have long stereotyped single, childless women as model potential managers. But a new generation of dual earners may be starting to shatter that view. A 1993 study by researchers at Pace University and Rider College shows married women earning more than single women, perhaps, the study suggests, because of husbands' support for their careers.

—February 14, 1996

Work Gets Wilder as Employees Insist on Stable Family Life

D avid Lewis might have been any involved dad of the '90s when he walked into his daughter Mary's Charlotte, N.C., day-care center one recent Friday afternoon, greeted the excited toddler and took her home.

Just one thing made Mr. Lewis' day-care run noteworthy: He arrived by plane from his office 700 miles away.

Since transferring to St. Louis four months ago, Mr. Lewis, a senior vice president of a NationsBank unit, has been commuting home weekends to avoid uprooting Mary, two years old, and her sister Elizabeth, seven, too abruptly. Though he's living out of a suitcase until August, Mr. Lewis and his wife felt disrupting Elizabeth's first-grade school year was out of the question.

Employees are going to extraordinary lengths to sustain the quality of family life through major career moves.

Rising value placed on family, coupled with mounting concern about kids' development, have made family ties the leading obstacle to relocation. Three-quarters of 165 employers surveyed by Atlas Van Lines cite family ties as the most common reason employees reject transfers, up from 55% last year and a "dramatic change" from three years ago, when cost of living was the most frequent obstacle, Atlas says.

Growth in the number of single parents is speeding the trend. When Naomi McKenzie, a former area vice president for Marriott in Chicago, refused to transfer to Portland, Ore., a few years ago to head the company's school-services unit, Marriott moved the division headquarters to her.

A single parent of two children, then five and six, Ms. McKenzie didn't want to give up her support network, including her sister, church and longtime sitter. "I couldn't risk my children's development and proper upbringing for the job," she says.

Since becoming president of the unit (and doubling sales there), she has passed on the same flexibility to her own executives, allowing her vice president, sales, to remain in California for the sake of his family.

Where families used to casually uproot kids until they reached high school, a growing number object to moving even small children. In the Lewises' case, "there was just no discussion" of disrupting Elizabeth's teacher and peer bonds midyear, Mr. Lewis says.

Instead, he stays as involved as possible in shared parenting with his wife, an accountant for a Big Six firm, by commuting weekly. "There's nothing more rewarding" than time with his kids, he says.

At Toyota Motor Sales, a father of two preschoolers, ages two and four, recently accepted a transfer to the West Coast from the Midwest. But a year or two from now, he told Toyota managers, he and his wife might resist a move to avoid disrupting their kids' education, says Bill Agopian, a human-resources consultant for Toyota. "If [employers] are struggling with any kinds of policy things, it's these softer issues," he adds.

Such concerns are slowing the pace of transfers. When Dow Chemical announced last year it was transferring employees at a Granville, Ohio, facility to Midland, Mich., most chose to commute to the new location to avoiding moving their families until the end of the school year, says Mark Forbes, Dow's manager, global relocation. In response to such concerns, Dow two years ago lengthened the period of time it reimburses employees for commuting expenses.

The extended commutes are forcing some extraordinary lifestyles. When Wharton "Zie" Rivers, a former MCI vice president in Alexandria, Va., got an alluring job offer from Chicago-based Ameritech more than a year ago, his reluctance to uproot his family almost drove him to turn it down. He and his wife had seen their older son struggle to sink roots and make new friends after a previous move, and they wanted to avoid that stress for their younger son Reggie, 16.

Instead, until Reggie graduates next year, Mr. Rivers has embraced a commuting lifestyle that might reduce a less-motivated executive to rubble. As president of Ameritech Network Services, he works "relentlessly," one subordinate says, five days a week in his suburban Chicago office overseeing 33,000 employees, then hops a jet for Washington, D.C., every Friday afternoon. During soccer season, he then travels with his family to Reggie's far-flung soccer tournaments.

One weekend, he worked late Friday in his office on a knotty question involving area codes. After a weather-delayed flight that arrived in Washington at 11 P.M., he slept three hours, drove 200 miles with his wife to a soccer tournament and watched a weekend of games, staying in touch with his office nonstop via pager, phone and laptop. After taking a Sunday-evening conference call in his car in a restaurant parking lot, he joined his son's team for dinner. Back home, he did laundry, grabbed four hours' sleep and headed to his office Monday for a 13-hour workday.

Is it worth it?

"It might sound hokey," says Mr. Rivers, a Vietnam veteran and former aide to the Joint Chiefs of Staff. "But you only have this opportunity once to see your child involved in some very wholesome activity." Though he admits fatigue, he adds, "to have a good balance between things going well at work and things going well at home, you feel pretty good."

—July 16, 1997

Business Travelers Reshape
Work Plans in Rush to Get Home

B usiness travelers with families will do almost anything these days to get more time at home.

One sales manager for a chemical company, a father of two preschoolers, arrives at out-of-town meetings at the last possible minute and rushes to catch red-eye flights back home to Chicago. He challenges nearly every request to travel on business and often says no.

He doesn't want his name used because he is "flying under the radar," he says—bypassing his company's cost-cutting travel agency, which pushes low-fare stopovers and side trips to remote airports. He insists on booking speedier connections himself.

"You have to challenge the system; you've got to push back on it all the time. If I didn't, I'd be on the road absolutely every day," the sales manager says. The point? Time with family. On a list he carries with him, he says, are his life priorities: "Family is first, myself is second, and business is third. That's the way I live."

No one measures the role of family ties in shaping business travel. But with a record 32% of adults traveling on business last year, according to the National Business Travel Monitor, the tension between travel and family is rising. "There's a general sense that things have gone totally out of control, that we're moving at warp speed. People are saying, 'I've got to slow down,' " says Peter Yesawich of Yesawich, Pepperdine & Brown, which conducts the Travel Monitor survey with Yankelovich Partners.

Vickie Driver, lead researcher on the Survey of Business Travelers by the Travel Industry Association of America and OAG, a travel-information and systems concern, says when business travelers are questioned in depth, the rush to get home surfaces as the No. 1 factor in picking flights. "You think it's going to be the fare or the frequent-flyer miles. But it's always the schedule. They're all trying to get home faster."

That tension is affecting employers. One-third of companies surveyed by Travel Management Group, Alexandria, Va., mandate that employees choose the lowest fares, which often require stopovers or Saturday-night stays, says Travel Management's Tom Wilkinson. However, none refuses to reimburse travelers who break the rule. One way to "foment a rebellion," he says, "is to require people to spend more time away from their homes."

Bottom line: Travelers' rush to get home is probably a net plus for companies. The yen for personal time can be a stronger motivator for efficiency than any corporate edict. Travelers with family ties are quick to eliminate nonessential trips, shorten visits and embrace alternate methods, such as videoconferencing. As CFOs strive to rein in soaring travel costs, such concerns may be another factor in the drop in annual business trips per traveler, to 5.3 last year from 6.5 previously.

Paul Gottsegen, a product marketing director at Compaq, used to jump at travel opportunities early in his 10-year tenure there. But now, with a wife and with children ages five and 2½ at home, he looks hard at every trip and rushes home as soon as his business is done.

Even consultants, the road warriors of the business world, are pushing for more home time. Employees at one big firm "fight hard" to end weeklong client visits at 2 P.M. or 3 P.M. Fridays, says Chris Essex of the Center for Work and the Family, a Berkeley, Calif., consultant on work-life balance. They resent it when clients block plans that would get them home "at a decent time."

Debra Thompson, a Tucson, Ariz., consultant-trainer and mother of five, refuses Saturday-night stays if they interfere too much with family life; she once lost a client over the issue. She offers discounts to clients willing to book appointments to coincide with others nearby, so she can combine several trips into one.

Despite their powerful motivating influence, family stresses are still largely unaccounted for in business travel and surface only in indirect ways. The World Bank found in a study of its globe-trotting employees that male travelers filed 80% more medical claims than nontravelers, and female travelers 18% more. On further study, the bank found the "psychological disorders" cited most often in the excess claims were frequently rooted in the stresses travelers faced returning home. "The more you probe, the more the issue of separation from family comes through," says Bernhard Liese, a Bank official.

Some travelers drive themselves so hard to eke out family time that they defeat their purpose. When a Maryland engineer stopped home for 24 hours between treks to Switzerland and Los Angeles, he was so wiped out that his family felt worse. "He was crabby and irritable and fell asleep on the couch," says the engineer's wife. "My son said, 'We would have done better if he hadn't come home.' "

Beyond such stresses, anecdotal evidence suggests more business travelers are making tough choices in favor of family. Compaq's Mr. Gottsegen loves his job, and his family is used to his heavy travel. Nevertheless, for the first time, he recently canceled a planned business trip. Just off a stint on the road, he was ready to leave again on a Sunday when his wife fell ill with the flu. Realizing she'd have a difficult time alone with the kids, he axed his plans. "I really had to figure out what the right balance was," he says. The surprise: "It all worked out fine."

—March 18, 1998

Families Are Facing New Strains as Work Expands Across Globe

In the ranks of globe-trotting expatriate spouses, Melissa Reiquam is a long-distance runner.

Ms. Reiquam, a former veterinary-clinic manager, jumped at the chance to move to the Central Asian state of Kazakstan for 2½ years with her husband Steve, an agribusiness consultant for a nonprofit group. She took in stride the region's poor medical care, earthquake risk, tense political climate and lack of reliable phones, electricity and airlines. She made friends and found a job she liked on the staff of the U.S. embassy, and then as an art teacher.

But even Ms. Reiquam has her limits. When she got sick from the food one night on a business trip with her husband into the wind-blown mountains of neighboring Kyrgyzstan, she had to race several times to the only bathroom at the home where they were staying—an outhouse. Shivering in 20-below weather, she was attacked en route by a huge guard dog, snarling, barking and straining on its hind legs at the end of its chain just inches away from her.

That night, Ms. Reiquam says, she decided one tour of duty on the global economic frontier was enough. When her husband was offered another posting by a management-consulting firm in Moldova, she sent him on his way alone.

The hottest emerging business destinations—China, India, Brazil, Russia and Mexico—are also among the toughest in many ways for U.S. employees and their spouses and kids, says a study by Windham International and the National Foreign Trade Council, both in New York.

Spouses' careers and concerns about kids are the leading reasons employees refuse international moves. Families' failure to adjust is also the No. 1 reason transfers fail, says the Employee Relocation Council. Richard A. Smith, head of an intercultural-consulting unit of Prudential Relocation, says family problems not only can cut assignments short, but also can cause a transferee to perform poorly, damaging a company's business prospects overseas.

Growth in emerging markets is complicating the picture. One U.S. employee in Central Asia wrote me out of concern that his employer would force him to come home early because his wife was pregnant. (She returned to the U.S. without him.) Other families worry about routine medical care for kids or about polluted air, says Jane Holston, Pensacola, Fla., author of *Smart Moves for the Relocating Family.*

More married expatriates are leaving their spouses behind, Windham says, and fewer expatriates (57%, down from 62% in 1994) are bringing children. Married expatriates are declining, too, Windham says, suggesting a shrinking of the candidate pool. In a study by Arthur Andersen Worldwide, based in Chicago, few of 400 expatriates surveyed said they would take an assignment if their families strongly objected or couldn't come along.

Dividing families seldom works well. Stephanie West LaCount, a Moraga, Calif., relocation consultant, says when her husband temporarily left her and their two children behind to take assignments in Angola and Kazakstan, the separation caused heavy family stress. With her husband trotting the globe, "I suddenly became a single parent of two teens," she says. With a spouse that far out of touch, "it feels like they're dead."

Mike Loewe of Relocation Partners, Troy, Mich., says he sees a 90% divorce rate among expats who try to sustain long-distance marriages.

More expatriates are finding a middle road. One chemical-marketing executive assigned to China brought his wife and baby to Singapore, where he could visit, she could work and caring for their baby would be easier, says Prudential's Mr. Smith.

Another promising trend is the emergence of a hardy breed of "global couple" who relish adventure, support each other, home-school their children if necessary and get involved in meaningful activities wherever they are stationed. Eager to savor a new culture, Sam and Tracy Williamson of Gainesville, Fla., agreed two years ago to move to Vietnam, where Mr. Williamson manages IBM's operations. Ms. Williamson, an attorney, never considered staying behind, she says.

In Vietnam, she found a job with the Hanoi office of a New York law firm. (It's often easier for U.S. transferees' spouses to find work in emerging economies than in developed nations, says Windham's Michael Schell.) The couple is savoring life in their Hanoi neighborhood, which Mr. Williamson calls "an adventure; your senses are challenged every day." Three weeks ago, Ms. Williamson gave birth to a healthy baby boy in Singapore. The Williamsons say they are open to other overseas postings.

An appetite for adventure outweighs dual-career hurdles for such couples. Ron Benson, an oil-company marketing manager, and his wife Diane, a petroleum engineer for another firm, both sought transfers to Southeast Asia, Ms. Benson says via e-mail. When Mr. Benson was offered a post on Borneo, she took a leave from her job. They are relishing the "slower-paced, friendlier" culture, he says. Ms. Benson adds: "This lifestyle is like a return to the 'college of life,' and it is very invigorating." (She still hopes to land a job with her company in Borneo.)

Spotting such couples will be increasingly crucial for employers. One-third of 162 firms surveyed by the Employee Relocation Council expect international relocations to surge in the next five years.

—November 12, 1997

Sought-After Workers Now Have the Clout to Demand Flexibility

For more than a decade, work-family advocates have been pushing flexible work arrangements, promising better output and a more diverse work force.

Not much happened as a result. Work-family arguments just didn't inspire most managers to action.

Now, the strong economy and tight labor market are accomplishing what 10 years of proselytizing could not. As competition for skilled workers mounts, the workplace is getting more flexible, fast. Some companies are even hiring telecommuters off the street—something that just didn't happen in the past.

My own survey of 16 big employers in various industries shows 13 reporting a significant rise in the past year or two in use of flexible work arrangements, though the numbers are still small in comparison with total work forces. Silicon Graphics has hundreds of workers in nontraditional setups, compared with fewer than 100 a couple of years ago. At Bristol-Myers Squibb, alternative schedules have more than doubled in the past couple of years, also to hundreds of employees. Bausch & Lomb, Champion International, Boeing, Compaq Computer and others also report increases.

"There has been a very quiet momentum" toward flexibility, says Barney Olmsted, of the nonprofit New Ways to Work in San Francisco, who has been tracking work patterns for more than two decades. The trend reverses a recent decline in flexibility following big layoffs.

The limits on what companies will do to lure skilled workers are expanding fast. When Apple Computer's Newton unit was increasing its staff in Cupertino, Calif., it wanted top-flight people like Keith Chiavetta, a software engineer in West Branch, Iowa, who had founded, then sold, his own high-tech company in college. But Mr. Chiavetta wasn't about to leave Iowa, where he and his wife have family and deep roots. So Newton readily granted his request to telecommute part of each week.

"You don't hire Keith and think about having him move to Silicon Valley," says Anita Grunwald, Mr. Chiavetta's supervisor. Though Apple has always been flexible, the company wouldn't have been as quick to allow such a setup in the past, she says. To lure the best people, Apple also makes time and space for employees' outside interests. One takes time off to play in a symphony and others bring their dogs to work. (Ms. Grunwald's greyhound, Bandit, beds down near her desk.)

More employers are making flexibility an explicit part of their recruiting pitch. Hartford Financial Services Group, Hartford, Conn., started running ads this month in Vermont, inviting computer programmers and analysts to "live where you are, work for us." The company plans to hire up to 20 telecommuters in a pilot program. Résumés are flowing in by e-mail and fax, says Vi Beaudreau, head of Hartford's advanced technology group. Hartford also wooed several new employees to its Denver regional office by promoting a compressed work week.

Offers of flexibility are showing up in internal job postings. At Baxter Healthcare, managers lately have sweetened 500 internal postings with offers of possible part-time, telecommuting, job-sharing or compressed-work-week status, a sharp increase from the past, says Alice Campbell, director of work and life at Baxter. "They're basically trying to market the position, saying, 'I'm flexible.' "

Bosses are doing backflips to retain workers, too. When Judy Metzner's husband was transferred to San Diego, the Citibank mortgage-banking vice president quit—or tried to. Her bosses persuaded her to telecommute instead. The trend reflects a growing awareness among employers that as wages and salaries rise, time can also be a compensation tool. Assuming competitive pay, the quality-of-life benefits afforded by nontraditional work arrangements appeal to today's rushed, lifestyle-conscious workers.

Employers also are finding their "new contract" with workers— the one that kills off lifetime employment and places responsibility for career advancement squarely in the laps of employees—comes with a rider attached: Workers are taking charge of their workstyle.

"They're saying, 'I'll get your job done, I'll do everything I promised, I'll keep my end of our new bargain. But I'll do it on my terms,' " says a manager for a telecommunications company.

Other factors are at work. Flexible scheduling has been around long enough that managers are getting used to the idea. And cost pressures have made managers more willing to tamper with tradition.

Angela Panzarella, vice president, investor relations, at Bausch & Lomb, would like a full-time staffer in her department but can't justify adding one. So she signed on a staffer from another department who wanted part-time work and is restructuring the job to suit her. Cost cuts "compel us all to look at our needs and be creative about how we're going to fill them," Ms. Panzarella says.

Is the traditional workplace going the way of the buggy whip? Not likely. But Alan Reynolds, the Hudson Institute's director of economic research, does see a future shortage of workers willing to commute to a 9-to-5 job.

With employees increasingly "in the driver's seat," he says, bosses will have to be "very sensitive to the needs and wants and desires of their individual workers—more sensitive than they have been in the past."

—September 17, 1997

Families, Communities Can Benefit from Rise in Home-Based Work

The trend toward working at home has grown to the point where it could begin to transform home and neighborhood life. Whether it actually does so, though, is an open question.

Today, one in every eight U.S. households, has at least one adult working full-time from home, for himself or an employer. That number will rise to one in every five households by 2002, driven by a tight labor market, growth in computer networks and changing worker values.

The forecast is based on three projections, one on telecommuting by Jack Nilles of JALA International, Los Angeles, in a coming book, *Managing Telework;* another on home-based self-employment by Ray Boggs of IDC/LINK, a New York market-research concern; and a third on household growth by the Census Bureau. The fastest-growing segment of home-based workers, full-time corporate telecommuters, will rise by 14% a year through 2020, according to Mr. Nilles. The former government spacecraft designer coined the term "telecommuting."

Visionaries like Mr. Nilles have long hoped that more home-based work would strengthen families and neighborhoods weakened by long commutes and the expanding work day. And interviews with pioneers on this workplace frontier—longtime telecommuters at three trend-setting companies, Hewlett-Packard, IBM and AT&T—suggest it can make a difference.

Kids can benefit from increased parental presence. Kay Atkinson's normally high-spirited teenage daughter took an emotional nose-dive and attempted suicide three years ago. Fortunately, Ms. Atkinson had just landed a work-at-home post for Hewlett. That gave her flexibility to closely manage her daughter's treatment and supervise her and her friends after school, all while getting her work done.

Ms. Atkinson partly credits her work-at-home status for letting her seek out a correct diagnosis of her daughter's problems and support

her through her recovery. The teenager has bounced back and is again getting top grades.

Kids can pick up a healthy work ethic from work-at-home parents. After watching her father work from their Logan, Utah, home as a human-resource researcher for IBM, Jeff Hill's daughter chose survey research as her first job.

Lee Ann Kuster of AT&T says her family is "more involved" in her work because she telecommutes.

Home-based workers can knit neighborhoods together. When a storm dumped two feet of snow on the roof of Patrick Schlight's neighbor, a 69-year-old widow, he took a break, climbed up and spent 45 minutes shoveling it off. Many of his elderly neighbors "like the fact that I'm around," says Mr. Schlight, an IBM manager in Salt Lake City.

When Mr. Hill feels like gathering with friends at the water cooler, he meets his neighbor across the driveway. When the neighbor, a college financial-aid adviser, was offered a new job in another city, he avoided moving by striking a part-time telecommuting deal. Such flexibility allows people to sink deeper roots, Mr. Hill says.

The trend also can ease the "people-like-us" syndrome—the tendency to socialize only with people of similar status and income. Neil Norris, a manager for Hewlett in Woodstock, Ga., has his office near his bedroom; when he works late, he takes his laptop to a nearby Waffle House to avoid disturbing his wife.

Over the years, he has met "all kinds of people" he would probably never encounter in his subdivision or an urban office, he says. One 21-year-old Waffle House regular sought Mr. Norris' advice on franchising his yard-care business. Another, an ex-Marine, asked Mr. Norris' counsel on retiring in Mexico. When Mr. Norris built a playhouse for his kids, the whole coffee shop crew wanted to see the photos he scanned into his laptop.

Better parenting and role models for kids, closer-knit neighborhoods and communities? It all sounds great, raising hopes of reversing trends that began with the Industrial Revolution. But realizing those benefits is by no means a sure bet.

Two '90s-style clouds loom on the horizon. One is the pressure on home workers, both self-imposed and from employers, to increase productivity. Bosses' expectations that home-based workers will pro-

duce more make it easy to justify closing the home-office door and descending into workaholism. The resulting "absent-while-present" state can pain loved ones more than a long commute.

Second, home-office technology makes it so easy to ignore time zones and geographic boundaries that work seeps into nights and weekends. The global marketplace feeds the work-all-the-time mentality.

One telecommuter, an international money manager for a Wall Street investment house, found herself so nailed to her phone, fielding calls from global clients, that she was forced to quit to save her family life—a luxury not all telecommuters have.

All that raises the specter of society's discovering a balm for neglected neighborhoods and families without applying it. Mr. Hill describes the paradox: "Teleworking does lead to flexibility. So you'd think that teleworking would lead to better work-life balance. But what happens, on average, is that people work so many more hours that on the whole, they're not any better off.

"The key isn't in the practice," he says. "It's in the individual making use of the practice to have a full life."

—May 13, 1998

Work and Family Go Mobile
and Wreck Your Sense of Balance

W hen Kellee Harris drove to a client's office to pick her up for a presentation over breakfast, she thought she had everything under control.

Ms. Harris, president of MarketSpark, a Portland, Ore., marketer, had been up since 4 A.M. preparing. Her suit was perfect, her materials tucked into her briefcase, her small children dropped safely at preschool. Only as her client appeared and began walking toward her car did Ms. Harris glance into the back seat and see lurking there the threat to her well-honed professional image:

Naked Barbies. Eight of them, limbs askew, grinning from a sea of granola crumbs left by her two preschoolers. Panicking, Ms. Harris dived over the seat and jammed the dolls into seat pockets, under seats—anywhere they couldn't be seen. "It blew my mind," she says. She feared her client, who hasn't any children, would wonder, "What in the world was going on back there?"

Work and family are meeting more frequently in the family car, and the result is often a head-on collision. Six million Americans work from automobiles most of the time, a number expected to rise 25% in the next five years, says Yankee Group, a Boston research concern. And 90% use the same cars for work and personal needs, says L.B. Gschwandtner, editor of *Personal Selling Power* magazine.

The result: "We're like turtles," toting the paraphernalia of multiple roles around on our backs, Ms. Gschwandtner says. In addition to a phone, office supplies, maps, brochures, computer gear, briefcases and products, Ms. Harris' Volvo carries a car seat, diapers, wipes and toys for her three children, as well as a lint roller to pick up hair from the family's 150-pound Saint Bernard.

All that gear makes the mobile office a crucible for work-family conflict. Erica Swerdlow, owner of EBS Public Relations, Northbrook, Ill., was rolling down the highway with her two small children in her Jeep Cherokee, talking with a client on her car phone, when her two-year-old's car seat came unbuckled. "He freaked, screaming, 'I'm going to fly through the window!' " Ms. Swerdlow says. Flustered, she started scraping her fingernail across the phone mouthpiece and yelled to her client, "We have a very bad connection. I'll have to call you back!" then hung up to resolve the crisis.

When a car serves both work and family, something has to give. Gary Moore, a Crescent City, Calif., sales representative who used his family car on a previous job, had to cancel appointments every time one of his children got sick and had to visit a doctor. "I'd call and say, 'I can't make it,' and not say why. It was a nightmare," says Mr. Moore.

Other mobile workers erase all boundaries between work and family. When school is out, Jean Taylor, a Washington Court House, Ohio, sales rep for *Farming* magazine and Primerica Financial Services, uses her Astro van as a rolling summer camp for her 14-year-old daughter, who reads beside her or helps her plan sales calls.

But it is hard sometimes for even the flexible Ms. Taylor to balance everything. When she uses the van to drive her daughter and her friends somewhere, she must shift eight boxes of sales files to one side. One windy day, she pushed things too far. When she opened the van door, a mountain of books and fliers fell out, and "stuff started blowing up the road," she says. The clutter poses professional stresses, too. From the outside, the tinted windows of Cynthia Pearson's car conceal the car seat, crumbs and Power Rangers figures strewn by her three children among her files. "If you don't look too close, you can't see what's cookin' inside," she says.

But when the Columbia, Md., pharmaceutical sales representative had to chauffeur a prominent, nattily dressed physician to speak at a client hospital, he brushed off the seat in disdain before sitting down. "I thought, 'OK, I'm going to have an awful day. This man thinks I'm a slob,' " she says. "I apologized all the way."

Indeed, even more than a deskful of family photos, the gear in a mobile office "screams very loudly" about the driver's values, says Sharon Morris of Performance Solutions, a Fremont, Calif., consultant. While helping a traveling bakery-product sales manager organize his trunk, Ms. Morris found bats and baseballs strewn atop his supplies, smashing his samples and brochures. He hastened to make light of family matters, explaining, "Oh, I just happened to coach a Little League game last night," she says.

But Ms. Morris wasn't fooled. "What mattered most to him," she says, "was right there on top."

Some mobile workers try hard to keep their cars' work and family roles separate. Others hire consultants like Ms. Morris, who separates and orders work and personal stuff with products like a Velcro-equipped organizer for the trunk and a car seat "desk" that anchors a laptop and other gear, made by Mobile Technology Products.

But Roger Stephenson, a Cassopolis, Mich., land surveyor, thinks he's found the perfect mobile marriage between work and family. In his "MO-V"—a van equipped by Mobile Office Vehicle, Zeeland, Mich., with desk, computer, files, printer, copier, phone and fax— he and his wife, Hazel, can work or do errands hassle-free. When Hazel takes the MO-V shopping, Roger stays in the parking lot and draws surveys. "There's nothing," Mr. Stephenson says, "you can't do out of this van."

—February 22, 1995

Telecommuter Profile: Productive, Efficient . . . and a Little Weird

If you dream of quitting the rat race for a mountain in Sun Valley or a beach in Aruba and working from home, this column is for you.

Surveys show telecommuting raises productivity and morale, and cuts commuting time and office-related costs—assuming you can do your job from anywhere and you like working alone.

After deciding four years ago to try for a better work-family balance by working from home, first as a freelancer and then as an Oregon-based telecommuter for this newspaper, I find that the flexibility works like a tonic and eases my own juggling act. But I've discovered another truth about long-term, full-time remote telecommuting, one to which the surveys hold not a clue: I am getting weird.

As much as I like it, all this working alone at home by phone and computer is causing persistent changes in the way I relate to people and places around me. Though most of the changes probably arise from my own peculiarities (I have plenty), some may have meaning for others dreaming of an escape to the virtual workplace. With that in mind, I've been keeping a journal on the changes.

Feb. 8: I struggle to break out of a slump. Career anxiety hovers—an unfamiliar feeling to someone who has never worried much about climbing the corporate ladder. I know telecommuters live and die by the rule, "I produce, therefore I am." My morale plunges on the corollary: "I don't produce, therefore I am not."

I have to admit that face time—time spent being seen at one's desk, a pretense that I've made fun of in the past—works two ways. Managers too preoccupied with it can be unduly rigid, but it's nice to be credited with being on the job when crawling to your desk is all you can manage.

Today, my bosses can't see me laboring at my computer; for all

they know, I'm out climbing Mount Hood. When I go to bed, I
dream I have been reassigned to the Philadelphia bureau. My newspaper operates no Philadelphia bureau.

April 19: I always enjoyed easy-going relations with my neighbors
in the past, but now my role-juggling confuses some. After seeing
me rushing from my car to my house and watching delivery people
come and go, a neighbor confides that she long suspected I was an
agoraphobic having an affair with the Federal Express man. Today, I
scare two kids by answering the door in my telephone headset.
Later, a friend knocks just as I am drawn into coverage of the tragic
Oklahoma City bombing. "There are nine!" she announces happily.

"What do you mean?" I reply, rushed and distracted.

Her face falls. "Puppies. We have nine puppies," she says, backing
away. Too late, I realize I have forgotten her joy over a pet's expected litter. Though I apologize, the moment is lost. Telecommuters' presence is supposed to be an asset in their communities,
but today I am hardly "present"; I feel instead like a Type-A Typhoid
Mary, spreading stress where it doesn't belong.

May 23: Today, both my computer keyboards jam. I race to my
computer-services company, where my car breaks down in the parking lot. To the bewilderment of onlookers, I abandon the car (tow-
ing it can wait) but make sure I have a loan keyboard before I catch
a cab home.

I am becoming fanatical about maintaining my home-office
equipment, the sandbag dike between me and le deluge: isolation
from my employer.

Aug. 9: Freed from such temporal boundaries as commuting or
the need to wait until the people around you wake up, the home-
based worker gains a great advantage: time-zone flexibility. From my
West Coast home, I regularly work an East Coast day, starting early
to improve my access to people there. This week, I forget to factor
sleep into my schedule. After work Monday, I take a red-eye flight to
New Jersey to make a speech, then fly back Tuesday night in time to
make several calls to Europe before dawn today.

After three days of working in six time zones, I am wiped out. My friend the Federal Express man (we are just friends) laughs when he arrives with a 2 P.M. delivery to see me through my office window dozing at my desk. By evening, as I bathe my kids, five and seven years old, I learn they have made up a song, "Mean Old Mommy," which they sing to drown out the sound of my yelling.

Aug. 11: In the office, coworkers used to kid me into easing up, and commuting was a buffer, too. But now, as I move seamlessly from home to work and back, I forget to turn off my rapid-fire, demanding workstyle. As I talk with my daughter after day camp, she grows reticent and protests, "Mom, you're asking me too many questions!"

Aug. 18: The bottom line, I think, is that a long-term remote worker must have a strong incentive to make the arrangement work. In my case, working at home eases my own particular work-family conflicts. I know others who like such work because they travel all the time anyway or are building a house on the San Juan Islands in their free time.

But as telecommuting grows, predicts Gil Gordon, a Monmouth Junction, N.J., management consultant, the vast majority of salaried home workers will strike a more fluid balance than mine, spending a day or two regularly in a central or satellite office and the rest of the time at home or in a mobile office.

I must stop now. I think I hear my boss on my voice mail; she seems to be saying something about Philadelphia.

—August 23, 1995

Madison Avenue May Need to Alter Image of '90s Telecommuter

I t's the middle of the workday and you're in your office, working on the phone, voice mail and e-mail. Do you know where your business contacts are?

Chances are better than you think that they're telecommuting from home. Chances are also good, if you can believe advertisers, that they haven't showered all day, they're holding a baby under one arm and they're wearing bunny slippers.

Bunny slippers?

After a dip in the mid-1990s, a sudden sharp rise in telecommuting has thrust this workstyle onto the national advertising scene. But while telecommuting has reached levels not expected until 2003, its image, as reflected in recent ads, remains firmly mired in stereotypes of the past decade.

One entertaining ad currently running for MCI, for instance, shows a working mother madly working from her home office via phone, pager, modem, fax and e-mail, wearing jammies and bunny slippers all day while driving hard bargains with the men in wingtips back at the office. Never does she shower, even after working out.

Another ad, aired earlier this year for Advanced Micro Devices, portrays another power-wielding mom, this one in chic professional attire, who makes underlings back at the office squirm via teleconference while caring for a baby in a crib nearby. At one point, she peers cheek-to-cheek into her computer with the placid child tucked under her arm.

It's great that Madison Avenue is finally paying attention to a workstyle with so much promise for easing work-family conflict. (Staples Inc. has been running humorous ads about home-based business owners, an older trend, for some time.)

But while the attention is welcome, the new ads focus too narrowly on women, and portray them as sloppy or caring for kids while working.

"Are the commercials cute and funny? Yes," says Ellen Reilly of Port Strategic Consulting, New York. "Are the ad people coming in and mucking it up? Yes."

So, are telecommuters all slobs with questionable work habits? Well, honestly, with 11.1 million corporate employees and contractors laboring at least part-time from the privacy of their homes, according to researcher FIND/SVP, who really knows what they're wearing or how they smell?

To pierce the veil around this expanding workplace frontier, I conducted my own survey of a dozen experienced telecommuters:

- Eleven of the 12 had showered. "Just because I'm a telecommuter doesn't mean I don't shower and I sit around in my pajamas all day long," sniffs Russ Glover, an AT&T manager. "I get up and do the same hygiene things I normally do."

  The only self-described "scumbucket" in the bunch, a top-producing stockbroker who asked not to be identified, says that like the woman in the ad, she doesn't have time to shower.
- None was wearing bunny slippers. Shorts, T-shirt and bare feet were the attire of choice for six. Mel Privett, a programmer for Edward D. Jones, dons one of his employer's T-shirts every day.
- Not one was holding a baby. All the parents of young children had child-care help, and parents of older kids forbade them to intrude on their offices.

  "Unless there's blood or smoke" in the house, one telecommuter tells her teens, "don't come in."

The bottom line: Telecommuters are a casual but clean, organized, focused lot who draw firm boundaries between work and home—the same boundaries that are blurred by the ads, says Jeff Hill, an IBM telecommuter in Logan, Utah.

If anything, telecommuters are even more poised for action than their corporate-office colleagues. Shelley Comes, a quality consultant who telecommutes to her employer from a Garberville, Calif., farm, says she keeps a loaded rifle handy in her home office in case bobcats or wild dogs attack her goats.

"I keep my boots on," she says, "because I never know when I'll need to grab the .22."

The advertisers say they got their message across. Advanced Micro says its ad showed how using its chips in new technology makes telecommuting affordable, and also conveyed a businesslike, professional image.

MCI says its ad is a realistic portrayal of a telecommuter who works hard but, thanks to technology, "has the freedom to decide whether to take a shower before work or wear bunny slippers," says John Donoghue, MCI's senior vice president, marketing. He adds, a little wistfully, "There are days I'd like to wear bunny slippers and not take a shower."

What does the future hold? Fewer stereotypes from Madison Avenue, we can hope, as the image of telecommuters catches up with reality. Despite the ads showing the contrary, telecommuters are 67% male and only 46% have children at home, says FIND/SVP's Thomas Miller.

And the future will also, no doubt, bring more growth in telecommuting, as both men and women take aggressive advantage of technology to lead richer and more balanced personal and family lives.

Full disclosure: I'm a telecommuter. I shower every morning, I only work in my jammies before dawn, and I own neither a rifle nor bunny slippers. To any workstyle questions beyond that, I take the Fifth.

—August 20, 1997

These Telecommuters Just Barely Maintain Their Office Decorum

I thought I'd captured the full range of work-at-home workstyles in an Aug. 20 column on telecommuters, but it turns out some folks are more liberated than I had dreamed.

I got on my high horse that week about TV ads portraying at-home workers as pajama-clad slobs with little regard for separating home duties and work. Not true, I said, they're conventional workers with firm work-home boundaries.

Well, I have since learned from readers that some folks don't fit my version of the truth. A sampling of letters:

"I understand your concern about the TV ads depicting an inaccurate image of telecommuters, but on the positive side, the ads do at least challenge the myth that you can only be productive in 'the appropriate business trappings.' In all the ads I've seen, the teleworker is shown to be a high performer.

"We struggle so much with measuring performance quality that we often resort to relying on the look of work—'face time'—rather than the results. Remote work of any kind challenges this practice, raising anxieties in managers and nonmanagers alike. Abandoning the old face-time measurement is difficult, but successful teleworkers are leading the way. I think the advertisers should be congratulated for getting people talking about telecommuting and depicting it as a productive, flexible, fun way to work.

"As for my personal telecommuting style, I dispense with the pajamas and bunny slippers, opting instead to work naked for the first hour of phone calling and e-mailing, then shower. Do I miss nylon stockings and the rush-rush of the office? NO. Do I feel better about my performance? Absolutely! Do I think having the freedom to work where, when and how you choose might work for others? Definitely. Change is always an opportunity for learning."

Cynthia C. Froggatt
Froggatt Consulting
New York

Ms. Froggatt: I might feel better about my performance if I worked naked, but I don't think I'd feel better about much of anything else, given the toll gravity has taken on my 46-year-old physique. I don't think my neighbors would be uplifted either, faced as they are with the big, curtainless window between my home office and the main drag in our subdivision.

Your point about face time, though, is a good one. Freed from the burden of commuting or looking presentable, many people actually work harder.

"As a consultant working from my home on a mountain, I don't fall solidly into either of the dress-code camps you delineate. You might find my case an interesting third way.

"Each morning, after my two-hour telephone 'rounds'—checking my voice and e-mail at 7:30 a.m., responding and making calls—I go cycling for two to three hours, shower and go back to work. Until my wife gets home at 7 p.m., the house is quiet except for the tapping of the computer keys.

"The most stressful part of my day comes from that wave of panic when I hear the FedEx deliverywoman stepping onto my downstairs deck, starting up the stairs to the main floor. Why panic? I don't have any curtains. And since my house is the highest house in the neighborhood, high above the mountain pass, I'm often in my birthday suit in the morning before I ride, succumbing to the temptation to send one more piece of e-mail. The stomping of the FedEx folks catches me in my moments of deepest concentration. At first thump, I sprint upstairs for some clothes!"

Phidias Cinaglia
Summit Park, Utah

Mr. Cinaglia: And I thought I'd already covered every conceivable angle on workplace stress. Do you ever worry about low-flying planes?

Clearly, you are just barely making it across that fine line to presentability when your courier calls, raising questions about whether there may be others out there like you who aren't bothering to run for cover at all. I asked Federal Express if its employees see a trend. "I don't think I have an answer that will help," says spokesman Greg

Rossiter, "except to say that, clearly, with more people working from home, it stands to reason that more of the type of situation you are describing could occur." Though he asked couriers whether they have encountered customers in the buff, he adds, "I haven't heard from anyone who is willing to admit it."

My favorite no-clothes story came from Jeff Hill, an IBM telecommuter in Logan, Utah, who works fully clothed at all times. He tells it to illustrate the importance of maintaining boundaries between work and home:

> *"I was downstairs in my den, recording my office voice-mail greeting. Working from home, you have to have a professional-sounding voice-mail greeting, so everyone knows you're hard at work.*
>
> *"Across the hall from my office is the laundry room. My wife was folding clothes at the time, and my daughter Emily, who is six, had just gotten out of the shower. She couldn't find any clean clothes in her bedroom and came down to the laundry room to find some. As my wife greeted her, the voicemail I produced sounded like this:*
>
> *"Male voice: 'Hi, this is Jeff Hill with IBM.'*
>
> *"Female voice: 'Look at you! You have no clothes on!'*
>
> *"Male voice: 'I'm not available right now . . .' "*

—September 24, 1997

Part Six

EMPLOYERS REACH OUT

As recently as a few years ago, most employers viewed child-care, elder-care and flexible-scheduling initiatives as window dressing, cheap efforts to gain good publicity and little more.

Carol Lay

Now, the tightening labor market, coupled with employers' widening search for tools to sustain productivity gains, have changed all that. More employers are exploring ways to aid employees' work-life balance as a route to their own goals: Firmer employee commitment, higher output and a warmer reception on Wall Street.

These columns cover initiatives by employers that reflect that new viewpoint. In many cases, bosses are finding that making workplace strategies mesh with one of employees' most powerful human impulses, the urge to lead a rich and sustaining personal life, can pay off in measurable ways.

Enter the "New Hero": A Boss Who Knows You Have a Life

Thearrival he topic, managing employees with work-life conflicts, is hardly at the top of most corporate agendas, but it had eight top-rated managers in a focus group at Merck on the edge of their chairs.

Asked how employees respond when their bosses handle work-life issues with flexibility and respect, the managers sound like a Greek chorus. "An increase in loyalty, a willingness to work very hard. And there's a productivity improvement," says one senior director. Three others murmur agreement: "I believe it." One adds: "It's a motivational tool."

"So why don't more managers do it?" the moderator asks.

The results "aren't measurable," a manager replies. A vice president adds: "You just have to believe it."

The dialogue sheds light on the lonely ground occupied by many skillful managers these days. Many are turning out three times as much work with half as many people as in the past. Yet the "soft," almost instinctive, managerial skills that often best motivate employees—building trust, respecting others' values, honoring their personal lives—aren't talked about much in Management 101 or in corporate goal-setting.

The focus group at the drug maker's New Jersey headquarters was part of a larger research effort that aims to close that gap. The Wharton-Merck Roundtable, a group of about 20 managers from big employers and professors from leading universities organized by the Wharton School and Merck, is identifying the skills needed by individuals and managers to achieve life balance and help others do the same. The results will be published in a resource guide; Merck, Cigna and Marriott International and other members plan to use the findings in management training and planning.

Merck's director of human-resource strategy, Perry Christensen, sees the skills as "the wave of managing in the future." As command-and-control management techniques go out of favor, "there's a 'new hero' manager we want to come out of the woodwork," he says. "A lot of people exercise these skills behind closed doors. We're trying to bring the practices out in the open as models" of enlightened management. In the first of two columns on managing work-life issues amid heavy layoffs, here are some of the 10 skills identified by the Roundtable, with focus-group examples of their effects:

Reward performance and productivity, not necessarily time spent working.
Working killer hours and traveling 30% of the time, including weekends, one Merck research manager used to get mad at a previous boss when she had to report to her desk at 8 A.M. Monday. The supervisor (who has since left Merck) expected lots of face time, no matter how little sleep employees got as a result. The research manager kept up her performance but her attitude took a dive. She felt, "OK, I'll do the best I can, but you're not getting any more from me." In a symbolic gesture, she kept her office door closed.

Her next boss, in contrast, made goals clear, then told the employee, "I trust you to get your job done." The result: "I was completely loyal to her and much more enthusiastic about my work," says the research manager. (She has started keeping her office door open again, too.)

Live by your values and encourage others to live by theirs.
Lori Kaufman and Linda Hoffman have different styles of managing working motherhood. After maternity leave, Ms. Hoffman was tormented by the long separations from her baby required by her high-pressure job. Ms. Kaufman says jokingly she is seen as "more of an ice queen"; she has cared for her two kids without missing a beat at work.

Despite their different styles, Ms. Kaufman, senior director, corporate accounting, didn't criticize Ms. Hoffman, an accounting manager, when she turned to Ms. Kaufman for help easing her conflict. Instead, she mulled the problem, lying awake that night until, in a midnight brainstorm, she solved it with a plan for Ms. Hoffman to job-share. Ms. Kaufman's support "amazes me," Ms. Hoffman says; it averted performance problems Ms. Hoffman feared she might develop, and inspired loyalty to Ms. Kaufman and Merck as well.

Build relationships based on trust and respect.

Senior financial analyst Diane Schweizer didn't expect to get time off when her toddler needed tonsil surgery during Merck's year-end rush. To her surprise, her boss Bob Underwood, controller for Merck's European operations, "just looked at me and said, 'Your daughter comes first,' " Ms. Schweizer says.

The gesture fostered intense loyalty. Later, she was leaving on a long-planned vacation at the shore when Mr. Underwood's assistant called for help preparing data for the head of Merck's European operations. Without hesitating, she "popped into the car and I was there," she says. "You don't think twice" when such a boss needs help, she says.

Fourteen other focus groups at Merck, Allied Signal and Johnson & Johnson yielded similar examples. Stewart Friedman, a professor at Wharton and a Roundtable co-organizer with Mr. Christensen and Jessica DeGroot, says the results shed light on a pressing question: "How do you generate commitment in an era where presumably, loyalty is dead?"

If the skills were applied broadly, he adds, "the potential business impact is big."

—May 8, 1996

Family-Friendly Jobs Are the First Step to Efficient Workplace

Consider this: Various units of a company achieve 30% fewer employee absences, shorter customer-response times and on-deadline completion of a new product for the first time. What management tool sparked the gains?

Empowered work teams, perhaps? Threats of layoffs? How about planning based on employees' work-family needs?

Since you're reading this column, you probably answered correctly that it's the latter. The finding is from studies at Xerox, funded and set for publication this fall by the Ford Foundation.

Many people assume you have to make case-by-case exceptions to usual business practice, and probably hurt the business, to take employees' family concerns into account. The Ford studies suggest the opposite can be true: By reversing the usual process—by defining "family" as all employees' personal concerns, then using employees' wishes for better-balanced lives as a starting point for restructuring jobs—managers can uncover a powerful incentive to streamline work.

The findings are causing a stir. Lotte Bailyn, a member of the research team at Xerox and a professor at MIT's Sloan School, is getting dozens of speaking requests and drew raves from the audience of executives when she presented the results at a March conference of clients of learning-organization guru Peter Senge.

The approach "promises to have great power in revealing deep sources of waste and inefficiency," says Dr. Senge, author of *The Fifth Discipline* and head of MIT's Center for Organizational Learning. Using work-family concerns as a starting point "holds tremendous potential payoff for more productive workplaces and more integrated human beings."

In three Xerox units, researchers asked employees, "What is it about the way work gets done around here that makes it difficult for you to integrate your work and personal life?" In Webster, N.Y., 17 engineers, under pressure to get a new printer to market in 18 months, said there was no way they could get their work done in a reasonable amount of time. All wished for more quiet time and more control over their lives.

By starting there, researchers got the engineers to take a critical look at how they used time. They began keeping hourly logs, wearing watches that beeped to remind them. To the engineers' surprise, they found they spent 52% of their time meeting with each other or interrupting each other. Though the talks were helpful, most weren't urgent, says Leslie Perlow, a researcher, now at the University of Michigan, whose book on the project will be published by Cornell University Press. Some engineers were coming in at 3 A.M. or staying until 10 P.M. to get time to concentrate.

The team agreed to set aside morning quiet times when interruptions were banned. The result: "Everyone felt very positive about their productivity," says Angelo Caruso, a technical specialist. A division head credited the experiment with the division's first on-time product launch in history, and the team won an internal Xerox award.

The benefits spilled into home life. Kelly Lindenmayer, a manager and mother, says her team experienced such a "huge improvement in motivation and satisfaction" that "the emotional benefits carried over to the family," helping her improve her relationship with her husband and her family life.

In a separate study, about 40 Dallas-area sales and service people had been trying to work together to serve customers. But the two groups, deeply divided by different cultures and territory boundaries, had a hard time even talking. Salespeople's free-wheeling style clashed with service reps' conservative culture. They blamed each other for problems.

But the two groups shared a powerful incentive for change: a desire to reduce stress and improve their personal lives. By focusing on that, the researchers helped them come together, says Tommy Greenhill, an operations manager. "It took the edge off" their differences and "gave us a broader vision," he says. Eager to improve their lives, the groups starting sharing information and making joint calls. Sales passed projections, and Mr. Greenhill says customer-response times posted an "incredible" improvement.

At a Dallas administrative center, many of the 240 employees were troubled by work-family conflicts. In a first step, controller Jim Edwards gave them some control over their schedules; nearly half modified their hours. Absenteeism plunged 30% and morale improved. The changes made everyone more comfortable discussing the way work gets done, providing a valuable platform for a second step: a shift to empowered work groups. "I like to break the chains of tradition," Mr. Edwards says, and the work-family approach provides the fresh perspective needed.

Merck, among others, is drawing on the research in organizational planning. A Midwestern manufacturer is testing the approach, says Work & Family Connection, Minneapolis consultants. Though developing the know-how to apply the research "will take many years," Dr. Senge says, it may yield "significant achievements" for those who try.

—May 15, 1996

Employers Are Finding It Doesn't Cost Much to Make a Staff Happy

What makes an employee decide to stay with a company? With worker turnover at eight-year highs, according to the Bureau of National Affairs, that may be the $64,000 Question of the late 1990s. The cost of replacing a good employee ranges from half to several times a year's pay, depending on the job.

Many assume raising pay is the only way to keep job-hoppers from hopping. Obviously, paying rock-bottom wages during low unemployment won't spark much loyalty. But handing out raises is costly and doesn't always work with today's increasingly diverse, lifestyle-conscious work force.

Some companies are finding other, nonfinancial ways to keep people, with measurable results. A sampling:

Allowing manageable schedules.

Grappling with 80% turnover, managers at Guardian Industries' 800-employee Auburn, Ind., automotive-glass plant decided "we needed to listen to the folks and find out what they felt would work better," says Mike Farrell, the plant's human-resources manager.

The message: Rotating shifts, which had workers switching from days to nights and back every few days, were making their sleep, child care and social lives too hard. Guardian switched to fixed, 12-hour day and night shifts and turnover fell by half, Mr. Farrell says.

Hotel-industry turnover can top 100% annually. But at Nashville's Opryland Hotel, managers of a 300-worker food-service unit kept quit rates "surprisingly low" by allowing servers to choose shifts when possible, says Carl Weinberg, a principal in Coopers & Lybrand's human-resources advisory practice and a consultant to Opryland. More broadly, Opryland also "structured the employment deal" to lure stable employees, offering child care and shortening the recruiting process to snare the best candidates, Mr. Weinberg says.

Rewarding longevity.

A.G. Edwards & Sons shuns the brokerage industry's megabucks signing bonuses. Instead of rewarding those who are just joining, Edwards rewards those who stay, says CEO Ben Edwards.

"Anyone who has left a big bonus on the table to join Edwards has more than made it back in the next four or five years in our profit-sharing and retirement plans," he says.

Edwards also shuns the industry's star system, broker quotas and pressure to sell in-house products, stressing customer service instead. The firm recruits people who share those values, then promotes from within. The result: 8.8% turnover, compared with an industry average of about 12%.

Providing flexibility.

Amid feverish competition for talent in the information-technology industry, turnover at American Management Systems was about 16.5% last year, below the 25% to 30% industry average. Judy Tinelli, vice president, human resources, largely credits the company's culture. AMS has long stressed flexibility and respect for its 8,000 employees' lives outside work. In a tight labor market, she says, "the groundwork we've laid on work-life balance issues, and the way we treat our employees, really come to support you." Another sign: Many former employees return; 4.5% of AMS's new hires are re-hires.

Making workers feel valued.

The reasons employees remain loyal differ dramatically among companies, says Ray Baumruk, a consultant with Hewitt Associates, Lincolnshire, Ill. When Hewitt surveyed employees in a customer-service unit of a 6,000-employee credit-card-processing concern, many said they weren't happy with the quality of their work lives and didn't feel valued. Though the company had good benefits, its practice of having the workers share common office space, rather than assigning private spaces, made them feel like "cogs in a wheel," Mr. Baumruk says.

Employees weren't particularly happy with their on-the-job relationships, either, especially with managers. The company provided
private workspaces, created work teams and started training and se-
lecting managers with greater care. Turnover fell to about 15%
from about 35% to 40%, leading to savings that outweighed the increased real-estate costs, Mr. Baumruk says.

Improving communication.

The turnover rate in the 24-hour back offices of the financial-
services industry can run 40% or more. In a 350-employee account-
processing unit at NationsBank, line managers tackled a turnover
problem in a personal way. Bosses took part in a 24-hour "expo" on
the banking firm's long list of benefits, including a child-care subsidy proven in internal studies to lower quit rates among users. They
staffed tables as late as 1 A.M. on a Saturday morning to explain the
benefits to off-hours workers. Benefits usage went up. "The power of
a supervisor talking to an employee one-on-one is profound," says
Kim Hains, a senior vice president.

Managers also were trained to communicate with employees in a
way that builds stronger relationships with the company. Instead of
slapping probation on a worker who was often tardy, one manager
asked first what was up. When he learned the worker was sharing
child care with a spouse on a different shift, squeezing commuting
time, the two simply agreed on a later starting hour.

The result of the combined changes: a 25% drop in turnover.

—November 19, 1997

Some Employers Find Way to
Ease Burden of Changing Shifts

When Cherry Semiconductor moved last year to overhaul the schedules of 600 shift workers at a Rhode Island chip plant, it got an unwanted result: an organizing drive by the Teamsters union—a rarity in the nonunion semiconductor industry.

The Teamsters eventually backed off, partly because Cherry calmed workers with informational meetings with a consultant. "We can understand how people were angry," says David Tomanio, human-resource manager at the plant. The company altered weekend schedules, disrupting lives.

Emotions are running high around shiftwork scheduling these days, and it's no wonder. The rate of shift-schedule changes is accelerating as plants and factories switch to 24-hour, seven-day operation and streamline shift schedules to raise their returns. Many are switching to 12-hour from eight-hour shifts and replacing fixed shifts with rotating ones. The goal is to distribute skilled employees evenly among shifts and ease communication between shift workers and day management.

But some of the schedules people are being ordered to work in the new 24-hour economy are horrendous. At one manufacturing plant I visited in Alabama, employees worked a rotating cycle of eight-hour and 12-hour day, evening and night shifts. Sometimes they worked all three shifts within three weeks; other times they got only one weekend off a month. Life on those shifting sands was taking a heavy toll, visible in the exhausted faces and chaotic lives of the workers.

"It's hard to have a life when your hours are always changing," says a union official at another company's plant, in Illinois, where management forced a rotating-shift schedule. The change wiped out the employee bowling team, golf league and softball team and disrupted families' lives and child care. Workers at both plants asked the companies not be named for fear of reprisals.

Now, some employers are taking a new approach. While companies in the past mostly rammed shift-schedule changes down employees' throats (guaranteeing workers will unite in hating whatever schedule is adopted), some are starting to involve employees in finding the best compromise between business imperatives and workers' physical, social and family needs.

"Management is getting so much heat from the floor they're having to take a different approach," says Bill Sirois, chief operating officer of Circadian Technologies, Cambridge, Mass., shiftwork consultants.

To begin, employers lay out basic requirements such as hours of operation, distribution of skilled workers among shifts, number of time-eating shift "turnovers" a day, employee availability for training, and so on. They educate workers about the physiological and social effects of shift-schedule alternatives, then let the workers vote. The result is often a schedule that is better for everyone.

Employees at a Shelbyville, Ind., glass-fabricating plant operated by Pilkington Libbey-Owens-Ford had been on rotating 12-hour shifts for about a year when serious problems surfaced. The schedule moved the plant's 500 workers from day shifts to nights and back again every few days, and they were exhausted. Managers were seeing product-quality problems and high accident, absenteeism, turnover and illness rates.

Though the setup allowed a lot of days off, most workers were too tired to enjoy them. Workers' kids were making heavy use of the company's employee-assistance program, seeking counseling for troubles at home, says David Barchick, Pilkington's senior human-resource manager.

"Mom and Dad were never around, or if they were home they were sleeping or just dead tired," he says.

The company opened up the problems to employee discussion, surveyed workers and educated them about shiftwork options. The survey showed half the employees lacked enough family time or energy for romance or recreation; 40% said their spouses were lonely and their families were complaining that the employee had grown irritable.

Based on the survey, workers were offered several new scheduling options; 89% voted for fixed 12-hour shifts, with everyone assigned to either days or nights. The company reaped big rewards: Turnover fell to 9% annually from 32%, health-benefit costs plunged, productivity rose and the plant went from having the worst safety record in its group to winning a companywide safety competition.

Involving employees in picking shift schedules isn't easy. The process never yields consensus; workers' individual lives and preferences are too diverse. And settling on a new schedule always raises powerful emotions, even if a majority agrees. At Shell Martinez Refinery, 85% of workers voted to change to rotating 12-hour from eight-hour shifts. Even then, the transition is proving a big adjustment for many. "You have to spend some time talking to people, communicating with them" about such changes, advises Larry Heasley, the plant's human-resource manager. "If you don't, the emotions can get ahead of you." Nevertheless, Mr. Heasley believes the people most affected by a schedule should help choose it. At one plant, says Circadian's Jim Stam, "one manager insisted, 'Come on, Jim, there must be one schedule that's the right schedule for this industry.' I said, 'Yes, it's the one that the people in the plant pick.' "

—March 25, 1998

Workplace Experts Offer
Some Advice for Small Employers

C an an employer help workers with child-care problems if it's not General Motors?

With so much talk about family-friendly policies focusing on the giants of industry, Derek Morrison, president of Morcroft Capital, a fast-growing, 31-employee medical-equipment leasing firm in Fairfield, N.J., would like to know. In a letter to me, Morcroft raises questions germane to thousands of small businesses: Does it make sense for a small employer to provide child care? Should it collaborate on a child-care center with other businesses?

Mr. Morrison already is positioning Morcroft as an employer of choice. He pays entry-level and junior back-office people more than his labor-market competitors. Benefits are good, including health insurance, a 401(k), flextime and casual dress; 75% of Morcroft's hires come from employee referrals.

But Morcroft is at a demographic threshold. Many employees are starting families; half will need child care in a few years, says Michael Crofton, general counsel. Already, one new mother is "shell-shocked at the high cost of day care." Messrs. Morrison and Crofton worry that she and others facing the same problem will quit. That's no small concern: It takes two years to get administrative employees up to speed, and labor markets are tightening.

What to do? I took Morcroft's case to seven leading work-life consultants. First, they recommend more study of employee needs. Nearly everyone will say yes if asked, "Do you think it's a good idea for the company to open a child-care center?" But people's actual child-care preferences are quirky. Holding focus groups may uncover problems Morcroft hasn't thought of, such as an unmet need for more neighborhood-based sitters, says Charles Rodgers of Work/Family Directions, Boston.

The local public child-care resource-and-referral service (provided by calling Child Care Aware toll-free) can flesh out the picture with data about community shortages and costs. The consultants also suggest Morcroft hook up with either the local resource-and-referral service or a private referral vendor, to secure child-care referrals, counseling and workplace seminars for its employees. (Private vendors help with a wider range of work-life issues.)

One thing Morcroft can count on: The cost of child care will continue to be a problem. People making less than $30,000 a year, as some Morcroft employees do, typically spend 25% to 30% of their household income on child care, a painful bite, says Arthur Emlen, professor emeritus at Portland State University.

Nearly all the consultants suggest Morcroft subsidize employees' child-care costs, perhaps on a sliding scale. A subsidy might be structured as a flat payment of about $100 a month, says Leslie Faught of Working Solutions, Portland, Ore.

Tom's of Maine, a 70-employee maker of personal-care products, gives child-care subsidies to lower-paid employees, enabling them to pick higher-quality child care of the type they prefer, a spokeswoman says; the program costs the company about $9,000 a year.

Should Morcroft plan a child-care center? The consultants were cool to the idea. Morcroft expects to grow to 50 employees in two years, and it would like to establish child-care services at the lowest possible cost. One problem: Employer-sponsored child care is usually more expensive than community care; companies are both quality-conscious and concerned with reputation. Another obstacle, of course, is Morcroft's size. With 50 employees, a center might expect to draw only seven to 10 kids at most, Dr. Emlen says.

That doesn't mean a small on-site center is out of the question. VCW Inc., a Kansas City, Mo., insurance firm, opened a center for only four children in 1989, when it had 30 employees. CEO Cheryl Womack "felt very strongly about providing peace of mind" to parents, a spokeswoman says. Today, VCW has 75 employees and 12 kids in its center.

To open a small center, Marguerite Sallee of Corporate Family Solutions, Nashville, says Morcroft would need 1,000 square feet of space, $50,000 to equip it and roughly $50,000 a year to run it. Liability insurance is easy to get at preferred rates.

More caveats: Opening an on-site or near-site center is a long-term commitment; closing it could hurt morale. Also, states regulate child care and often have stringent rules on outdoor play areas and other amenities. For near-site centers in neighborhoods, zoning can be an obstacle.

Consultants were chilly, too, to the idea of collaborating with other employers. A freestanding center usually needs to enroll at least 40 to 60 children to avoid "drowning in red ink," says John Place of Dependent Care Connection, Westport, Conn., meaning Morcroft probably would have to assemble a lot of partners.

A better route, says Sandra Burud, Bright Horizons Children's Centers, Cambridge, Mass., might be to form an alliance with a high-quality center nearby, financing improvements in return for employee discounts and priority access.

Meanwhile, Morcroft should fortify the competitive advantage it already has: its employee-friendly culture. Tyler Phillips of Partnership Group, Blue Bell, Pa., suggests equipping people to work at home when possible and considering various flexible-work options.

—September 25, 1996

Some Employees Get a Free Rein and Work Fast, Efficiently

T he customary way of organizing the workplace hasn't changed much since the Industrial Age. The typical company still opens offices, assembles workers at desks and hands them their marching orders.

A few mavericks are changing all that.

They are outliers—small companies run on the bet that you can get skilled people to work better, faster and cheaper by letting them work where and when they want, right from the starting gun. While the idea won't fly on an assembly line, some service and professional businesses are trying it. A few examples:

Bookminders' competitive secret is its work force: mostly experienced, skilled, college-educated mothers of young kids who can't find decent part-time jobs. The four-year-old Pittsburgh firm does weekly bookkeeping for businesses. Founder Tom Joseph, a former Westinghouse manufacturing engineer, equips and trains his 10 employees to work from home, then turns them loose to service the firm's 50 clients. With his offer of flexible part-time, home-based work, he is mining a deep vein of workers.

Job seekers call him every week; his help-wanted ads draw hundreds of responses. Overhead for his "cottage corporation" is low, and employee turnover is almost nil. The result: Bookminders is profitable and projected 1995 revenue will top $250,000.

Bookminders jobs are marginal; pay is for work completed, and there are no benefits. But the jobs are still a cut above most part-time work.

After an eight-year break from the work force to raise two children, the only part-time work former IBM customer-service representative Ann Strasser could find paid $5 an hour and would have required her to be at the office when her kids get home from school. Now she averages $12 an hour and sets her own hours.

Shari Powell, an experienced bookkeeper, couldn't find a part-time office job that would pay for the child care, wardrobe and commuting it would require, she says. But her Bookminders job has enabled her and her husband to pay debt, buy a van and pay for music lessons and soccer for her two kids. Such workers, Mr. Joseph says, "are the heart and soul of what we do."

Qwest Consultants employs the same kind of high-priced people big consulting firms do. The difference is Qwest gives them the freedom to say no.

While working 90-hour weeks for the consulting firm Towers Perrin, Rochelle Moulton saw her personal life take "a nosedive." She realized many of her coworkers also wished for more control over their work.

So a year ago, she and David Glueck, another former principal at Towers Perrin, started Qwest, where people with "an overwhelming desire to work flexible schedules" are the norm rather than the exception, she says.

The new Chicago firm's 18 human-resources consultants are mostly refugees from big competitors where 80-hour weeks are common. At Qwest, they work two-to-four days a week in roles designed to challenge them; they are freed from the administrative and marketing tasks required by big companies, focusing exclusively on the firm's 15 clients, from Kraft General Foods to Brunswick.

They are paid by the hour at varying rates, depending on their expertise and experience. But they also are free to turn down projects without blowing potholes in their career path. "When a consultant says no, it's a no-fault no," Ms. Moulton says. Saying no offers a chance to lead a multidimensional life. Though most of Qwest's employees have young children, one volunteers at a homeless shelter and another runs a fashion business on the side. Even as CEO, Ms. Moulton has cut her work week to 70 hours to pursue other loves: biking 200 miles a week, ballet dancing and pro bono work. "It's incredible what you can do with 20 hours a week," she says.

Primetime Publicity & Media's people work from anywhere—from a farm in Kansas to a lakeside home in Charlotte, N.C.

The freedom helps lure to the public-relations firm top employees, mostly former reporters, producers and editors weary of burnout schedules or heavy travel. Elaine Carey joined Primetime last year from her Los Angeles home after 17 years as a foreign correspondent for major newspapers. Now she can oversee her 11- and 13-year-olds while making calls for clients through the day and evening, she says.

The setup keeps costs so low that Primetime can meet another goal: billing clients only for results in the form of media coverage, says CEO Dick Grove, a 27-year PR veteran. The firm has 25 clients, and revenue has doubled in four years to a projected 1995 level of about $2 million.

Though Primetime offers benefits, employees' pay is also based on results. That's a plus for Bill McAndrew, a former manager for NBC News, whose annual income in five years at Primetime has hit "the $100,000 range," a career high, he says. Meanwhile, he enjoys being with his son, age three, on breaks from work in his suburban New York home.

All that makes the firm an oddity in a business where lavish offices and expense-account lunches are common. "We've come across [applicants] who insist on putting on a pair of braces and a tie and white shirt and have a huge desire to ride elevators to work," says Mr. Grove, who runs the firm from his Lawrence, Kan., farm. "Most of those people don't fit very well in our company."

—November 22, 1995

Rooms with a View and Flexible Hours Draw Talent to WRQ

As more employers scramble to lure skilled workers, Seattle software maker WRQ Inc. is recruiting on the razor's edge. Based in the fastest-growing pocket of one of the nation's fastest-growing industries, the 674-employee maker of connectivity software must vie with high-tech companies nationwide to lure increasingly scarce engineers and programmers.

If that isn't bad enough, WRQ must make its recruiting appeal heard over the giant sucking sound that is Microsoft hiring. Just over Seattle's Capitol Hill from WRQ's headquarters, the software giant, based in Redmond, Wash., has tripled Seattle-area employment since 1990 to 12,000 and is hiring 2,000 more workers this year. Even for Microsoft, with an alluring stock plan famous for transforming employees into millionaires, finding skilled workers is "our chief obstacle to success," a spokesman says.

But WRQ has a trump card of its own in the talent market—employee-friendly policies—and therein lies one of the most stringent tests I've seen of the appeal of workplace culture. In contrast with most of the software industry, with its culture of work-crazed excess, WRQ is a nice place to work where people are expected to enjoy their lives. "WRQ has carved out a niche as a place where family life and personal life are very important," says Rita Ashley, a Seattle executive recruiter.

How the firm fares in the coming years, as the Baby Bust dominates the market for new hires, will say much about the value of an employee-friendly workplace.

So far, WRQ's reasonable and flexible hours, team management and family-friendly policies, including time off to volunteer, have enabled it to attract and keep high-quality, experienced employees.

Its annual turnover of 10% is about half the industry average and far below the 50% some firms are experiencing. It employs more women than most software companies. And the privately held firm,

239

which posted a 17% revenue gain in 1996 to $130 million, has been consistently profitable and has a reputation for good products and service. "The first word that comes to mind in association with WRQ is quality," says Seattle recruiter Sonja Carson.

WRQ usually doesn't compete head-to-head with Microsoft for talent. Because its work teams deal directly with its big-company customers, WRQ recruits more experienced workers than most software firms need, and its workers tend to be older and more settled. "We always tease people when they go to WRQ that they're more interested in lifestyle than workstyle," one recruiter says. Also, WRQ's management-by-consensus style drives some Type-A techies crazy.

Nevertheless, WRQ's two new office buildings on Seattle's Lake Union have drawn many visitors intrigued by their worker-friendly atmosphere. The buildings have work spaces flooded with natural light from a 10-story atrium; massage, napping and breast-feeding rooms; and balconies overlooking the lake.

For Wall Data, a software maker competing directly with WRQ for talent, "WRQ is a tough nut to crack," says Don Rooks, Wall's human-resources manager.

Having a life outside work comes naturally to WRQ co-owners Doug Walker and Craig McKibben, mountain-climbing buddies who founded the firm in 1981 with three other partners who have retired. Mr. Walker, CEO, father of a nine-year-old girl and an avid outdoorsman who bicycles 20 miles to work, integrates work and personal life. During a recent trip to WRQ's Singapore offices, he took time off to climb Mt. Kinabalu in Borneo.

Behavior that would clash with the culture of most software firms comes naturally at WRQ. Software developer Kathy Boscole, a mother of three, still remembers the moment seven years ago when she made the decision to join WRQ. During a job interview with WRQ's partners, Mr. Walker's daughter, then a toddler, knocked on the window of the conference room, entered and sat on her father's lap. "It was just a natural thing to blend family and work," Ms. Boscole says.

Like other firms, WRQ has had to step up recruiting, adding internships and visits to campuses, where its message plays well. When Mr. Walker speaks to students, says WRQ recruiter Jane De-

Paolo, they "don't just see a computer nerd. They see a guy who has a life."

WRQ's appeal is strong, too, to young fathers in the software industry who want to spend time with their children. (Even Bill Gates has been leaving work earlier since the 1996 birth of his daughter.) Systems engineer Leroy Jenkins, 31, a former Microsoft contractor who joined WRQ two years ago, says that as much as he enjoyed the work he did at Microsoft, his 13-hour workdays there, and being on call around the clock, were too much for him, his wife and his new baby. "It just wasn't worth it," he says.

WRQ's fortunes in the red-hot recruiting market will depend partly on how badly new hires want to balance work and personal life. So far, it's fair to say more employers will be looking over WRQ's shoulder. As demand for technical talent mounts, work-life concerns "are going to become the Achilles heel of the high-tech industry," predicts Susan Adler Funk, president of Diversity Difference, Seattle, who has studied some of the nation's biggest high-tech companies. "This is an issue employers are going to have to face."

—August 13, 1997

Insurance Firm Cracks Tight Labor Market with Flexible Hours

For managers in St. Paul Cos.' information-systems unit, a labor shortage is a day-to-day reality.

Amid unemployment of only 3% in the Minneapolis-St. Paul area, competition for skilled systems workers is "brutal," one manager says. Newspapers and Web sites run thousands of ads for skilled systems people; some workers get two headhunter calls a day.

Yet St. Paul, a big insurer not known as a high-paying employer, has single-digit turnover among information-systems workers, compared with roughly 15% to 20% elsewhere. When St. Paul employees depart for greener pastures, they often come back. The insurer even lured a couple of recruits recently from Andersen Consulting, a firm known for its recruiting acumen. Why? Flexibility is a major reason. Rather than icing its alternative-scheduling policy during 1990s layoffs and cost cuts, as many employers have, St. Paul spent 1½ years overhauling it to make it work better for the business.

The result is a state-of-the-art approach that makes flexible scheduling a key to unlocking tight skilled-labor markets. All staff employees have access to alternative schedules, providing they can show the change would work well for bosses, customers and coworkers.

To St. Paul information-systems employees, who are about half men and half women, flexibility is as good as money in the bank. One programmer told a headhunter recently that any new employer would have to offer him $10,000 a year more to compensate for the loss of a compressed work week. "Headhunters can come along and offer much more money to work for some other company, [but St. Paul is seen] as a great place to work," says David Healey, a veteran Minneapolis recruiter.

In overhauling alternative scheduling, St. Paul solved many of the problems that discourage other employers from abandoning the old 8-to-5 regime. Here's how:

The entitlement mentality: Some employees assumed in the past that flexibility gave them the right, forever, to work the schedule of their choice. Paradoxically, flexibility was making the business rigid, says Wayne Hoeschen, senior vice president, information systems; "People thought if they had a four-day week they never had to work more than those four days."

So a volunteer employee committee, working with Paul Rupert, a flexibility consultant with Boston-based Work/Family Directions, wrote a new plan saying employees have to "give flexibility to get flexibility." Employees must change their hours if work demands change. Managers review alternative schedules at least yearly.

At first, employees complained that schedule changes had so many strings attached, Mr. Hoeschen says. "Some asked, 'Now you're saying, more is expected of me?' " he says. "Our answer is, 'Yes, more is expected of you.' "

The ghost-town syndrome: In the past, Tuesday through Thursday were "core days" when employees had to be in, making staffing too thin on Fridays. So the committee ended core days, letting managers base schedules entirely on business needs. The result: More employees on compressed weeks are taking midweek days off. For programmer analyst John Fagnant, that means he can bike and roller-blade on Wednesdays, when paths aren't crowded. Fridays, he provides needed customer-service coverage at work.

The fairness problem: Employees used to be confused about how alternative schedules were handed out. "New people would wonder, 'Do I have to wait until [a colleague] retires to have flexibility? Or is it only for people with young kids?' " says Mark Klein, vice president, underwriting systems, and head of the committee. So the committee gave everyone access to a work-arrangement application form that asks how any proposed change will help meet customer needs.

At first, some employees turned in the forms with the question about business benefits left blank. "I'd say, 'OK, go back and try it again. Think about it from the customer viewpoint,' " says manager Scott Moesle. It was "an awakening" for employees.

Manager overload: With nearly everyone on nonstandard schedules, paper-and-pencil tracking of vacation days was a nightmare. So the committee created an on-line, time-off tracking system based on hours worked that reconciles oddball schedules with the company benefits plan. The system makes it easy to change schedules quickly, says Diane Cushman, manager, work-force partnering.

Controlling poor performers: Many managers feared slackers would seek more leeway under an open-door scheduling policy. Some did, but bosses have found the new application makes it easy to say no and apply pressure to shape up.

When a problem employee asked Kathryn Jorgensen, an information-systems manager, for a schedule change, the written application framed a discussion about the employee's performance problems and "made it easy for me to say this wasn't going to work," she says.

In 1997, St. Paul will roll out the plan to all of its 9,000 U.S. employees.

—November 13, 1996

A Crucible in
Balancing Job and Family

When Denise Buonopane, a partner at Deloitte & Touche, sat down to advise rising star Mary McCarthy-Coyle on her career, the talk wasn't about her consulting skills.

Instead, Ms. Buonopane conveyed a '90s-style message: Cut your work hours to make time for a personal life, she advised Ms. McCarthy-Coyle, who was putting in 100 hours a week—and wasn't happy about it. The goal: to keep Ms. McCarthy-Coyle from burning out and quitting.

That advice is heard surprisingly often these days in fast-track professions like accounting and consulting. For decades, big firms in these fields have fostered a workaholic culture so intense that requests to work a 40-hour week were often met with a pay cut. That climate has served firms well, producing high client-service standards and a reputation as a training ground for top recruits.

But increasingly, the culture is also a curse. Women and dual-career couples are the primary recruits in many professions, and many aren't willing or able to sacrifice personal and family life. Their resistance is driving turnover, particularly among women, to damaging levels of 25% or more, hurting client service and diverting huge amounts of employee time to recruiting and training.

Few firms have tackled the problem with more energy than Deloitte, based in Wilton, Conn. Concerned that 25% annual turnover among its female employees was draining talent and, increasingly, that male employees were becoming dissatisfied with workaholic lifestyles, the firm has promoted an avalanche of programs in the past 1½ years, from flexible scheduling to gender-awareness training. Monday, Deloitte won an award from Catalyst, a leading women's advocacy group, for its efforts. In many ways, the 15,000-employee firm is a crucible for a cultural change that is being attempted at a growing number of companies.

Deloitte's experience has taught a major lesson: transforming a rigid culture takes time. The last frontier is the minds of over-achievers like Ms. McCarthy-Coyle, who must not only trust that their employer's new policies are more than rhetoric, but change their own expectations of themselves if any significant change is to occur.

"It's a slow process," says Deloitte CEO J. Michael Cook. Despite proclamations that the accounting and consulting firm wants part-timers and would make them partners, "the reaction was, 'Yeah, right. Tell me when that happens so I can fall over dead,' " he says. This year a part-timer in its San Jose, Calif., office was named a partner.

Some progress is measurable; turnover among women is down to 15% from 25%, the same as men. Ms. McCarthy-Coyle, 33, a man-ager, had been with Deloitte about three years—a stage when many young fast-trackers flee—when Ms. Buonopane and other partners reached out. With their support, she halved her work hours and, for the first time since she joined the firm, started planning social activities on evenings and weekends. Without those changes, Ms. McCarthy-Coyle says, "it would have been difficult to stay with the firm for the long haul."

Ms. Buonopane's own example is a powerful influence. An 11-year employee and mother of three children under four, she some-times works seven-day weeks. But she is expert at drawing the line, refusing weekend travel and even turning down a project manager's order to report every Sunday afternoon to a client's offices. When the same manager started phoning her home at 11 P.M. on Sundays for a conference call, she stopped answering the phone.

Deloitte has workshops to get people to talk to one another about such issues. The biggest task, says Gale Hiering Varma, human re-sources director in the firm's Parsippany, N.J., office, is to help em-ployees "accept the challenge of, 'I've got to manage my own work-life balance,' vs. thinking that 'The firm makes me work this way,' " she says. "That happens slowly. My target is a five-year shift in attitude."

By many measures, it will take at least that long. Chris Foster, au-dit manager in Deloitte's Tulsa, Okla., office, had been working seven-day weeks and traveling heavily for seven years before he hit the wall. He and his wife, an information-systems project manager who also travels a lot, were worried "that our careers were pulling us away from each other," he says. They also were expecting their first child. In desperation, Mr. Foster told his boss, "I have to find something else to do." To his surprise, he was offered an 80% work schedule that has allowed him to avoid "the advanced stages of burnout," he says.

Mr. Foster says the tallest hurdle was his own fear. "I felt I was washing my career down the drain. It took a lot of soul-searching" to modify a work ethic learned from his parents to suit the realities of a modern two-career family, he says. Once begun, the balancing act takes day-to-day effort. Elizabeth Rader, Deloitte's first part-time partner and mother of two toddlers, says she struggles to "instill in myself the discipline to say no occasionally." Turning down some extra duties offered recently "felt like an unnatural response," she says.

Yet such personal choices are the basis of broader change. "We're trying to bring about some very fundamental cultural changes here," Ms. Rader says. "We don't have all the answers, and we're not there yet. But we're moving in the right direction. We're truly on the cutting edge of professional workplace culture."

—December 14, 1994

Accounting Firms Battle
to Be Known as Best Workplaces

Who would have thought it could happen?
The spectacle of all the top firms in any one business duking it out for status as the No. 1 employee-friendly workplace could have existed in the past only in the hallucinations of a Dilbert-style burnout case.

Yet that's exactly what is happening now among the Big Six accounting giants. All the firms, hurt by raging turnover (particularly among women) and a shortage of experienced talent, are vying to keep workers happy. They are competing to get on best-employer lists and are promoting a blizzard of new initiatives, from flexible schedules to novel career tracks.

Amid all the hoopla, actual progress is slow, particularly in advancing and retaining women, who are half of accounting recruits but only 7% to 10% of Big Six partners.

But as the skilled-labor market tightens, similar rivalries may heat up in other fields. Meanwhile, the Battle of the Big Six has created a crucible for workplace innovation. Some of the lessons so far:

Flexibility works. Treated as window dressing in many industries, flexible work arrangements are proving a powerful retention tool. Deloitte & Touche says its flexible setups are a major reason people stay with the firm.

That echoes a new 614-employer survey by Watson Wyatt Worldwide ranking flexible schedules as the most effective retention tool, better than training, above-market pay and stock options.

Deloitte, KPMG Peat Marwick, Coopers & Lybrand and Price Waterhouse all have carved out a high profile on flexibility, but Ernst & Young is gaining fast. Ernst has set up an innovative database on its various flexible work arrangements, with 450 user profiles. Separately, a self-assessment quiz helps employees figure out which (if any) flexible schedule is right for them.

The database drew 7,000 hits in its first month out and has helped drive a sharp increase in flexible work arrangements—to 6% of Ernst & Young employees, the highest percentage reported by the Big Six.

Clients aren't the only cause of overwork. The Big Six firms have long blamed demanding clients for workaholic cultures. The old idiom, "If a client says jump, the only right answer is, 'How high?' " has been a powerful rationale for burnout hours and rigid career tracks.

But now, in a Big Six version of Pogo's "We has met the enemy, and he is us," the firms are discovering that much of the pressure for overwork is coming from inside. An Ernst study of 300 top performers who quit found men and women alike citing reasons relating to a lack of life balance. They said, "Our clients aren't demanding it, it's our own partners," says Deborah Holmes, head of Ernst's new Office of Retention.

Ernst is piloting a plan to eliminate pointless overwork. The pilot will explore ways to deepen employees' communication about work priorities with both partners and clients, eliminate needless pressure and help people break from voice mail and e-mail during vacations.

Alternate career paths help employees get a life. The Big Six's old, rigid up-or-out career path has long discouraged anyone who wanted to slow down for a while—to go back to school, raise a family, or just write poetry. But Price Waterhouse has broken the mold with a "new career model" that makes room for all that. Among other things, it allows part-timers to become partners, a practice that is shunned in the top ranks of most businesses, but that has been embraced by most of the Big Six.

Reward results, not face time. Some firms are replacing overtime pay with pay plans that peg compensation to performance in meeting individual or group targets. Arthur Andersen is installing one such gain-sharing plan. "We've removed the idea that you have to work a lot of overtime to be successful," says Denny Reigle, named a year ago to the new post of managing director, human resources and recruiting, for Andersen in the U.S.

How is it all working? Deloitte, Ernst & Young, Coopers and KPMG all claim annual turnover is declining, based on unaudited numbers provided by the firms. Deloitte and Ernst claim turnover below 20%, compared with more traditional levels of 23% to 25% at other firms.

And the Big Six pitch is playing well with Generation Xers jaded by the juggling woes of their parents. Anita Hutchinson, a University of California, Berkeley, graduate who just joined Coopers & Lybrand, says she gave life-balance concerns a 50% weighting in picking an employer. "I don't want to be working so hard that I can't enjoy my twenties," she says. "I don't want to have a midlife crisis at 25."

Steve Judd, 28, a recent Ernst & Young recruit who just became engaged, says the firm's emphasis on flexibility has cast his future in a new light. "Originally, my thought was no way" could anyone be an involved father while working in the Big Six, he says. "Now, I'm thinking, 'Maybe I could try it.'"

Setbacks may loom if planned mergers between Price Waterhouse and Coopers & Lybrand, and KPMG and Ernst & Young, put so much pressure on fees that the firms have to push burnout hours to compete.

Would the Ms. Hutchinsons and Mr. Judds of the world stick around in that environment? Stay tuned.

—January 21, 1998

Part Seven

CARING FOR THE AGED

One out of four employees in the U.S. have provided care for aged relatives and loved ones in the past year, a number likely to grow to two out of five by 2002, according to the 1997 National Study of the Changing Workforce by the Families and Work Institute.

Carol Lay

About one-third of caregivers find they must take time off or cut back at work to attend to elders. Within a few years, demographic trends will likely have made elder care a bigger factor in U.S. productivity than child care.

The frailty or illness of an aged loved one can raise unnerving emotional issues, immersing a caregiver in a sea of confusion and worry. And elder-care needs are complicated, often waxing and waning in periodic crises separated by long periods of calm. Those realities can have a major and often traumatic impact on a caregiver's personal and work life.

These columns offer advice and insight from elder-care experts and experienced working caregivers to the elderly. They identify issues that require advance planning, sources of help and ways to foster family cooperation. Trends in employer elder-care policies are addressed. The columns also cover issues peculiar to our mobile society—caregiving for family members from afar, hiring geriatric care managers and, in an increasingly popular option, transferring your aged parents with you to a new job.

With Elder Care Comes a Professional and Personal Crisis

For many years, Jeanne McLaughlin cleared every hurdle she met.

An honors graduate in economics from Stanford University, she earned two master's degrees and rose through the ranks of a major oil company to become a senior tax adviser. She also had two children. Throughout her 16-year career, says her boss Tom Lyden, she was "highly valued and dedicated to her work."

Then Ms. McLaughlin hit the wall: Both her elderly parents fell ill almost at once—her mother with brain disease, her father with pancreatic cancer. The ensuing months dissolved into a blur of doctor visits, trips to chemotherapy and days spent researching treatments. Gradually, in what Ms. McLaughlin calls "a life-changing experience ... my career became secondary." She recently took early retirement at age 42 to gain more flexibility to care for her parents, with plans to start a consulting practice.

Elder care is derailing more high-powered careers these days. In the past, aged relatives were a marginal workplace problem because women, who did most of the caregiving, held mostly marginal jobs—if any. But now, more fast-track caregivers are emerging as women rise in corporate ranks and men take on more family duties.

The trend is a wild card in the workplace; no one can tell how or when an elder-care crisis will hit. Once it does, relatives find that good home health aides, adult day care or assisted-living facilities are scarce or booked. They often must take over the elder's financial affairs at the same time. About 25% of caregivers, studies show, are forced to take a step backward at work.

Three years ago, Annette Tomarazzo's father developed neurological disorders that stripped him of his mental abilities so quickly that she had no opportunity to plan for his care. So Ms. Tomarazzo quit a promising job as an operations manager for a Manhattan stockbroker and took a 25% pay cut to work in New Jersey for a discount broker to be near him during the day.

For two years she used her vacation to be with her father. He has since entered a nursing home, and Ms. Tomarazzo is back on track with a stock exchange post.

Not only are elder-care needs hard to manage, but they can bring to the fore thorny family issues that an employee may have long ignored. One manager for a telecommunications concern, who was dedicated to her career and traveled extensively for her job, had little contact with her aged mother for five years. Then her mother's husband died, and the elderly woman began wandering the streets at night, searching for her own dead mother.

Overwhelmed by guilt and embarrassment at losing touch for so long, the manager panicked and stopped going to work. For days, she stayed in her mother's house around the clock. The family could afford a home health-care aide; "there were things that could be done," says Barbara Wolfgang, an elder-care consultant for the Partnership Group who counseled the manager. "Isn't it amazing that she didn't even think of them?"

"It's a familiar song," says Donna Wagner, vice president, programs, at the nonprofit National Council on Aging. "You can be competent in every other part of your life and be blowing this one."

Many of the qualities that make someone a great employee—perfectionism, commitment, thoroughness, loyalty—also can draw them deeply into the details of elder care. For Ms. McLaughlin, managing her parents' care herself was "an ethical issue. When you look at the elderly population and how much they've contributed to society, don't they deserve that? My parents gave me their time, and I feel I should at least try to return that in part."

Researchers have found that an ailing elder might need any of 300 combinations of services in passing from one life stage to the next, says Barbara Lepis of the Partnership for Elder Care, a nonprofit consortium of employers and New York City's Agency for the Aging. Services include day-to-day home care and meals as well as day-care, assisted-living or nursing-home facilities.

Some caregivers can manage the super-human workloads that result. When an adult day-care center that enrolled her mother threatened to close, Marilyn McCumber, a Glendale, Calif., attorney who was already working six-day weeks, bought the center. She continues to operate it, oversee her mother's care and sustain her law practice.

The grief of watching a loved one's decline can drain the hardiest professionals. A New York TV production-company executive, who has beaten breast cancer and raised two children alone, says caring for her mother, who has Alzheimer's disease, is harder. "I can't conquer it. I'm powerless. I can't get my mother to listen, to understand. I feel like I'm being sucked into the vortex. It's like being caught in some large, uncontrollable phenomenon like a tsunami or a hurricane," she says.

The good news: A growing number of people, called "pre-caregivers," have begun planning for elder care, Ms. Lepis says. These pre-caregivers, often helped by employer-paid seminars, are talking with relatives before crises strike, learning early signs of geriatric ailments and studying options for elder housing and care. Also, Ms. Wolfgang says, children are learning from their parents and will be better prepared for the increasingly prolonged demands of old age. "This," she says, "is a groundbreaking generation."

—November 9, 1994

Planning Ahead for
the Inevitable: An Elder's Illness

K.C. Burns was stepping into his car at his Hartford, Conn., workplace, ready to leave with his wife for a weekend in Vermont, when the call came.

"K.C., your mother is on the phone!" a coworker yelled frantically. Mr. Burns ran back into his office at Aetna Life & Casualty and got the news: His 83-year-old father, who had looked fine just a day earlier, had lapsed into a deep coma. Thus was Mr. Burns' life transformed for the next 1½ years. He adjusted every aspect of his days, from his work schedule to his free time, to help his parents.

Elders' health crises often strike family members like lightning, with little warning and nearly the disruptive force. If you are a working adult, odds are that you, too, will assume elder-care responsibility at some point. Like me and most others in our youth-crazed culture, you may be in denial about this. But the numbers are irrefutable: At least 16% of the work force is already providing elder care. The ratio of the frail elderly to middle-aged people is expected to rise 75% by 2030. Life spans are lengthening, and family members provide 80% of care for the aged.

"Almost everybody becomes a caregiver sooner or later," says Marilyn McCumber, a Glendale, Calif., attorney who cares for her mother.

This column begins an occasional series on elder care in which four experts—Jeffrey Abrandt, a New York elder-law attorney; Katharine Hazzard, work-family manager for John Hancock Mutual Life Insurance; Barbara Lepis, director of the Partnership for Elder Care, a consortium of the New York City Agency for the Aging and several employers; and Donna Wagner, vice president, programs, National Council on the Aging—and others will offer advice on common dilemmas facing working caregivers. In this column and next, they focus on planning ahead.

Mr. Burns, who is Aetna's human-resources manager, can attest to the need for planning. His father, who had pancreatitis, was in a coma for six weeks, but has battled his way back to near-recovery. Mr. Burns says his and his mother's lives were made harder by the fact that they knew nothing about his father's wishes regarding medical treatment, nor about his insurance, assets or finances. So they had to scramble for the information they needed to manage his care.

As a first step, Ms. Wagner recommends finding out what kind of care your elder wants. Respecting his or her wishes "is more than just an ethical issue," she says. Studies in the late 1970s at Yale and Duke universities showed that nursing-home patients stay healthier if they are given some control.

Being prepared to assert the older person's wishes can be crucial. When Carolyn Johnson's 75-year-old mother was hospitalized after a bad fall, her doctors began laying plans for nursing-home care. But Ms. Johnson, a 46-year-old Baltimore social-science researcher, felt "everything was happening too fast. I said, 'Wait a minute, let's talk this over,'" she says. Knowing her mother preferred to stay home, Ms. Johnson insisted on it. "Being at home has been a great help to her emotional, mental and physical well-being," she says.

Also crucial is securing the legal right to carry out an elder's wishes if he or she is incapacitated, Mr. Abrandt says. Delegating power of attorney to a relative usually allows him or her to sign documents and manage assets. The power of attorney should be "durable," meaning that it remains valid after the signer becomes incompetent. An older person also can opt for a "springing power of attorney," which takes effect only when certain conditions are met—when the person is certified incompetent, for instance.

Family members also may need to make health-care decisions. This right can be conferred in 27 states through a health-care proxy or health-care power of attorney; in 12 other states, a durable power of attorney serves this purpose, Mr. Abrandt says. The better-known "living will," recognized by 47 states, performs similarly. But many attorneys favor the more flexible health-care power of attorney; living wills usually define only narrow circumstances when a family can act.

Neglecting these documents can lead "to real catastrophe," Mr.

Abrandt says. In the case of a New York family, the aged mother had made clear that she didn't want to be kept alive if she fell into a coma. But the family lacked medical power of attorney. When the mother lost consciousness with no hope of any recovery, the family had to seek a court order to disconnect the life-support systems and let her die as she had wished—a "time-consuming, expensive and emotionally debilitating" ordeal, he says.

Ms. Lepis also recommends boning up on your elder's affairs. She gives relatives a list of documents to track down, including a will; Social Security card; life, health and home insurance policies; tax returns; and savings, credit, safety-deposit, military and real-estate records. Having the data, she says, "is like life insurance. You may not ever need to use it, but it's there if you do."

(Financial planning for long-term care is beyond the scope of this column. But it's crucial to begin early by learning about long-term care insurance, Medicare and Medicaid rules in your state.)

As for Mr. Burns, both his parents now have living wills, and he knows their financial and legal affairs thoroughly. If another crisis should arise, he says, "this time, I'm ready."

—March 22, 1995

Identifying the Issues
That Go into Deciding
About Care for Elderly

I t was a moment Frances Walton would like to forget. Her 84-year-old grandmother, "the love of my life," had dementia and could no longer live in her own home. As family members discussed her care, Ms. Walton says, her grandmother "turned to me and said, 'Frankie, can't I come live with you?' "

Ms. Walton, a mother and school secretary, had already been caring for her grandmother around the clock at great cost. The older woman's night wakings and demented behavior had Ms. Walton frazzled; she was exhausted and losing weight. Her husband and son were frantic with worry about her, and Ms. Walton's doctor had warned her that she would fall seriously ill if she didn't get some rest.

Torn, "I said no," Ms. Walton recalls. "Then I went home and cried buckets."

The needs of ailing elders pose ethical dilemmas that require identifying and weighing the values, needs and wants of one person against those of others. The choices are growing ever more complicated and demand an organized approach so that the outcome is agreeable to most of those involved.

The dilemmas may range from how to arrange in-home help for a needy but resistant elder, to whether to place a reluctant but feeble parent in day care so you can work.

At issue are such questions as when you're morally and legally obligated to make a decision on someone else's behalf, and how you can do so and still respect that person's lifestyle choices, says Denise Brown, owner of Tad Publishing, Park Ridge, Ill., and publisher of "Caregiving" newsletter.

Such dilemmas are coming up more often, for three reasons. As more people enter old age in good physical health, ailments of the mind, such as dementia, are taking center stage, raising questions about how to keep someone safe when they are physically able but mentally incompetent.

Also, two in three caregivers are now employed and many live far from their elders, eliminating the obvious choice in tough situations: providing around-the-clock care yourself. Finally, new medications can slow the progression of disease and prolong people's care needs.

As baby boomers age, the number of people facing such dilemmas "is going to explode," says Steven DeKosky, chairman of the medical and scientific advisory council of the Alzheimer's Association.

A 10-step decision-making process, developed by medical-ethics researchers, can help, Ms. Brown says. Briefly, review the situation and gather all the information you can. Identify the ethical issues and professional and individual values of all involved. Identify values conflicts. Decide who should decide. Identify possible actions and likely outcomes. Then, choose a course of action, carry it out and evaluate the results.

Though Ms. Walton's dilemma forced her to weigh conflicting interests, the solution was in everyone's best interests: She regained her health and was able to continue to play a big role in the care of her grandmother, who went to live with a daughter.

Soon, Ms. Walton faced another dilemma when her mother, then in her 70s, could no longer drive safely but refused to stop. Ms. Walton confronted her one day when her mother took the car and wound up stranded, confused and frightened after the car broke down. "I don't want you to hurt yourself and I don't want you to hurt someone else," Ms. Walton told her mother. "I'm sorry to tell you this, but I don't want you to drive the car anymore." She cushioned the blow by keeping her mother's car tuned up and using it to drive her on errands, telling her, "This will always be your car."

Such ethical dilemmas often serve as crucibles, affirming our most deeply held values. Linda Combs, a former banking manager, worked hard to achieve her post as an assistant U.S. Treasury Secretary in the Bush administration. But she gave it all up in 1991 when her father was no longer able to care alone for her mother, who has Alzheimer's.

"One phone call I'll never, ever forget," she says, was from her father to her Treasury Department office, saying he was overwhelmed. "I can remember standing there with the phone in my hand, looking over at the White House" from her office window, "and saying, 'Dear Lord, why are You giving me these great opportunities here, yet I'm so needed back home?' "

She moved to Winston-Salem, N.C., near her parents, and soon faced another dilemma: She and her father wanted to keep her mother at home, but the toll of overseeing her round-the-clock care was destroying her father's health. In a sad talk over her kitchen table, Dr. Combs told him, "You know, Daddy, we have to look out for your well-being. Would you like me to see when we could get a room at the nursing home?" Near tears, her father agreed, and the decision allowed him to continue living on his own for a time.

The root answer to such dilemmas is "knowing who you are," says Dr. Combs, who gives seminars on leadership and has written a book on Alzheimer's, *A Long Good-Bye.* In her case, she was sticking to guiding principles of compassion and commitment to valuing family, honesty and integrity.

—December 10, 1997

A Worker's Guide to Finding Help in Caring for an Elder

As a senior consultant for Coopers & Lybrand, Carolyn Cotton has a wealth of information at her fingertips, from a library to computer databases. But a brief message on Ms. Cotton's office voicemail one day reduced her to frantically searching the Yellow Pages.

The call was from a social worker at a hospital where her mother was recovering from a broken hip: "Your mother will be discharged tomorrow. You need to arrange 24-hour-a-day care for her."

"I was panicked," Ms. Cotton says. "I didn't know if I was going to have to provide care myself, if I could find someone else to do it or how much it would cost." Though we live in the Information Age in a nation with a premier health-care system, information for people who care for the elderly is scattered and hard to find. The first resort of many caregivers in a crisis—the Yellow Pages—offers little help tapping the network of elder-care services and professionals.

The long-term care system "is a maze that is so complicated," says Katharine Hazzard, work-family manager for John Hancock Mutual Life Insurance. This column, the second in an occasional series on dilemmas facing working caregivers to the elderly, is a road map to information you need to plan ahead.

A good starting point is the federally funded network of 675 area agencies on aging, which track services and finance programs for aged people who live at home. A toll-free line, the Eldercare Locator, can identify the one nearest your elder.

The agencies don't help screen or choose services, though. When Carolyn Johnson, a Baltimore social science researcher, needed home care for her 75-year-old mother, she found that some of the programs listed with her aging agency had two-year waiting lists. Many "were never intended to serve the large numbers of elderly," she says.

Private telephone resource-and-referral services can sometimes cut red tape. The best ones are sponsored by employers; after a coworker referred Ms. Cotton to Coopers & Lybrand's R&R service, provided by the Partnership Group in Blue Bell, Pa., a counselor helped delay her mother's hospital discharge and find a home-care aide. Coopers, Aetna Life & Casualty and John Hancock are among a tiny percentage of employers that offer elder-care R&R.

For people without access to an employer program, Children of Aging Parents, a nonprofit Levittown, Pa., group, can provide some referrals by mail. Some hospitals, senior centers and nonprofit groups such as local Alzheimer's Association chapters also have information. And private geriatric-care managers usually charge about $15 to $60 an hour for helping research and plan care.

In a hopeful sign, new resources are emerging. A new National Alliance for Caregiving, a Bethesda, Md., partnership of four big aging organizations with funding by Glaxo, last month announced plans to open the first national resource center for caregivers to the aged. Also, Child and Elder Care Insights, a Rocky River, Ohio, dependent-care consultant, plans to make parts of its elder-care database available on the Internet within a few months.

Networking is crucial. Barbara Lepis, director of the Partnership for Elder Care, a consortium of employers and the New York City Agency for the Aging, recommends building a support system including the elder's neighbors, clergy, friends, doctors, accountants and other advisers. Experts also recommend touching base early with an elder-law attorney and a geriatrician. Upon signs of serious illness, or by age 70 to 75, most people should see an attorney to investigate, among other things, options for financing long-term care, suggests Jeffrey Abrandt, a New York elder- and health-law attorney. Medicare usually pays for less than most people assume, and Medicaid eligibility guidelines are "a minefield," he says.

Though K.C. Burns' parents had wills, they were healthy, and no one thought of planning for a long illness. The result: When Mr. Burns' 84-year-old father fell gravely ill and spent nearly a year in a nursing home, the Aetna human-resources manager found himself awash in "unbelievably complicated" legal issues applying for Medicaid. He wished then he had laid the groundwork with a lawyer, he says, "rather than being in a crisis mode."

The National Academy of Elder Law Attorneys, Tucson, Ariz.,

screens and sells a list of attorneys for $25. State bar associations, agencies on aging and R&R services can give referrals.

Tapping a geriatrician can ensure that an older person's medical care is on track, says Donna Wagner, vice president, programs, National Council on the Aging. Old people have special medical concerns. Marilyn McCumber, a Glendale, Calif., attorney who is caring for her Alzheimer's-afflicted mother, didn't know until consulting a geriatrician that the thyroid medication her mother had been taking for years was too harsh for elderly patients; a geriatric specialist switched her to a milder drug. "People always take their children to a pediatrician. But it doesn't occur to us that the same kind of specialization is needed when people hit the other end of the age spectrum," Ms. McCumber says.

Planning for a loved one's final years is increasingly important, Ms. Lepis says. As life spans lengthen, "people are spending 20, 30 or 40 years" in old age, often requiring several kinds of assistance, she says. "It's like another phase of life."

—April 5, 1997

More Family Members
Are Working Together
to Care for Elders

I f Catherine deSaules, age 75, needs long-term care in her final years, one thing is certain: Her children and grandchildren will provide it.

There are several possibilities. Catherine's daughter, Pat deSaules, a Princeton, N.J., executive recruiter, has bought a town house with an extra bedroom for Catherine. Another daughter, Marie, changed jobs and moved to New Jersey from Pennsylvania to be near her mother. One of Marie's daughters bought a house near Catherine's with extra space for her. The family has toured assisted-living facilities, and all five of Catherine's children, including three sons, plan to support her in old age.

Why all the cooperation? The deSaules know more about long-term care than most; they cared for five years for their father, who died last year. Their experience of managing his care was so difficult that "we all agreed we would plan ahead for my mother," Pat deSaules says.

The first major study of long-term elder-care trends suggests the deSaules aren't alone; cooperation among siblings and other relatives is increasingly the rule in elder care. In a trend analysis for the National Alliance for Caregiving, Donna Wagner of Towson University, a leading elder-care researcher, found households with at least one caregiver present tripled since 1987, compared with a 21% rise in the elderly population. "In America, caregiving truly is a family affair," Dr. Wagner says.

While an increase in caregiving for the elderly has been widely predicted, the study suggests the trend is broader than expected, signaling a wider impact on the workplace, too.

The trend, however, is also shallower. Caregivers today are less

likely to help with essential daily activities such as bathing and dressing and more likely to be doing lighter tasks such as shopping and
bill-paying, based on previous studies by the alliance and the American Association of Retired Persons. That may be because old people
are living longer, in healthier condition, or because people are
quicker to define themselves as caregivers than in the past, Dr. Wagner says.

The pattern of shared, lighter duties doesn't hold for many families caring for elders with heavy needs, including dementia, where
the caregiving burden still typically falls on one family member, says
Lynn Friss Feinberg of Family Caregiver Alliance, San Francisco, a
nonprofit organization.

In any event, the increased family cooperation is likely driven by
several factors. First, in more families, all adults are employed and
unable to stay at home with an aged relative, forcing siblings to work
together.

One California family, with three sisters and a brother, have cared
for their ailing parents for four years. At various times, each of the
four—a computer salesman, a public-relations consultant, a medical
student and an executive recruiter—has provided personal care and
helped with bills, doctors' visits or shopping for their parents.
"We've been tight our whole lives, and this has made us even
tighter," one sister says.

Second, the rising cost of nursing homes, assisted-living facilities
and in-home care is forcing many families to plan ahead. Nursing-
home costs have risen roughly 20% in three years to an average of
$46,000 a year, based on government and industry sources; assisted-
living facilities offering personal care have ranged from about
$20,000 to $48,000 recently.

Joan Gruber, a Dallas financial planner specializing in the elderly,
insists on meeting adult children of her clients. As the elderly live
longer, financial planning increasingly means "saving the kids from
a pile of Mom's bills," she says.

Finally, worries about changes in Medicare and Medicaid are also
driving families together. In the deSaules family's case, a Medicaid
reversal left the family holding the bag for an unexpected $23,000
nursing-home bill after their father's death.

Though the family had been told informally by Medicaid officials that their father would likely qualify for Medicaid, Pat deSaules says, officials after his death denied payment for his seven-month stay in a Medicaid-eligible nursing home. (Ocean County, N.J., officials responsible for the decision declined comment but granted the family a hearing on the case earlier this month.)

The experience so embittered the family that the deSaules have rearranged their lives to share their mother's care in a home setting. "We're doing our own thing as a family, and we're not the only ones," Pat deSaules says. "A lot of people see the handwriting on the wall." Indeed, some 40% of people whose parents are still living say they support them financially, or expect to, up from 22% in 1994, says a survey by Yankelovich Partners for Phoenix Home Life Mutual Insurance.

The implications for employers: More employees will need information, time and money to meet elder-care needs. Workplace information services—consultation and referral, caregiver fairs and seminars—will be used more. More workers will be weighing long-term care financing; Hewitt Associates, Lincolnshire, Ill., says 8% of 1,050 employers it surveys annually offer group long-term care plans to employees, up from 2% in 1990.

And perhaps most significant, more workers will be using the federal family-leave law. A 1997 study by the National Alliance for Caregiving shows 11% of employed caregivers had taken unpaid leave.

—July 23, 1997

Brother and Sister Bond
As They Care for Aging Parents

L ike most teenage brothers and sisters of the '60s, Judy and Dan Ahern grew up in different worlds.

Judy, two years older, was the A student, Dan the sports star. She danced to the Beatles in her room while he played football in the streets of their San Francisco neighborhood. He complained about her music; she warned him to keep his "goony friends" away from her dates. After high school they split, Dan to the University of California at Berkeley and a job in advertising, and Judy to a clerical job, marriage and a house an hour from the city. For 33 years, they never shared an important decision.

Then their mother got Alzheimer's disease.

That single development plunged sister and brother into a crucible of shared decision making and despair as their mother, a warm-hearted woman who loved laughter, Frank Sinatra and "the one-armed bandits" of Nevada's casinos, slowly lost her capacity to remember, speak or behave normally, and their father grew too depressed and ill to care for her.

Stressful elder-care situations are notorious among social workers and gerontologists for driving a wedge between adult siblings, who often disagree over long-term care, managing parents' assets or divvying up care duties. This is the story of a brother and sister who grew closer instead, their lives forever changed in a pressure cooker of juggling jobs, child-rearing and painful decisions for their parents.

"The first thing that happens is that the family disintegrates." That's the prediction Mr. Ahern heard, soon after his mother fell ill, at a support group for caregivers of brain-impaired adults. He and his sister, by then Judy McLean by marriage, resolved that things would be different for them. Over the next six years, that resolve was tested repeatedly.

With counseling and referrals from Family Caregiver Alliance, San Francisco, a pioneering nonprofit support organization that has helped hundreds of groups develop similar programs nationwide, the siblings planned for long-term care, dividing their parents' modest assets so long-term care costs wouldn't bankrupt their father. They separately visited different long-term care facilities and were dismayed by what they saw. They nearly enrolled at a board-and-care home, then learned from an advocacy group that a woman had fallen down the stairs there and lain injured on the floor all night. Other places reminded Mr. Ahern of *One Flew Over the Cuckoo's Nest.*

They decided to stick to in-home care for a while, but that brought other hassles. Ms. McLean, who was juggling a part-time job and raising two children, fired one aide for accepting overseas collect calls on her parents' phone.

To share decisions, the siblings talked by phone as often as five times a day. Mr. Ahern gained new respect for his sister. At one point, their father, a strong-willed former college athlete, refused needed hospitalization for various ailments. Mr. Ahern, who is 6 feet 1 inch tall and also played college sports, couldn't budge him. But his 5-foot-5-inch sister, Mr. Ahern says, "walked up to him and put her finger in his chest and said, 'You need to do this and you're going!' " The father complied.

After much persuasion, their mother agreed to attend adult daycare to give their father respite. But after a year, she was expelled for the unruly behavior typical of Alzheimer's victims. Mr. Ahern canceled client calls that day to race to his parents' house. He found his father in tears, struggling to care for his mother. With both parents declining fast, "it was like triage," he says. "We had to make a specific choice: Who can we save?" Both siblings dreaded the nursing-home decision; Mr. Ahern especially wanted his mother to remain home.

In a tearful discussion in Ms. McLean's backyard, she helped him accept the inevitable. Their mother, she reminded Mr. Ahern, had confided to Ms. McLean that she didn't want her children to suffer caring for her. Painfully, he agreed to move ahead.

In the ensuing months, Ms. McLean saw a toughness in her brother she hadn't seen before. Though the nursing home they chose had a good reputation, their mother fell and injured herself three times there. One winter day, Mr. Ahern arrived to find the heat off and his mother sitting unattended, her nails blue with cold.

Outraged, he called state inspectors and threatened to sue. The nursing home fixed the heat problem and asked Mr. Ahern to run training sessions for the staff on what it's like to be a patient's family member.

Though their mother died in 1993, Mr. Ahern, 41 years old, and Ms. McLean, 43, continue to care for their father, 75, in his home. Mr. Ahern, who has married and had a daughter, has become a long-term-care activist of sorts, testifying before California lawmakers and becoming a director of Family Caregiver Alliance. As the nation ages, "the future is families pulling together through [such] organizations" to solve long-term-care problems, he says. He also enrolled in night law school; he hopes to combine advocacy for the elderly with practicing law.

Ms. McLean, too, finds herself leaping to the aid of families with ailing elders. And both live with a new awareness of their mortality.

"You think you have a lot of time," Ms. McLean says. "But in one blink of an eye, your whole life can change."

—January 17, 1996

Caring for an Elder from Miles Away Raises Stress Level

I t was the kind of conversation you dread if you live far from an aging parent.

Judy Hines' mother, in her late 80s and living alone in New York, was pressing Ms. Hines to move there to care for her. Ms. Hines, a science journalist with a career, marriage and household to maintain, suggested instead that her mother move to a retirement community near her in Lovettsville, Va.

Angrily, the older woman accused her daughter of trying to "warehouse" her. "She was making me feel very guilty," Ms. Hines says. (She now knows her mother's uncharacteristic demands were symptoms of suspected Alzheimer's disease.)

Balancing work and elder care can be a challenge at any distance, but caring for an elder from afar has a unique psychological edge. "Long-distance caregivers," as they are called, often walk a fine line between doing too much for an elder out of guilt, anxiety or poor communication, and doing too little—in effect, denying the toll that aging takes.

More people are walking that line as the population ages, families fragment and employees transfer far from family. No solid data exist; but assuming 12% to 15% of the work force provides elder care, roughly 2% to 6% of workers care for elders who live more than an hour away, based on various studies and calls received by resource-and-referral services.

How to cope? Here is some advice from experts and experienced caregivers:

Come to terms with the distance. Most elders prefer to remain in their communities. John Boyle, Pleasanton, Calif., and his brother in Florida were deeply worried about their aged mother living alone in Boston with a heart ailment after their father's death. The brothers tried long and hard to get her to move in with one of them, and she finally agreed to move to Florida. But just before she was to go, she fell ill and died in a nursing home.

In retrospect, Mr. Boyle believes he underestimated her desire to stay near where her husband was buried. No matter how bad you feel about living far away, he says, you must respect an elder's wishes.

Pay attention. Katharine Hazzard, work-family manager for John Hancock Mutual Life Insurance, advises making a mental checklist during visits. Do friends call often? Is your elder driving safely? Is the refrigerator stocked with good food? Is the mail full of letters from charities, a sign that your elder may be giving money to anyone who asks? Learn to distinguish normal signs of aging from red flags. Any abrupt physical change should be a concern; "Mom's not going to go suddenly from forgetting somebody's name now and then to not knowing what day it is," says Angela Heath, a Washington, D.C., consultant. Watch out for signs of malnutrition, depression and adverse drug side effects or interactions.

Some problems can be solved with straight talk. Paul Conrad was dismayed when his elderly mother in Kansas City started having trouble paying bills and falling prey to scams. Though he briefly considered moving her out of her house, the retired San Jose, Calif., computer analyst sat down with her instead and said, "Mom, you're not going to be able to stay in your house if you keep spending all your money." He now helps her budget her money and oversees some of her finances.

Plan ahead. When crises arise, the added complication of distance can make elder-care demands a black hole. Boston entrepreneur John Wilson has been trying since April to secure a good housing arrangement in Asheville, N.C., for his father, who is hospitalized with Alzheimer's, and his mother, who needs less care. He has made a half-dozen trips, driving 15 hours each way, but has hit repeated obstacles. His corporate events-planning business has suffered, and he has been so stressed that his doctor increased his blood-pressure medicine.

You've read it here before: Legal, financial and long-term planning for elder care is crucial, and long-distance caregivers need to lay even more plans for travel and time off work. Save family-leave or personal days, make backup child-care plans and start a travel fund. If your boss is supportive, explain your elder-care role. Two good resources: Ms. Heath's book, *Long Distance Caregiving;* and *Miles Away and Still Caring* (American Association of Retired Persons).

Set up backstops. If your elder is frail but living independently, a few simple safeguards can ease anxiety and avert crises. Household safety checks and "personal emergency response systems" that send distress signals when an elder can't reach the phone are among them. Barbara Lepis, director, Partnership for Elder Care, a consortium of employers and the New York City Agency for the Aging, recommends finding a neighbor or friend who will agree to be "your eyes and ears on the spot." Donna Wagner, vice president, research and development, National Council on the Aging, recalls a Bridgeport, Conn., man in his 80s whose only child lived on the West Coast. As the man grew more frail, a neighboring university student and his wife took such an interest that they arranged for him to move into an apartment below theirs.

Know your limits. In complex cases, you may need professional help. Ms. Hines hired a geriatric care manager who coordinates her mother's care, including a housekeeper and a companion. The arrangement has restored family peace.

—October 18, 1995

Take Steps to Ensure Your Care Manager Meets Elder's Needs

For people who work and also care for an aged family member who lives far away, it sounds like a perfect solution: Hire a geriatric-care manager to handle all your elder's needs.

Amid a spate of glowing media coverage portraying care managers as "surrogate family," geriatric-care management is booming. Membership in the National Association of Professional Geriatric Care Managers, Tucson, is up 50% from a year ago. Indeed, a good care manager can do "a world of good," says Angela Heath, a Washington, D.C., consultant, providing services from assessing an elder's needs to overseeing long-term care.

But as the field grows, a healthy dose of consumerism is long overdue. Pressed by the often overwhelming demands of elder care, some families are falling prey to care managers who are inept, overpriced or unethical. "It's a big consumer issue. Anybody can hang out a shingle and call themselves a care manager," says Vicki Zoot, a consultant for CNA Insurance Cos.

Some care managers, usually nurses, social workers, gerontologists or counselors by training, give bad advice in areas where they lack expertise. Arabella Dorth, a word processor for a San Francisco law firm, relied briefly on a San Diego care manager to oversee her Alzheimer's-afflicted mother. Ms. Dorth needed to secure the legal right to manage her mother's affairs. But the care manager, instead of helping her take the relatively simple step of getting power of attorney, filed a legal petition for a highly restrictive type of conservatorship designed to lock up criminally insane people. Dismayed, Ms. Dorth fired her.

At $50 to $110 an hour, care managers' fees can mount fast. A New York social worker was socked with $10,000 in vaguely worded bills by a care-management agency for overseeing home-health services for her aunt in Connecticut for about a year. "I didn't monitor them well enough," the social worker says. "It was an expensive lesson."

Be wary of potential conflicts of interest. There is controversy in the field over whether people who call themselves geriatric-care managers should accept referral fees from nursing homes or other care facilities. (Most don't.) If the so-called care manager isn't also charging the consumer for supposedly impartial advice, there's no conflict. But collecting both management fees and referral fees poses potential conflicts that can be expensive for consumers.

Steve Barlam, owner of Senior Care Management, Beverly Hills, Calif., and head of the national association's grievance committee, recalls an advertising manager who came to him because her mother, in her 90s with a variety of ailments, wasn't faring well in a nursing home she had recently entered. The client had been referred to the home by another care manager, who received a fee from the nursing home but also charged the client $500 for advice.

Indeed, Mr. Barlam found the nursing home, a large facility, wasn't giving the mother enough one-on-one attention. But the aged woman was too frail to move again, so the client had to hire a companion—on top of paying for the nursing home.

The profession is moving rapidly to set standards. The 800 members of the national association subscribe to rigorous ethics and standards. And a new National Academy of Certified Care Managers, with funding from CNA and others, plans certification exams starting in 1996.

Meanwhile, to find a good care manager, ask for referrals from the association and interview several candidates about their experience, credentials and fees. Care managers should disclose all income sources and any personal financial interest in long-term care facilities. If a care manager handles an elder's money, he or she should have a proven track record as a fiduciary agent and someone should oversee outlays, says Jeffrey Abrandt, a New York elder-law attorney.

At best, geriatric-care managers do perform much like family. In southern Florida, care managers at Rona Bartelstone Associates, Fort Lauderdale, took aged clients into their own homes during Hurricane Andrew. In Falls Church, Va., a care manager with the

Ann E. O'Neil agency cheered up an aged client during a dreaded move into an assisted-living facility by bringing her baby along; the child's presence was "wonderful therapy," Ms. O'Neil says. In Pacific Grove, Calif., a care manager for the Cresscare agency befriended the bartender at the Elks Club to enlist his help curbing an 82-year-old client's tendency to have too many beers there every afternoon.

If you can't afford a care manager, many federally funded Area Agencies on Aging will provide a free needs assessment or make referrals to needed services. To limit costs, many clients hire care managers for a one-time needs assessment; for about $125 to $350, a care manager will visit an elder at home and make recommendations. Some employers, including IBM and Hallmark, sponsor assessments for employees. The service made a difference for Paul Conrad, a retired IBM computer analyst in San Jose, Calif. After his mother's longtime companion in Kansas City died, she was so troubled that he worried about whether "she was hanging in there OK." A care manager reassured him that though she was grieving, she was managing her household well. For a long-distance caregiver, Mr. Conrad says, it was "the quickest way to get a little peace of mind."

—October 25, 1995

You May Want to Take the Parents with You to That New Posting

As much as I hate packing boxes and saying goodbye to friends, one of the toughest things about my family's cross-country move two years ago was leaving my mother-in-law.

Before you all rush to recommend counseling or send your favorite mother-in-law jokes, please note that I am part of a trend. An Atlas Van Lines survey set for release today shows more employees are resisting leaving elderly relatives behind when offered transfers, and many are bringing them along.

Family ties, in which elder-care concerns are a growing component, are for the second straight year the leading reason employees turn down relocation, Atlas says; 64% of employers name it as a reason employees rejected transfers last year, up from 53% in 1993. The next biggest obstacles: spouses' jobs, cited 62% of the time, and cost of living in the new location, 53%.

More employers are stepping into the breach by offering to move elderly relatives with the transferee or provide other elder-care help; 24% did so last year, up from 16% in 1993, Atlas says. Employees are using the services heavily; Work/Family Directions, the biggest supplier of employee elder-care referral services, says questions about finding elder housing and other relocation issues are up sharply.

What's going on here? Clearly, America's fragmented families aren't rebanding into tribes. But the population is aging. Workers' ties with elders loom larger as downsizing batters their bonds with employers. And relocation is cutting a wider swath as some companies move entire units as part of re-engineering.

While in my case my mother-in-law is thriving where she is with many other family ties, community activities and a home she loves, a growing number of today's mobile families see taking elders along as a sensible option. This column, third in an occasional series on elder-care dilemmas, examines that strategy for transferees.

Assuming your elder relative is at least partly independent, moving together can work well if it's what the elder wants. When Deborah Beatty and her husband asked her 76-year-old mother-in-law to move with them on a transfer to Houston from Monroe, N.Y., she at first resisted leaving her own house in Monroe.

But after the family built a small cottage for her in the backyard of their new home, Ms. Beatty's mother-in-law sold her house and began spending winters in Houston and summers at her daughter's home in New York. She found new friends in Houston, and with her cottage nearby, she "has the option to join us whenever she wants to," says Ms. Beatty, executive vice president of a Houston steel-fabrication concern.

In most cases, though, the odds weigh against success. While every family is different, research shows elders who move far to be near children tend to make "really poor adjustments. They leave their memories and their support system behind," says Barbara Lepis of the Partnership for Elder Care, a consortium of employers and the New York City Department for the Aging.

For a move to succeed, an elder must be willing to reach out for new ties. One manager for a telecommunications company relocated his father to Colorado from Texas only to see him withdraw, shunning senior activities, says Donna Wagner, vice president, programs, for the National Council on the Aging. "He was totally isolated, and of course he was unhappy and made additional demands on the family." Another concern is that Medicaid rules vary state by state, says Jeffrey Abrandt, a New York elder-law attorney, affecting the affordability of services you may eventually need, such as home care.

Using a transfer as an excuse for moving an elder in with you may seem best in the short term but often causes longer-term tensions. Ms. Lepis suggests considering these prerequisites: Can the elder take a back seat in running the household and find new friends and interests? Does your partner or spouse really like the idea? Do you enjoy the company of the elder? A guiding principle, experts agree, should be encouraging elders to remain as independent as possible for as long as possible.

The alternative to moving together—staying in touch from afar—raises another set of issues for a future column. Whatever you decide, it's reasonable to ask your employer for some time to weigh your options, says Jane Holston, a Pensacola, Fla., consultant and author of *Smart Moves for the Relocating Family*. (Atlas says half of the employers allow two weeks or less to decide on a transfer offer.)

And no matter how hard you try, the outcome isn't likely to be perfect. When Debbie Rowland and her husband moved to New Jersey from Houston, they insisted that his new employer relocate Ms. Rowland's 62-year-old mother, too, and bought a house in New Jersey with room for a basement apartment. But in the midst of selling both their houses in Houston, Ms. Rowland says, her mother decided not to go along, fearing she could be swept into successive transfers for her son-in-law's career. Ms. Rowland instead helped her resettle in her hometown of Madison, Wis.

"It's not a perfect situation for either her or us," says Ms. Rowland, who worries about her mother and misses her. But "if she had moved with us, she would have given up her own life. And she was a little too young for that."

—May 24, 1995

Part Eight

ACROSS THE GENERATIONS

Until recently, work-family conflict has been treated mainly as a concern of baby boomers, the first generation in which women scored broad, steep advances in the paid work force.

But as the giant post-World War II generation advances into middle age and their children grow older, the picture is changing. Generation Xers are bringing to the workplace the fresh,

Carol Lay

grounded-in-reality and often iconoclastic view of an age group that spent a lot of time in day care. The generation behind them, the baby boomlet, is old enough to give voice to honest opinions about the work-life balance their parents have struck.

And as boomers pass through midlife, they are re-examining the values that drove them in their early years and, in many cases, over-hauling their lives in search of a new balance.

These fascinating cross-generational dynamics are the focus of this section of columns. As the columns show, the quality of parents' jobs has a big impact on kids. The life-balance struggles of today's teenagers are beginning to rival their parents'. A new generation of skilled job seekers is posing new challenges to recruiters by demanding flexibility and family accommodations from the starting block. Several columns focus on the increasingly honest and often painful dialogue among the generations over the best ways to balance work and family.

It's the Type of Job You Have That Affects the Kids, Studies Say

The hour is late when a friend, sipping coffee after dinner, begins talking about her kids.

Over her employer's pleas that she stay, she recently quit a rigid, frustrating executive job at a firm to start her own business as a real-estate manager in New Jersey. Some big clients have followed her unsolicited; she is working hard, feels in control of her life again and is happier than at any time in memory.

What she didn't foresee, she says, are the changes she is noticing in her daughter, age five. The child used to be miserable during her first hour at school, her teacher has told my friend, withdrawing to the fringes of the group for hours. Now, her daughter comes to school skipping and singing and jumps into class activities right away. The only apparent cause, my friend says, is that she, the child's mother, feels better about her work and her life. In the past, with job frustrations consuming her, she says, "my life was a frenzy. I was so intense that I didn't have time to hear and observe my kids."

Parents seldom think of children as having a stake in their work beyond the paychecks brought home. But new research suggests children are deeply affected by the quality of parents' work lives.

A study by three researchers, first disclosed last month in a work-family meeting with Vice President Gore, found fewer behavioral problems in children whose mothers' have control over how, where and when their work gets done. The same effects appear in children of fathers who say they are satisfied with their work.

"Kids are the unseen stakeholders in the American workplace," says Stewart Friedman, director of the Wharton Life Interests Project at the University of Pennsylvania and one of the researchers. He and co-researchers Jeffrey Greenhaus, professor of commerce and engineering, and Saroj Parasuraman, a management professor, both at Drexel University, plan a book on the sweeping interrelationships between work and family.

In the past, most studies about kids and the workplace focused on whether a mother's working outside the home hurts children, a question that is far too simplistic. Jobs differ; some drive you nuts, make you impossible to live with and pay so little that you can only afford lousy child care. Others lift your self-esteem, impart new skills and enable you to buy enriching care for your kids.

Assuming all jobs have the same impact is like assuming that driving a car affects everyone the same. If you have a safe car and drive it well, you and your family will benefit. If your car is a wreck and you drive it badly, you'll probably injure both yourself and your passengers.

Not surprisingly, the past studies found no consistent link between kids' development and the simple fact of mothers' employment. But new research is looking in a more realistic way at how parents' work affects kids. The findings: Whether they like it or not, employers have a big role in raising kids.

In their study of more than 800 managers and professionals, Drs. Friedman, Greenhaus and Parasuraman found that the greater a mother's degree of authority, freedom and control over decision making on the job, the fewer behavior problems in their four- to 17-year-old kids. A 28-item index was used to measure such child behaviors as shyness, withdrawal and aggressiveness.

The researchers also found that the amount of time parents spend working isn't linked to their children's behavior. What does have an impact is how much parents' work tensions taint home life. Parents whose jobs don't distract them from family when they are home, or interfere with their psychological involvement with their children, have better-behaved kids.

Separately, Toby Parcel and Elizabeth Menaghan of Ohio State University have found in several studies that children of mothers with more complex, responsible jobs have better home environments and, in turn, behave better and perform better over time on verbal, math and reading tests, after controlling for mothers' own education and mental skills. And Ellen Greenberger at University of California, Irvine, and others have found that parents with more stimulating, challenging jobs are warmer, less harsh and more responsive in their parenting.

Parents know all this from experience. On a previous job in a banking concern where everyone put in lots of face time, Susan Cannon grew so frustrated with office politics that she had to struggle when she got home to be emotionally available to her toddler. Now, as co-founder of Global Marketing Partners in Glendale, Calif., she is free to call her own shots. Though she is still working long hours, "I'm so happy and fulfilled, I feel as if I'm parenting better than I ever have," she says.

Anne Lawler, a Seattle attorney, says the rigid culture at previous employers sometimes made it hard to respond to her kids' needs. Now, at a law firm she helped found, she has control over her time. She is able to drive one of her children to midday tutoring sessions, improving both his grades and her communication with him. During their drives, he opens up and shares concerns that he otherwise might not.

With such effects now documented in research, employers trying to create high-quality workplaces can take pride in a spinoff benefit: They're helping future generations of workers, too. It all gives new depth to that old term, "family-friendly."

—July 31, 1996

Playground Set Shows Signs
of Stress over Parents' Jobs

A nne Pauker was washing lettuce in the kitchen of her Aberdeen, N.J., home when she overheard her children playing a new game.

She and her husband had guests, and both families' kids—ages 11, eight and two six-year-olds—were playing with Barbie dolls. As Ms. Pauker listened, she realized Ken had lost his job and Barbie was counseling him on finding work.

The name of the game: "Outplacement Barbie." Parents in both families had been through layoffs, and to them, the game "says a lot," says Ms. Pauker, a management consultant. "It means the children are thinking about this."

As hundreds of thousands of heads rolled in corporate America in recent years, many adults haven't paid much attention to kids' reactions. In studying families of 100 layoff victims, Ruthan Rosenberg of Murray, Axmith & Associates, a Toronto outplacement firm, found that almost all the parents said their kids weren't affected.

"If parents get divorced, people are on the alert" to kids' fears, says Betty Carter, a Mount Vernon, N.Y., family therapist. "But no one is paying that kind of attention to children whose parents are losing their jobs."

Meanwhile, job insecurity has become part of playground culture, and the messages kids are getting are mostly negative. On a visit to my seven-year-old's school, I heard some kids yelling, "You're fired!" When I asked my daughter to explain, she said they were playing a game: Each child must walk perfectly straight down a long line; if you swerve or waver, you're "fired," she said. To get your "job" back, you try to walk absolutely straight along an even longer line, over and over until you do it perfectly. I said, "That sounds pretty grim. How does anybody win that game?"

"The only way you can win is to keep your job," she said.

In my own survey of 15 experts who talk with children everyday—

family therapists, psychologists and principals—two-thirds said they see kids wrestling with anxieties about their parents' jobs all the time. A few examples: When employers around Kennewick, Wash., laid off many parents, Terry Barber, principal of Amistad Elementary School, saw more kids sent to his office for misbehavior. Children are "much more in turmoil" at such times, unable to play peacefully or concentrate in class, he says. "They are taking out the tensions they sense from their parents."

Though a Florida couple pretended in front of their children that all was well after the father, a plant manager, was laid off, their eight-year-old could see them counting pennies and worrying about how he was doing on his new job, says Marilyn J. Mason, a Minneapolis psychologist. The child grew so anxious that he brought home failing grades. "The parents were devastated," she says; their overprotective tactics backfired and "only instilled shame."

Evan Imber-Black, director of family and group studies at Albert Einstein College of Medicine, sees teenagers of affluent families showing more than the usual rebellious behaviors. The kids, a type who a few years ago would have been excited about their future, are wondering, "What is this all about, anyway?" she says. Meanwhile, instead of addressing their children's doubts, the parents are "putting on the usual pressure about getting college applications in and all that," deepening the kids' sense of meaninglessness.

Job loss, however, can be a positive lesson in resiliency for kids. Ms. Rosenberg recalls a laidoff manager for a drug firm whose wife responded by calling a family meeting. She asked her husband to keep her and their four children, ages six through 15, informed about his job search. The family, in turn, found ways to support him. One child gave up her room so he could have an office. Two teens helped pare the family budget and got part-time jobs.

When the children complained about making sacrifices, their mother consoled them, then quickly refocused them on the benefits of pulling together. When the father went for retraining, the family talked about how everyone needs to adapt to change. When the father got a new job, "the whole family felt it was their success," Ms. Rosenberg says.

The bottom line: The power of families is enormous in mediating the messages kids get about job loss. In a study of 115 unemployed workers by Boston University and Jandl Associates, Lynnfield, Mass., some fundamental family strengths, including communicating, co-operating and reaching out for community support, determined whether family members fared well or fell apart after a job loss. At stake, therapists say, are kids' hopefulness and confidence about jobs and the world of work.

As a parent, I'm not ready for this. My husband and I have had our share of job changes and stints of unemployment in recent years, causing family stress. I'm not eager to add my kids' likely anxieties about job security to a parental worry list that already includes drug abuse, drive-by shootings and sex on the Internet. It's easier to repeat the same old saws—"A college degree is your ticket to success" or "The world is your oyster"—even though they don't work anymore, than it is to teach the resiliency and adaptability our kids will need as 21st-century workers.

But if the world of work is to be anywhere near as alluring to my kids as it has been to me, I'm not sure I have a choice.

—November 15, 1995

What Does Your Job Tell a Crystal Burch About Fulfillment?

A sk people about 13-year-old Crystal Burch, and they will tell you stories of her eagerness.

Every time she made it to third base in softball, recalls her longtime Little League coach, Darrell Bennett, she begged for a green light to steal home.

"'Can I do it? Can I do it?' she always asks," Mr. Bennett says. "Crystal is always pushing the envelope." When he gave her the go-ahead, the child—graceful as a gazelle at 5 feet 8 inches—would race down the base path and score. He counts her among "the cream of the crop." But like all teenagers, Crystal "could go either way" in the future, depending on how adults guide her, adds Mr. Bennett, a coach for 15 years. Any adolescent's fortunes are "a precarious thing." For most girls, the teenage years are a high-wire walk between determination and self-doubt, and Crystal Burch, daughter of a working-class family from the suburbs of Portland, Ore., is no exception. On this eve of the fourth annual Take Our Daughters to Work Day, this is the story of Crystal's particular tightrope act, and how her exposure to corporate America has helped her keep her balance.

Crystal's early lessons about work came from her family's training in the School of Hard Knocks. After her grandfather lost a leg in a construction accident, her grandmother, Lauraine Burch, raised four children on her paycheck from a Dairy Queen. Crystal's mother Nancy, one of 14 children of a mechanic and a mother who worked various jobs, is a supervisor at a packaging plant. An athletic woman, Ms. Burch still comes home tired; recently, she cut her arm so badly at work that it required five stitches. Crystal's father Mike picked farm crops and moved irrigation pipe from age eight, then rose through the blue-collar ranks to production manager for Anthro Corp., a computer-furniture maker. After 14 years of marriage, the couple recently saved enough to buy a cottage-style house in the town of Aloha, Ore.

Aware that the School of Hard Knocks isn't teaching many high-paying skills these days, the Burches hope for much more for their kids. "When I came of age, you could sneak onto a job and prove yourself. Today, you can't even get in the door without a college education," Mr. Burch says. Ms. Burch's green eyes mist over when she talks about her hopes for Crystal and her son, Nick, 11: not only college, but management jobs. Both worry about motivating Crystal to succeed.

Enter corporate America; here, in the form of Nike Inc.'s sprawling headquarters in Beaverton, Ore. Crystal's grandmother Lauraine broke into the white-collar world there 15 years ago in a clerical job and has worked her way up to assistant to the director of sports marketing; she has brought Crystal to every Take Our Daughters to Work Day since 1993.

The workplace exposure has been a powerful motivational tool. At Nike, Crystal saw people who work in suits and dresses, attend meetings, solve marketing problems. In Ms. Burch's office, she typed, filed and worked on computers, the first she had seen outside school. Unlike her mother, Crystal noticed, the workers there didn't have to lift 50-pound loads, nor did they seem to be in the remotest danger of getting hurt or even very tired. For the first time, she thought, "I don't have to work like my mom . . . I'd like to work my way up to be a manager, and maybe run my own business one day."

Clearly, Crystal is made of the same stuff that propelled her family out of poverty. When she decided she wanted to be a pitcher, she worked through the winter with Mr. Bennett to learn how. Already, she shows aptitude with computers. But role models became crucial again last year when the stresses of adolescence nearly derailed her. Her self-esteem took a dive when she transferred from her neighborhood grade school to a much larger middle school. She was bewildered by the crowded halls and the switch to five classes from one. Older kids kicked and jammed her locker, making her miss homework deadlines. In class, her habit of interrupting eagerly to ask questions drew scoldings.

For the first time, Crystal's GPA tumbled. "I got so mad," she recalls. "I would come home and take it out on the family. And I put myself down." Her parents met with her teachers. Near tears, Crystal told her grandmother, "I don't understand what's going on" in class. "I'm just not smart."

Again, the workplace provided a needed spark. Lauraine Burch had worked with Olympic athlete Jackie Joyner-Kersee on a promotion and shared the material with Crystal for an oral presentation in English. The track star's tale of overcoming asthma and early defeat by discipline and hard work intrigued Crystal. Grandmother and granddaughter worked through one weekend at Nike on the report, then Crystal practiced it for three days. Her grade: A-plus.

The success marked a turning point. Crystal has boosted her GPA to 3.0 and her spirits have lifted. Asked what she learned from Ms. Joyner-Kersee, she said: "You can do anything you want if you try hard enough."

Tomorrow, Crystal again will join as many as eight million girls at the workplace. Even the most resilient among them will need all the positive adult influence they can get if they are to make the leaps necessary to fill the skilled jobs of the future.

One of them may be watching you, looking for a green light.

Don't screw it up.

—April 24, 1996

Work-Life Issues Are Starting to Plague Teenagers with Jobs

W hen a service club polled 260 teenagers at a Falls Church, Va., high school about their biggest worries, guidance counselor Eric Kinneman expected fears about gangs or relations between the sexes to top the list.

He was surprised to learn "the No. 1 issue was jobs," finding good after-school jobs and making money. In a follow-up forum, he was surprised again by the intensity of the teens' job worries. "The kids were really frustrated" at how hard it was to find work reflecting their skills and abilities, he says.

Today's teens are wrapped up in work, and new research suggests that preoccupation has a dark side. The largest study so far of adolescents, a federally funded look at 12,000 students from grades seven through 12 by the University of Minnesota and the University of North Carolina, shows teens who work 20 or more hours a week during the school year are more likely to be emotionally distressed, drink, smoke, use drugs and have early sex. The results were controlled to eliminate the effects of poverty, family structure, race and ethnicity.

The study, released last month, also shows paying jobs taking a heavier-than-expected toll on high-school students' time. Among ninth through 12th graders surveyed, nearly 18% work more than half time during the school year. While no comparable data exist from the past, the government says only 17% of older teens, including high-school graduates, worked any number of hours year round in 1995.

Teenagers need job skills, of course, and many benefit from working during the school year. To save for college, Chris Friesleben's two sons, ages 18 and 22, worked through high school at a grocery and a dry-cleaning shop, the older one often topping 20 hours a week.

Both are doing fine, says Ms. Friesleben, a public-relations manager in Des Moines, Iowa. "I firmly believe my kids needed to understand that as a parent, I wasn't a walking ATM machine." Indeed, many parents encourage their teens to work, not only to make money but in hopes they'll have less time to drink, smoke, use drugs and have sex.

In determining how much a teen should work, "there's no magic formula," says Michael Resnick, a University of Minnesota professor and lead author of the study. But for most kids, "when you get to this half-time-or-more mark, it's just too much."

The bottom line, say experienced counselors, therapists and parents, is that the struggle for life balance, viewed as an adult concern, is emerging in an even younger generation, and the issues it raises are as challenging for teens as for adults.

Adolescents' needs are complex, says Kate Kelly, author of the *Complete Idiot's Guide to Parenting a Teenager*. "Teens already have a job, and that's school," plus homework, she says. Beyond that, they need time to do extracurricular activities, sustain family relationships, get the extra sleep teens need, "connect with friends, bond with teachers and feel accepted in their world."

Like adults, teens suffer when they can't control their work hours. One of Viana Rockel's two daughters, who held waitress jobs during high school, often had to scramble to find people to fill in for her during "can't-miss" proms and concerts. Sometimes, she missed out, says Ms. Rockel, a college administrator. Though Ms. Rockel thought her daughter was working too much, "once they get into a job, it's almost impossible for the parent to step in and cut back" the hours.

Bad working conditions can hurt a teen's morale and self-image. When Sharon Marco's daughter worked in a bakery, she was embarrassed by other employees who sat in a back room ridiculing customers and making rude remarks, and often came home upset.

Ms. Marco, a Colorado computer-systems coordinator, says family support was essential, including dinner-table talks and parental advice about setting broad emotional boundaries between work and the rest of your life.

Job flexibility is important, too. Ms. Friesleben attributes her sons' success to the fact that both had managers who allowed them time off for extracurricular activities.

Teens' struggle for work-life balance can be especially poignant for parents who may, at midlife, be questioning their own life choices. As Ms. Rockel watches her daughter, now in college, juggling job and studies, she says, "I wonder, how much of this did she learn from me, that you have to be busy every minute and overextended?"

For teens, the study suggests, the risks of work overload are even higher than for adults, threatening developmental deficits that are hard to make up in adulthood. Many need adult help to change direction. Mr. Kinneman met 10 times with a junior struggling to decide whether to go out for football or work at a hotel.

"The lure of the quick, easy, fast money on the front end was real hard to ignore," Mr. Kinneman says. "But at the same time, he was yearning to be connected more" to friends and school. With guidance, he chose football, and he's happy about it. Future research will document more precisely the causes of working teens' problems, such as fatigue, too much loose cash or negative influences by workplace peers, Dr. Resnick says. Meanwhile, it's not too soon for parents to take current evidence to heart. "As a parent," he adds, "I look at this and say, I'm going to do some serious thinking."

—October 15, 1997

Would Your Teen Give You High Marks on Career-Handling?

Adults are flooding the media these days with opinions on work-family matters. Toddlers' reactions to our collective balancing act are scrutinized in a torrent of child-care research.

But the voices of teenagers, the giant baby-boomlet generation on the cutting edge of work-family change, are largely missing. Its oldest members were entering school in 1983, the first year a majority of mothers of children under six took paid jobs. What has their experience been?

In this week's column and the next two, I'll write about round-table discussions I held last month with two groups of 15- to 17-year-olds in Lincoln, Neb., to find out how they would grade baby boomers' approach to work and family, how they plan to combine their work and family lives and how they manage stress.

Despite widespread criticism of working parents, most of the teens give their parents' generation high grades. But many (including some with a parent at home) describe their family lives as nearly barren of relaxed time together and say they wish for more leisurely time spent talking with their parents as peers. Though they expect it to be difficult, most vow to find a way to spend more time with their own children.

I chose Lincoln because it foreshadows trends predicted for the nation: It's the city with the highest proportion of working mothers in the state with the highest rate of maternal employment, according to Westat, a Rockville, Md., social-science research concern. That distinction is due to the city's high overall employment, strong work ethic and highly educated population. Thanks to Lincoln Public Schools officials who assembled 19 students from four schools, our discussions reflected a diverse mix of family types, income and ethnic origins.

I asked the kids to evaluate their parents' generation as a whole.

The majority gave their elders a B or so on their work-family routines. "As many things as they have going against them, they're doing a good job," says Chris Kingsley, 15 years old. He describes those pressures as multiple duties to "themselves, spouses, kids and taxes."

Several children of dual earners said they value the independence and perspective they say they've gained from having working parents. Marc Berger, a 16-year-old with a straight-A average, said his professional parents "bring two very different philosophies" to bear. "I wouldn't be where I am today, or who I am today, if it weren't for those varying influences from each of them." Some said the experience of staying home without an adult after school from the age of 10 or so "allowed" them to grow up sooner and fostered close sibling bonds.

Preschool memories were understandably hazy; and not surprisingly in a group setting, none of the teens aired bad experiences. Most of the children of working parents said they had been cared for primarily by parents working reduced or back-to-back schedules or by other relatives, rather than by professionals. (Nationally, more than half of working parents rely on themselves or other relatives for child care.) Several said one parent worked in a home-based job until they were 10 or so.

A handful of the kids, however, gave their parents' generation grades of C or D. Some parents "have the amount of money they want, but they're not seeing their kids. As a result, they don't understand us. They know they don't understand us, and they're thinking they should," says one boy, 15. In that, adds another 15-year-old, they're missing "the quintessential aspect of being a parent: attention and focus."

The teens understand the workplace pressures that keep their parents away from home so much. "The work force is growing so competitive, and their bosses are pressuring them. To keep up with their jobs and to advance, they have to spend their time there," says Dave Hansen, 16.

Still, they voice a nearly unanimous wish for more relaxed time with parents, not to hear rules, but to share stories and experiences. That mirrors a feeling among 70% of working parents that they lack enough time with their children, says the Families and Work Institute.

Drawing nods and murmurs of agreement, Abby Euler, 16, recalled a three-hour talk with her father one night at a coffee shop: "He listened to what I had to say. I listened to what he had to say. We didn't get into a fight if we had conflicting views. I learned a lot about him that night and it was great. I will remember that for a long time." Despite many adults' views of teens as remote, the teens said their parents' attitudes have a major effect on how they feel.

Such talks, Mr. Kingsley says, help teens make better choices. "Your parent might say, 'Look, I was stupid as a kid, too. Now that I'm older I know what I did was stupid and here's why.' " Many kids want "to talk to [parents] before putting themselves in a compromising situation."

Asked if they would spend more time with their own kids than their parents' generation has, a chorus of "Definitely . . . Absolutely . . . No question about it!" rang out. "I don't resent my mom for not being around much, but I would love to spend more time with my kids than she spent with me," says a 16-year-old whose single mother works "crazy hours."

Ronee Roach, 16, vows to be "Superparent": a parent who provides, but also has "that relationship with my kids, like they're my best friends."

—May 20, 1998

Teens Have Hopes for Flexible Careers but See High Hurdles

Nearly an hour into my roundtable talk with 10 teenagers about how they will find time for their own kids in the future, hopes are running high.

Jobs "will evolve to meet the needs" of future families, demanding less workday time at a desk, Chris Kingsley, 15 years old, predicts. Ronee Roach, 16, utters one word to explain how she will bend work around family needs: "Technology!"

But Chris Kills Enemy, 16, injects a skeptical note. Just minutes earlier, he points out, his peers were describing their home lives as rushed, stripped nearly bare of relaxed family time by escalating job and school demands. "We're moving fast as it is, and you know our kids are going to be moving even faster." High hopes, high hurdles: Those are the tense realities that frame teenagers' vision of the future. And it's a different frame than the one that bounded their parents' outlook at the same age.

This second of three columns on my talks with two groups of 19 Lincoln, Neb., high-school students, shows teenagers intent on building close families. In fact, their desire for relaxed, sustaining family relationships ran deeper than any I recall hearing from baby boomers as teens. "Family should be the most important thing," says Joel TerMaat, 16. "You make so much more difference in society by raising good kids than you do by just going to a 9-to-5 job. Society gains so much more."

But the teens envision their families of the future through a distinctly '90s lens. Steeped already in tough competition, both academic and athletic, these kids expect to have to compete for good jobs.

Many already feel financial stress, with a large minority of those I met working for pay after school. And with many of their parents putting in long hours at work, some of the teens expect jobs to become more demanding.

Financial stresses on Lincoln families are about average. The city's median household income of $34,014 is 4% below the nation, paralleling lower living costs. The teens I met come from a diverse mix of working families. Most live with two parents or a parent and stepparent, a majority of them in dual-earner homes. Two of the students' mothers are full-time homemakers. A minority live with employed single parents.

Most of the teens envision themselves in dual-earner households as adults, and many plan to delay childbearing in hopes of better equipping themselves to carve out time for their children while paying the bills. "I want to be very much established in my career, or working for myself, before I get into the family thing. When I have my kids, they are going to be the focus of my life," says Ebony Leary, 15.

Gender roles weigh lightly on these teens. Asked if they would consider a household where the father stayed home with the kids, several boys leaped at the idea; "I think that would be great!" said one. Katie Henkenius, 15, who plans a stint in the military before becoming a doctor, says she has thought about such a setup. Their response mirrors a national Whirlpool Foundation study showing that 48% of teenage girls see having an at-home husband as somewhat or very likely.

Some hope new technology will enable them to cross work-home boundaries with ease. But others are skeptical. "My dad works at home sometimes, and it doesn't make any difference, or not much," says a 15-year-old boy. "He's physically there, but mentally he's isolated. Mentally there's a door between us."

Many of the teens see the "traditional family," with a woman as full-time homemaker, from a hazy historical distance. One girl, 16, described its peak as "way back when women would stay home." None recognized the names "Ozzie and Harriet" when I mentioned them.

Some of the teens hope to have one parent stay home. "It's definitely best if a parent is caring for a child, as opposed to a nanny or au pair, or bringing the kid to day care," says Michael Johnson, 16. "It's a very privileged position to have a parent stay home with the kids. But if you can do it, you should."

The topic stirred a debate. "I disagree!" said Abby Euler, 16. Attending preschool while her parents worked taught her to think and learn independently, skills that help her today, she says. "My pre-school teacher was like a mother hen. She helped us learn. I think that was a great thing for my parents to do."

Others shook their heads at the idea of one breadwinner support-ing a household. The perfect family, says Patti Blair, 17, who works 35 hours a week at a fast-food restaurant to pay for her own food, clothing and other basics, would be "one where my kids don't have to work." Asked if she wants to stay home as a parent, she says, "I don't think that will happen."

Mr. TerMaat thinks it's easier to raise children well if one parent stays home, but he sees obstacles. If "both parents have to work a lot more" to sustain a household, as trends suggest, he says, "something is going to have to change . . . There has to be some social reform that would allow one parent to make enough money to support the whole family."

Barring such reform, he paints a pressure-cooker scenario: "The only thing I can look forward to is that I'd have to make a lot more money than the normal person in order to support the family. And I'd want a job where they couldn't afford to make me work in-stead of going to family functions. They'd have to respect that." He doesn't really know yet, he says, what kind of job that might be.

—May 27, 1998

Teens Are Inheriting Parents'
Tendencies Toward Work Overload

Several members of a group of peers are gathered to talk about the causes of stress in their lives. "We don't have enough time to do all the things" we need to succeed, says one. Another feels "bogged down with this ridiculous amount of obligation." A third gets one-on-one therapy to deal with stress.

These are baby boomers, middle-aged jugglers from the Sandwich Generation, right?

Wrong. They're 15- to 17-year-olds, members of the giant baby boomlet generation now on the cusp of adulthood.

With school, jobs, extracurricular pursuits and the quest for "the big resume" to meet heavy college-entrance demands all competing for their time, many teenagers are mounting a juggling act that rivals anything their parents might conduct. Add the normal raging adolescent hormones and peer pressure and you've got a recipe for angst.

In this third of three columns concerning roundtable talks with 19 Lincoln, Neb., students, many of the teens named "time management" as a top source of stress. Coping with overload was the topic that stirred the strongest emotional reaction. The stories the kids told—from staying up all night to finish routine assignments, to agonizing over falling grades because jobs crowd out homework— suggest many are making tough tradeoffs of a kind I never faced until adulthood.

Lincoln is no hotbed of teen stress. With its high employment and friendly Heartland culture, this university town of 209,000 manifests some of the healthiest dimensions of American society. Most of the kids I spoke with exemplify the value we place on hard work and achievement.

For some, there is a positive side to the overload. "It's a very experimental time," Marc Berger, 16, says. "I'm trying to experience as much as possible" to prepare for the future.

Nevertheless, the students emphatically describe the stressful "equilibrium" they strike and the compromises they make to cope with what they see as boundless demands on their time. One student, 16, handling a heavy course load, says, "I'm a perfectionist. I work over my limit. I'll stay up until 5 A.M. if I have to. I have to make [my work] as good as I know it can be." The student recently entered stress therapy.

A 15-year-old accepted a peer-tutoring position even though it meant cramming full all nine periods of her school schedule. Though unhappy with the heavy load, "it looks good on your résumé," she says.

Patti Blair, 17, who works full-time after school, says her grades have slipped because she can't start homework until late evening. Responding to a straight-A student's talk of homework struggles, she says, "That used to be me. I couldn't stand getting a B. Then once you get a job and start getting F's . . ."

"You learn to compromise," asserts a 16-year-old boy.

Ms. Blair says that after a while, a D looks good. She isn't alone. A survey of 1,200 students for Phoenix Home Life Mutual Insurance Co. found nearly one-third have jobs that interfere with studies. Asked if she felt frustrated, Ms. Blair says, "Like, 'God, I hate this?' Yeah." But she says she handles her own expenses at home, leaving no alternative.

The students who work often seek flexible jobs to make everything fit. Others drop activities they pursue only for enjoyment. Dave Hansen, 16, loves singing in his school's concert choir. "It's a good way to release stress. I put my heart into my singing," he says. But his heavy course load and time-consuming gymnastics regimen—his ticket, he hopes, to a college scholarship—have crowded out time for singing. Cutbacks don't always mean less work. When Ebony Leary, 15, signed up for three science classes, she felt so stressed that she got stomachaches before the toughest one. So she dropped an easier course "to give me more time to work" on the class.

Teenage symptoms of overload mirror those of adult jugglers. Separate studies of teens and adults show that those who feel stressed by conflicting demands tend to drink too much and get depressed.

But adults and kids aren't talking much to each other about the issue. Asked if adults give them credit for their balancing act, the nine teenagers in one group I talked to responded in a chorus: "No!" One adds, "They expect it." Nor do the teens pay much attention to adults' juggling act. "I realize my parents are under stress, but I haven't taken the time to ask them," says one.

"Parents and children are running on parallel treadmills," says Ellen Galinsky of the Families and Work Institute. She is interviewing 1,000 children for a book, *Ask the Children.* But no effort is made to slow the exhausting pace because no one talks about the stress. "There is no problem-solving," she adds.

Therein lies a lesson, at least for me: that a tendency to take on too much isn't just a family-care issue or a generational issue. It's a cultural habit. As time-use experts John Robinson and Geoffrey Godbey say in a 1997 book, *Time for Life,* we have forgotten in our rush how to savor the moment.

The Lincoln teens, by and large, will no doubt move on to lead successful adult lives. So what is the real cost of overload? Consider Marc Berger's response: "We're not getting the full satisfaction, the full rewards out of what we're doing. We remain separate, very aloof, from experiences ... not really connected" to what we're doing.

I couldn't have said it better.

—June 3, 1998

New Job Hunters Ask Recruiters, "Is There a Life After Work?"

C orporate recruiters are seeing a surprising trend this season on undergraduate campuses.

Questions about work-life balance—which in the past were saved for the final round of interviews, or never asked at all—are surfacing in job candidates' first-round talks with employers.

A sampling of questions asked by undergraduate recruits, from my own interviews with recruiters for 12 big employers:

1. Do people who work for you have a life off the job?
2. Do your employees get to see their families?
3. What support can you offer my significant other?
4. Do you offer flextime?
5. If my job requires too much travel, can I change without doing serious damage to my career?
6. Does the location you're hiring for offer (fill in sport of choice)?

The questions are coming from single and married recruits alike. Mark Buzek, 22 years old, a December chemical-engineering graduate from Ohio State University who had six job offers, isn't married. But strong ties with his parents, two sisters and a brother in Ohio, he says, led him to rule out offers requiring frequent relocation; he wants to continue babysitting for his sister's kids and watching his nephew's soccer and baseball games.

Sarah Schroeder, 22, a recent mechanical-engineering grad who got five job offers, cut off interviews with several employers who expect continuous 60-hour-plus work weeks. She picked Saturn Corp., she says, because of its "quality of work life" and flexibility, in addition to the challenge and responsibility of the job.

"Work is important to me and I really want to do my best," she says. "But that's not what I'm working for. I'm working to be able to afford the other values in life," including outside interests such as tennis, roller-blading, cooking, sewing and eventually a family.

Intel, which interviewed about 2,500 undergrads on 50 campuses this year, is hearing questions about life-balance concerns 50% of the time, compared with 20% five years ago, says Mike Foster, college-recruiting manager. For grads generally, says Marianne Mueller, assistant engineering dean at Ohio State, "quality of life issues are more in the forefront than in the past."

Some recruiters admitted they were turned off at first by the line of questioning, which sends up in flashing lights the old "slacker" stereotype about Generation X. But several say many of the candidates who asked these questions in the past ended up being top performers in their jobs. "The thing I found is that these folks can set their priorities within time limits," says Faye Ambrefe Omasta, who recruits management trainees for GTE. Gordon Welton, placement manager for Principal Financial Group, adds, "Somebody who comes to you with those kinds of questions is on the ball. They know what's important to them. They're passionate not just about their work, but about themselves."

Why are such questions surfacing now? Clearly, recruits are emboldened by the tightening labor market. But the trend also signals a major change. Where Baby Boomers were willing to defer family, interests and relationships until their mid-30s or later, after paying some career dues, Generation Xers "want work-life balance on Day One," says Maury Hanigan of Hanigan Consulting Group, New York, strategic staffing specialists.

Many grew up in households pained by work-life conflict. "These were the latch-key kids. They had stressed-out moms and dads who saw them for 20 minutes before they went to bed. Then their parents were laid off, and they said, 'This equation doesn't make sense to me,' " Ms. Hanigan says.

Susan Allen, a human-resource manager who recruits for Ceridian, recalls a 22-year-old information-systems graduate who asked her point-blank about the company's "organizational values" on work and family. "He said he never saw his father when he was growing up and he wasn't going to allow that to happen to his children."

And while Baby Boomers have typically kept silent on life-balance matters for fear of being seen as "uncommitted to the job," these new recruits see no point in pulling punches, recruiters say. "They're not willing to waste their time in the interview process by not talking about things that are important to them," says Brenda Hightower, a recuiter and utilities leader for Hoechst Celanese.

Recruiters are sorting out the implications. One supervisor plans to coach his staff to give upbeat answers. He wants them to be honest about the long work hours his company often requires without responding "in a very negative way." He says some recruiters wear their grueling work schedule like a badge of honor, an attitude that doesn't wash with many recruits.

Some recruiters tell positive stories. Ms. Omasta tells students about her setup with GTE, in which she telecommutes part time from her farm in Massachusetts.

As the competition for workers heats up, Ms. Hanigan says, more employers will need to tailor their recruiting, and the workplace, to the change. Otherwise, she says, they'll lose good candidates "who look at a frenetic work environment and say, 'This isn't worth it to me. I've got other choices. Better choices.' "

—January 29, 1997

Caregiver Duties
Make Generation Xers Anything
But Slackers

I f you think of Generation X as a disaffected crowd with tattoos and pierced navels, meet John LaVaccare.

When his mother fell ill with Parkinson's dementia complex and his father moved out, Mr. LaVaccare, then in his teens, changed career goals from science to business so he could avoid graduate school and help care for her.

He landed a job as an accountant at a Big Six firm and lived with friends in Chicago's trendy Lincoln Park area. But it was too hard to manage his mother's care, so at 23 he moved in with his mother in a nearby neighborhood. He missed out on the lifestyle of a successful young bachelor. But he hung in as a primary caregiver for four years, when family members stepped in so he could attend medical school. Does he regret the years of sacrifice? No, says Mr. LaVaccare, now 30 years old. "I felt helping out at home was more important."

There are a lot more John LaVaccares out there than you think. A new study of 1,000 people by the National Council on the Aging and John Hancock Mutual Life Insurance has surprised long-term care experts by showing that 24% of people under 32 have provided, or are providing, hands-on, long-term care to a family member or friend. That compares with 31% of the total population who has done so.

The study matches findings by Maury Hanigan of Hanigan Consulting Group, New York human-resource consultants, showing "a strong sense of family, and a high priority placed on family" among Generation Xers. Those values often surprise employers trying to hire or transfer young workers, she adds.

The study also proves, again, that stereotypes are nearly useless in predicting the family conflicts of today's work force. As families fragment, scatter and re-form in nontraditional patterns, grandchildren often find themselves caring for grandparents; that was the case among 59% of the Generation X caregivers surveyed.

Other factors: The AIDS epidemic and a trend toward adult children living with parents longer, says Leslie Faught of Working Solutions, Portland, Ore.

Behind the statistics lie poignant stories of young caregivers even more isolated than their older counterparts. "If you're 21 or 22 and you're caring for somebody who is ill, how can your friends relate to you? They're starting careers, going to school, getting married, and you're tied to a bedpan," says Suzanne Mintz of the National Family Caregivers Association, Kensington, Md.

In his 20s, Mr. LaVaccare missed the neighborhood basketball games and some of the dating his friends enjoyed. Though he was struggling to juggle caregiving with his demanding job, he didn't talk about his family role with coworkers. He became so immersed in it that he nearly lost his sense of self.

Only after he began using the resources at Alzheimer's Association, a national organization based in Chicago, did he understand "that I had my own life," he says. He attended a support group, where older caregivers encouraged him to meet his own needs. Now, as he completes medical school at University of Chicago, he says he's glad he realized "a terminal illness isn't a good focal point for your life at age 23."

Of all caregivers, the under-36 age group are the most likely to be depressed, says Lynn Friss Feinberg of the Family Caregivers Alliance, a nonprofit resource group in San Francisco. Among the caregivers the Alliance has helped, more Generation Xers than any other group needed additional medical care themselves and 25% had to quit jobs to provide care. Heather Urban, 28, an administrative assistant for a Boston nonprofit concern, was ready to interview for higher-paying jobs when her father, a 61-year-old widower, had a disabling stroke. To keep him out of a government-funded nursing home, she quit her job and moved to California to care for him.

After she brought her father home from the hospital, he grew depressed and began waking her up repeatedly through the night for help. Exhausted, "I started to just go mental," says Ms. Urban. "I was crying all the time."

Her father's doctor intervened, treating him for depression and insisting she spend at least an hour a day away from the house. She joined a swim class and a theater group. But she has given up dating. The men she knows "really weren't accepting of my situation," she says. She still misses the camaraderie of coworkers at her job; "I miss feeling like there's some reason for me to be, besides Dad."

Other Generation X caregivers must cut back at work at a time when they would like to go all-out for career. Helen Wong, 24, was working overtime at an environmental-cleanup company and hoping to land a job as a government auditor when her father had a stroke. Ms. Wong, who lives at her parents' home, was so swamped by insurance paperwork and helping her father that she cut back overtime.

When she got the job offer she had hoped for, she hesitated. It required travel. "What if something happens when I'm gone?" she worried. She took it, but schedules her days so tightly that she has no time for herself. On business trips, she calls home daily and keeps lists of "10,000 things" to do when she returns.

Ms. Wong sometimes yearns for a more carefree lifestyle. But she finds her parents' plight heartbreaking, she says. "People say to me, 'Why don't you just move out?' But if I did, I wouldn't have peace of mind."

—May 22, 1996

Families Are Feeling the
Generation Gap
in Work-Family Issues

In her youth in the 1950s, Diana Goldstein's family talked around the dinner table about how more women needed to finish college and find an occupation in case their husbands died young.

Today, the buzz around her family dinner table is on a new topic, says Ms. Goldstein, who is 56 years old: how to combine work and family. Last Thanksgiving, nearly a dozen relatives from three generations sat around her table over dessert, discussing when and how parents should return to work after childbirth.

The conversation between generations about work-family conflict is heating up—based on my mail and interviews with workers in their 20s and early 30s. Families are tackling subjects that weren't discussed much in the past. Many Generation Xers are laying plans for combining work and family further in advance than their parents. They face more financial hurdles to child-rearing, and more choices about how to blend work and family, than any generation before them. Many are working much longer hours straight out of college than the generation before them.

As the media and politicians seize on child-care problems as a social issue, work-family conflict has become fair game for family discussions. Many Gen-Xers "are having strong debates" with relatives "about what to do when they decide to start a family," Ms. Goldstein's daughter, Lisa D. Bauer, 27, writes in a letter to me.

In some families, the discussions crash and burn in the generation gap. Some older people fail to grasp the heavy responsibility many young women feel for paying household expenses. One 28-year-old secretary at a suburban Chicago bank pays half her modest household's bills, and is delaying having children while she looks for flexible work. She wants to avoid putting her baby in child care for the long office hours her current job demands.

But when her dilemma came up over dinner at her sister's house, her mother, trying to help, suggested she take a secretarial job in her brother-in-law's business—a position that pays less than her current job, too little even to cover child-care bills. "My mom said, 'If you worked for family, it would be so much easier for you to take [time] off with the kids,' " the secretary recalls. "I said, 'No, Mom, you don't understand. It would be worse.' "

For men, too, the crumbling of gender-role boundaries has been too swift for some families to navigate. Peter Scott, an avionics technician, and his wife, an accountant, decided early that whoever made less money would stay home with the kids. So child care falls to Mr. Scott, who loves being a full-time dad.

But some of his relatives, though supportive, were worried when they heard the decision. His mother feared the consequences of his jumping off the career ladder. Some men in the family lapsed into awkward silence. Work-family roles are changing so fast, says Stephanie Coontz, an author and family-studies professor at Evergreen State College, Olympia, Wash., that "we're in this transition with a kind of chasm between each generation."

Still, many parents find a way to play a strong supporting role. Ms. Bauer credits her mother with consistently encouraging her to coin her own work-family solutions. After five years in fast-track jobs on Wall Street, Ms. Bauer quit to become a financial planner, a career she hopes will provide both the income and control over her time she needs to raise a family.

Jennifer Prosek, 28, co-owner of a marketing firm, talks often with her parents, with whom she is close, about her long-term plans to marry and raise children. Like a growing number of young adults, she hopes to live near her parents and involve them in child care.

Over dinner together, Ms. Prosek's mother, 52, a teacher, told of a dream she had about life in retirement: "We were in your apartment. I was taking your two kids to the park and you were going off to work," Ms. Prosek says her mother told her. Both took pleasure in the image.

As my three Generation X stepchildren near the life stage where work-family conflict cuts deep, I fight the impulse to spout advice about child care, overload and so on. They're far savvier already about work and family than I was at their age, and I haven't uttered a word yet. I'd probably help them more by honing the example I set, than by forcing on them any 3-D map of the rough seas that lie behind me.

A better intergenerational model took shape around Ms. Goldstein's dinner table last Thanksgiving. As relatives, ranging from at-home moms to career-focused dual earners without kids, relaxed over coffee, one new mother, a speech pathologist with a two-month-old son, wrestled aloud with plans to return to work. Ms. Goldstein, a teacher who put her work on temporary hold to raise children, saw her ambivalence.

But Ms. Goldstein and the others refrained from giving advice, offering encouragement instead, and asking questions to help the mother sort her own values and responsibilities from the expectations of others. (She later decided to stay home.) In complex times, no parent can afford to be "opinionated and dogmatic," Ms. Goldstein notes. For young people wrestling with unique personal imperatives, "it is hard" to blend work and family, she adds. "This is an ongoing dilemma."

—February 11, 1998

Today's Young Women Are Redefining Debate About Working Moms

D ebra Ross has been thinking about how to combine work and family for much of the past 15 years.

Ms. Ross, 29 years old, was in her teens when she started considering flexible careers. When she graduated from college, she took a job with a start-up to learn entrepreneurial skills. At 25, she started her own programming and software-training business out of her home, to gain control over her time and workstyle. She and her husband, who talked while they were dating about child-rearing principles, hope eventually to work together in her Fairport, N.Y., business, so they can share at-home parenting.

Why all the groundwork? By the time they start a family as early as next year, Ms. Ross hopes to have created "an ideal environment for children to thrive." Combining work and family well, she adds, "requires a great deal of planning and deliberate attention."

Many women in their 20s are planning for working parenthood far earlier and more carefully than women typically did in the past. Informed by the often painful work-family conflicts of older women, they are deliberately arming themselves to the teeth, years before childbirth, to balance work and family on their own terms. Their weapons are red-hot skills, multiple degrees and entrepreneurial experience. Their goal is to carve out work-family balance on their own terms.

More young men are also interested in combining work and parenting, but they aren't planning ahead to the same extent. Young women see family "through a very different lens" than five to 10 years ago, says Roxanne Hori, career-management director at Northwestern University's Kellogg Graduate School of Management. They're "much more conscious of it."

Heidi Brennan of Mothers at Home, an advocacy group, says today's young women "aren't like baby boomers, who said, 'Of course I'm going to go back to work,' and then had this enormous

313

crisis" later. Instead, "women are more anticipatory," she says, sometimes contacting her group even before childbirth.

Some acquire scarce job skills to remain employable. One California woman who was planning for kids, left her secure job as a systems analyst for a big high-tech company. She joined a smaller
consulting firm to learn Year 2000 software, says Kevin Rosenberg,
managing director of Bridgegate, an Irvine, Calif., recruiter. A couple of years later, she had a baby and dropped out for 14 months.
She kept up her skills and rejoined her former employer on the
part-time schedule she wanted, he says. It is a plan-ahead pattern
Mr. Rosenberg is seeing often.

Others are getting multiple degrees to gain workplace clout. Jane
Kimble, 29, has a master's in electrical engineering and is working
on her M.B.A. at Simmons College. She hopes that when she and
her husband start a family, "I'll be unique enough, and add enough
value, that [my employer] will want to be flexible," says Ms. Kimble,
a manager for a telecommunications concern.

Others see advanced degrees as easing their re-entry to the work
force after a break for child-rearing. Louise Meyer, now home with
her children, ages two and five months, says she got an M.B.A. at
Northwestern's Kellogg School partly because she knew the degree
"would give me the credentials I needed to step in and out of the
work force, and get the flexibility I need for my family." She plans to
resume work in a few years.

Jeanne Lewis, senior vice president, marketing, at Staples, says
she was surprised when she was studying for her Harvard M.B.A. to
see how many women there said one of their goals was to take time
off for children. A Harvard M.B.A. "told future employers that they
were serious, that they were competent and that their career was important to them," she says.

Women earned 21% more bachelor's degrees than men in
1994–1995, up from 14% more five years earlier, says the National
Center for Education Statistics. Women also earned 23% more master's degrees than men, up from 11% more.

Many anticipatory mothers also focus on building a trusting relationship with one employer. Catherine Briggs, a product manager
for a food company, turned down other job offers for three years before she had her twins, because she wanted to build a track record.

The strategy worked; she works part-time now and has a lot of control over her hours. "I have the equity here, that people know I'm going to get the job done," she says.

Others craft flexible new businesses of their own. After acquiring human-resource expertise at a big company and consulting skills at a Big Six firm, Karen Wotherspoon now runs her own company, Startup HR, from her Newport Beach, Calif., home. She structures clients' programs via the Internet and spends only a day or so on-site with each. The setup will allow her to raise her 11-month-old son and a second child, due this fall, the way she wants. These women transcend the perennial debate over whether mothers should work. Most young couples today expect to share long-term breadwinner responsibilities. Against that backdrop, "women these days don't want to be told what to do. We want to have options," says Kari Schmitz, 29, a senior executive aide at a consumer-products company who is working on her M.B.A. at Simmons College. Combining work and family is the buzz among Gen-Xers, she says. While most women want or need income, fulfillment or both from work, she says, "children are our future and someone has to be there . . . for them."

—July 15, 1998

Executives Look Back on the Work Ethics Learned from Fathers

Family and work interact in far-reaching ways. If, as psychologists say, family behavior is the most powerful influence on children, the examples we set as workers will shape the workers of the future.

As Father's Day approaches, I took a look at how fathers influenced some well-known careers.

Thomas Watson Jr., who succeeded his father as CEO of IBM, once said his ambition "was to prove to the world that I could run on the same racetrack as my dad." The father of discount retailer Sam Walton was an avid trader who bargained hard for low prices. Lee Iacocca's dad, a stern patriarch, taught his son early to meet boundless expectations. Here are some of the things five CEOs recalled in interviews about their own fathers:

Bob Allen, AT&T: I learned from my father mostly by example. Most important in terms of business was the value of service to your customer and the trust established by always standing behind your product. He was a children's clothing retailer. . . . Though people never delivered in those days, many times he'd get in the car and deliver something to a customer.

I learned dependability. When I was 11 or 12, I worked after school doing odd jobs. One afternoon I went [instead] to the church basement to play basketball. I'll never forget seeing my father coming down those steps. He had walked all the way across town. When I saw the look on his face, I dropped the ball and said, "I'm sorry." I never missed a day after that. . . . I also learned that one should expect a lot [of people who work for you] but never more than one gives oneself. In that business, he did everything: sold to customers, did the books, took inventory, cleaned floors, washed windows. It was one thing that persuaded me I didn't want to inherit the business.

Larry Perlman, Ceridian: My father ran a production operation of several hundred workers. He had two offices, one up with the other executives and another right off the production floor. He spent more time with the workers on the floor than with the executives. He was an early example of a leader as coach.

I remember going hunting with him; I was about 12. I shot a pheasant in a field of tall corn. I hit it in the wing. I didn't want to try to find it in all that tall corn. But my dad said, "You shot it. You go get it." . . . We have consistently tried here to build a culture around getting [employees] to understand they have personal responsibility for their work and giving them the power to carry that out. My dad exemplified that principle.

Ron Compton, Aetna Life & Casualty: My birth father disappeared from the scene fairly early, and my mother remarried an insurance agent. In college I decided the real world was a useless place, and I was going to live the rest of my life in academia. I was a philosophy major, and a good one. But by my senior year, I was becoming more and more disillusioned.

One day I was eating breakfast with my stepfather. He rarely interfered in my life except when he thought it needed a midcourse correction. He said, "You aren't very happy, are you?" I said, "I'm miserable because the one thing I've had my heart set on isn't going to work." He said, "Have you ever thought about going into the insurance business?" [After] I did some interviews, I asked him, "How should I make this decision?" He said, "Decide which company will give you the best education." I said, "How do I know?" He said, "I'll tell you: It will be Aetna." That was 41 years ago.

Ralph Horn, First Tennessee National: I grew up on a little farm. My dad was in politics and real estate and teaching. He made my brother and me grow a crop from the time I was 10. When he bought us a present, he gave us a mule to plow. There was a real contrast between my dad and that old mule. Dad believed in three key things: Do your work before you play, be honest, and respect others' property and feelings. And that mule was lazy and disrespectful and meaner than a junkyard dog.

Early in my career, I took one day off from my new job at what was then First National Bank of Memphis. I was selling securities in the bond division and I hated it. I couldn't sleep at night. I decided to look for another job, but I was afraid that would make me a failure in my father's eyes. After a year, I started loving my job. If it hadn't been for him instilling in me the work ethic, I never would have stuck it out.

Mike Cudahy, Marquette Electronics: My grandfather started a meat-packing company and built it to 6,500 employees. Somebody once asked me, "Gee, Mike, you've got it made. Why do you work so hard?" And I said, "To show my deceased grandfather I'm just as good as he was." Because Irish families practiced primogeniture and my father wasn't the oldest son, he went off to law school. He became ambassador to Poland, U.S. minister to Ireland and ambassador to Belgium in 1939. The old man got out of there in one piece, barely, and came back to write for the *New York Times.* He was the only American reporter to interview Adolph Hitler [as the war expanded].

I became sort of a crusty character because of all that. I went off with a bold attitude, "The old man can do it, and my grandfather can do it, so why shouldn't I?" I look at people who start companies and are so easily defeated. I guess I didn't have that problem. After my partner and I founded the company, there were times when it looked like disaster. Having the spirit to keep going makes all the difference.

—June 14, 1995

Our Families' Tales Can Speak Volumes About How We Work

One sunny day in 1929, six-year-old William N. Sirois walked with his mother Martha to the gates of the Lewiston, Maine, mill where she worked. He watched as she crossed a footbridge to the door of the mill, turned and waved to him, smiling. Then she reported to her seven-day-a-week job spinning textiles.

It was the last time Mr. Sirois saw his mother. Hours later, she collapsed on the job and died of a ruptured appendix. She had ignored her warning pains because the company fired anyone who missed work for any reason. With the Depression beginning, Mrs. Sirois couldn't afford to lose her job. That final image of his mother, smiling and waving in the sunshine, was one Mr. Sirois carried with him throughout his life.

Nearly 70 years later, Mr. Sirois's son, William G. Sirois, still centers his career on the issues raised by that family story. As chief operating officer of Circadian Technologies Inc., a Cambridge, Mass., shiftwork consultant, he helps companies set up humane and effective workplaces. Though the younger Mr. Sirois didn't think about his grandmother when he chose his life's work, he says he suspects her experience was an unconscious factor.

Among all the ways family and work affect each other, the influence of family history on work-life choices is among the most interesting. Yet Americans rarely talk about it, seeing ourselves instead as free agents who can leave our families behind, if we choose, and get on with our lives on our own terms.

Family history helps shape our choices in relationships. Beth Sirull's father encouraged her mother to pursue a career in law, an unusual stance for a man of his generation. Then her father supported her mother's wish to enroll, at age 65, in a Yiddish Studies program at Oxford University in England. Similarly, Ms. Sirull's own husband has supported her pursuit of her dreams, first to quit her job and start her own Oak Park, Ill., marketing firm, then to write a book.

The influence of family experiences can extend several generations. Debby Hall's grandmother was one of the first telephone operators in the early 1900s. Her mother helped run a family poultry business and retired at 83. No wonder Ms. Hall, a vice president for Prudential Insurance Co. of America, says, "It never occurred to me not to work."

Family history also explains some unconventional work-life choices. Former American Express Co. President Jeffrey Stiefler and Silicon Graphics Inc. co-founder and chief engineer Rocky Rhodes stunned acquaintances by abruptly resigning or sharply scaling back powerful careers at their peaks. Both men felt their time with their fathers had been cut short by premature death. Informed by the loss of their fathers, each acted to nail down more time with family, before it was too late.

The power of family history is explained in family systems theory, a psychological perspective developed by pioneering therapist Murray Bowen in the 1970s and popularized by author-therapist Monica McGoldrick in her 1995 book, *You Can Go Home Again.* This set of principles holds that people and their problems don't exist in a vacuum, but as part of a broad family system. Like all systems, changes in one part of the family system affect other parts. Family patterns of working, relating and dealing with stress can reverberate through generations.

Understanding family systems theory isn't just an exercise. It heeds George Santayana's warning that those who cannot remember the past are condemned to repeat it.

Dr. McGoldrick, director of the Family Institute of New Jersey, says understanding the past can free you to change your future. She encourages people to become researchers on family history. "Look for transformative stories"—instances when a family member reacted to a bad or traumatic event in a creative, constructive or healing way—"or ways to make stories into something transformative for yourself."

Consciously or unconsciously, many people strive to transform family history. Evan Imber-Black, a Manhattan family therapist and author of *The Secret Life of Families,* tells of a man who realized he became a policeman to address the sins of his grandfather, whose crime sprees had shamed the family.

Old family stories can explain the special meaning some people derive from their work. While the younger Mr. Sirois had other jobs, as an engineer and a consultant on productivity and ergonomics, "something just magically clicked" when he began shiftwork consulting in 1992, he says. "It all made so much sense. It was about stopping building workplaces that hurt people."

Reflecting on family experiences also can help solve what is, for many, a puzzle: how to balance work and life. Valerie Young was commuting far to a corporate job she disliked when her mother, a university janitor, died of a heart attack at age 61—just five months before her long-anticipated retirement. Four months later, Dr. Young quit her job. Now, she runs her own Northampton, Mass., publishing, consulting and training firm. In that, she has gained a sense of control and fulfillment her mother never had, she says.

"She died with a million projects she was still going to do. In my attic I still have boxes of her recipes, pieces of quilts she was going to put together someday." By reordering her life so she could enjoy it in the present, she says, "I feel like I honor my mother."

—April 29, 1998

Recommended Resources

Barnett, Rosalind, and Caryl Rivers. *She Works/He Works.* Harper San Francisco, 1996. Based on a study of 300 dual-earner couples, the authors paint a new picture of two-income pairs as cooperative partners who share increasingly similar priorities in marriage, family and work.

Bravo, Ellen. *The Job/Family Challenge: Not for Women Only.* John Wiley & Sons, 1995. A resource guide on workplace rights, flexible schedules and other practical matters by the head of 9to5, National Association of Working Women.

Bua, Robert N. *The Inside Guide to America's Nursing Homes.* Warner Books, 1997. A former nursing home administrator and attorney rates 17,000 nursing homes and gives advice on how to make the best choice.

Burggraf, Shirley. *The Feminine Economy and Economic Man.* Addison-Wesley, 1997. This isn't light reading, but it frames an important new perspective on the crucial economic role played by the family in society.

Coontz, Stephanie. *The Way We Really Are.* Basic Books, 1997. The strengths and weaknesses of today's diverse families, as seen by the author of the best-selling *The Way We Never Were.*

Covey, Stephen. *First Things First.* Simon & Schuster, 1994. A fresh, thoughtful look at the art of time management by one of the nation's leading self-improvement gurus.

Covey, Stephen. *The Seven Habits of Highly Effective Families.* Golden Books, 1997. Dr. Covey applies his megaselling "seven principles of highly effective people" to home life, with many anecdotes from life with his own nine kids.

Edwards, Paul, and Sarah Edwards. *Working from Home.* Tarcher/Putnam, 1994. This home-office guide is one of many excellent works by the nation's best-known advisors in the work-at-home field.

Hersch, Patricia. *A Tribe Apart.* Ballantine Publishing Group, 1998. This intimate, three-year look at the lives of eight middle-class teens shows how parents err in pulling away from their teens too soon.

Hochschild, Arlie Russell. *The Time Bind.* Metropolitan Books, 1997. This provocative look at employees in a supposedly family-friendly workplace exposes all the denial mechanisms we use, from "downsizing" our emotional lives to living in the future, to kid ourselves into believing we're spending enough time with our families.

Kelley, Linda. *Two Incomes and Still Broke?* Times Books, 1996. A smart perspective on the costs of the dual-earner lifestyle.

Levering, Robert, and Milton Moskowitz. *The 100 Best Companies to Work for in America.* Plume, 1993. A reference guide to people-friendly employment practices by two of the nation's leading experts.

Levine, James A., and Todd L. Pittinsky. *Working Fathers.* Harcourt Brace & Co., 1997. Working fathers' most longstanding advocate offers practical advice and support for men seeking better balance and deeper involvement in family.

Matthews, Joseph. *Beat the Nursing Home Trap: An Insider's Guide to Choosing and Financing Long-Term Care.* Nolo Press, 1995. Hard-headed advice on a wide range of the most difficult elder-care issues.

Nilles, Jack. *Making Telecommuting Happen.* Van Nostrand Reinhold, 1994. The man who coined the term "telecommuting" maps routes around potential obstacles for people who want to work from home.

Raffin, P. Michele. *The Good Nanny Book.* Berkley Books, 1996. Lessons from 100 interviews with parents who have employed nannies.

Rechtshaffen, Stephan. *TimeShifting: Creating More Time to Enjoy Your Life.* Doubleday, 1996. Drawing on wisdom from various cultures and teachers, the author shows why and how we need to slow down and consciously savor each moment.

Shelton, Sandi Kahn. *You Might as Well Laugh.* Bancroft Press, 1997. Columns on parenthood by a working mother offer a fail-safe way to lighten up.

Sherman, James R. *The Caregiver Survival Series.* Pathway Books, 1994–1996. Twelve slim, appealing volumes offer wisdom, wit and advice on many facets of caring for elders and other dependent adults.

Tolliver, Cindy, and Nancy Chambers. *Going Part-Time: The Insider's Guide for Professional Women Who Want a Career and a Life.* Avon Books, 1997. A savvy guide to cutting your hours.

Index

ABOUT THE AUTHOR

SUE SHELLENBARGER's "Work & Family" columns have been appearing regularly in *The Wall Street Journal* since 1991. The former chief of the *Journal*'s Chicago news bureau, Shellenbarger has been writing and editing for the *Journal* for nineteen years. She has also served as a contributing editor and columnist for *Parenting* magazine and as a financial markets columnist for the Associated Press.